LAND
USE
PLANNING
Techniques of
Implementation

LAND USE PLANNING
Techniques of Implementation

T. William Patterson

Van Nostrand Reinhold Environmental Engineering Series

 VAN NOSTRAND REINHOLD COMPANY
NEW YORK   CINCINNATI   ATLANTA   DALLAS   SAN FRANCISCO
LONDON   TORONTO   MELBOURNE

Van Nostrand Reinhold Company Regional Offices:
New York   Cincinnati   Atlanta   Dallas   San Francisco

Van Nostrand Reinhold Company International Offices:
London   Toronto   Melbourne

Copyright © 1979 by Litton Educational Publishing, Inc.

Library of Congress Catalog Card Number: 78-26309
ISBN: 0-442-24203-4

Manufactured in the United States of America

Published by Van Nostrand Reinhold Company
135 West 50th Street, New York, N.Y. 10020

Published simultaneously in Canada by Van Nostrand Reinhold Ltd.

15 14 13 12 11 10 9 8 7 6 5 4 3 2 1

Library of Congress Cataloging in Publication Data

Patterson, Theodore William.
  Land use planning.

  (Van Nostrand Reinhold environmental engineering
series)
  Bibliography: p. 323.
  Includes index.
  1. Land use—Planning—United States.   2. City
planning—United States.   3. Regional planning—United
States.   I. Title.
HD205.1979.P37   333.7'7'0973   78-26309
ISBN 0-442-24203-4

This book is dedicated to the memory of my Mother,
Helen Lindsley Patterson

Van Nostrand Reinhold Environmental Engineering Series

THE VAN NOSTRAND REINHOLD ENVIRONMENTAL ENGI-
NEERING SERIES is dedicated to the presentation of current and vital
information relative to the engineering aspects of controlling man's physical environment. Systems and subsystems available to exercise control of
both the indoor and outdoor environment continue to become more sophisticated and to involve a number of engineering disciplines. The aim of
the series is to provide books which, though often concerned with the life
cycle—design, installation, and operation and maintenance—of a specific
system or subsystem, are complementary when viewed in their relationship
to the total environment.

The Van Nostrand Reinhold Environmental Engineering Series includes
books concerned with the engineering of mechanical systems designed (1)
to control the environment within structures, including those in which
manufacturing processes are carried out, and (2) to control the exterior
environment through control of waste products expelled by inhabitants of
structures and from manufacturing processes. The series includes books
on heating, air conditioning and ventilation, control of air and water pollution, control of the acoustic environment, sanitary engineering and waste
disposal, illumination, and piping systems for transporting media of all
kinds.

Van Nostrand Reinhold Environmental Engineering Series

WATER QUALITY MANAGEMENT PLANNING, edited by Joseph L. Pavoni

HANDBOOK OF ADVANCED WASTEWATER TREATMENT (Second Edition), by Russell L. Culp, George Mack Wesner and Gordon L. Culp

HANDBOOK OF NOISE ASSESSMENT, edited by Daryl N. May

NOISE CONTROL: HANDBOOK OF PRINCIPLES AND PRACTICES, edited by David M. Lipscomb and Arthur C. Taylor

AIR POLLUTION CONTROL TECHNOLOGY, by Robert M. Bethea

POWER PLANT SITING, by John V. Winter and David A. Conner

DISINFECTION OF WASTEWATER AND WATER FOR REUSE, by Geo. Clifford White

LAND USE PLANNING: Techniques of Implementation, by T. William Patterson

BIOLOGICAL PATHS TO SELF-RELIANCE, by Russell E. Anderson

HANDBOOK OF INDUSTRIAL WASTE DISPOSAL, by Richard Conway and Richard D. Ross

HANDBOOK OF ORGANIC WASTE CONVERSION, edited by Michael W. M. Bewick

LAND APPLICATIONS OF WASTE (Volume 1), by Raymond C. Loehr, William J. Jewell, Joseph D. Novak, William W. Clarkson and Gerald S. Friedman

LAND APPLICATIONS OF WASTE (Volume 2), by Raymond C. Loehr, William J. Jewell, Joseph D. Novak, William W. Clarkson and Gerald S. Friedman

STRUCTURAL DYNAMICS: Theory and Computation, by Mario Paz

Foreword

The search for justice and order in a complex, disorderly and frequently aberrant world is imperative. In our own country, all too frequently, we are hampered in such an effort by our own endless, self-adopted, conservative and frequently illogical traditions. A state boundary remains a bad habit. Thus it is also with counties and cities capped by the top nonsense, our capital, both a political myth and an anacronism. Examples are endless. What this book attempts is to find rationality within a giant, irrational framework.

Dr. Patterson's task obviously was not easy. He collates multiple issues and packs them skillfully within a land planning boundary and carefully documents the issues. Since there are an infinite number of possible spin-offs as well as internal mixes, a careful centroid is maintained to avoid as many distractions as possible. This is a major achievement in the ever-increasing welter of books on planning, the preponderant number of which seek nonexistent systems in swirling galaxies of episodes.

Technical literature dealing with legal events and shifting management tools inevitably faces increasing obsolescence as each year new federal, state and local legislation is enacted and legal battles are fought. Hopefully future readers of this book will recognize that its publication date is less important than the fact that the book provides the bases on which it should be possible to position future events.

I cannot forebear from making two comments. First, the record underplays the goals and objectives essential to valid land use planning. An example would be the Declaration of National Housing Policy contained in the Housing Act of 1949, which among its purposes was designed to provide "a decent home and a suitable living environment for every American family." The uncoordinated masses of land planning law and the infinitely complex management programs which have resulted exist without the consistency or the guidelines of a national land policy. The result is that even where individual states and their lesser jurisdictions, as well as interstate agencies, adopt policies and guidelines, as some have done and as noted by Dr. Patterson, only a fruitless, piecemeal result occurs. The fragments will never assemble themselves into a coherent plan. A national land use planning program such as died with the lamented National Resources Planning Board in 1943 is today a categorical imperative.

My second comment is also a query. Why is there so obviously a time and cultural lag among planners? There is little record to date of a developing interface between land use planning, pending energy crises and pending societal impacts of energy issues.

Traditional land use planning is about to undergo fundamental changes, which will undoubtedly be reported on in the next edition of this book.

CARL FEISS, AIP, FAIA
Gainesville, Florida

Preface

The success of urban and regional planning lies ultimately in the effectiveness of translating plans and policies into programs and projects which are effectively and satisfactorily carried out. Increasing concern among planners and their clients about the problems of bringing plans and policies into realization, have in the last few years led to both criticisms of the planning implementation process, and significant innovations in legal and organizational techniques and strategies involving both conventional means and unconventional means. The purpose of this book is to describe and evaluate most of the means available for carrying out land use plans with an emphasis on the more promising innovations. It is limited to looking at land use planning because in most settings this is still the predominant task of urban and regional planners.

The first chapter looks at the background and context in which planning takes place. Chapters two, three and four, respectively deal with the traditional tools, zoning, subdivision regulations, and other supplemental regulations and related development policies. Chapter five deals with financial planning which is becoming a critical tool in the guidance of development. Chapter six discusses the advantages and disadvantages of the use of special districts for planning, guiding and carrying out development. And the last two chapters deal with growth guidance systems and summarize the author's conclusions concerning possibilities for improving the land use plan and policy implementation process.

Designed primarily to serve as a text and reference book for students of urban and regional planning, the book will also be of value to professionals in their efforts to improve implementation processes.

The author is grateful to the many people whose contributions, experience and proposals have been drawn upon in putting this book together. In addition to sources acknowledged in this text the author is indebted to Professors Harold Michael, David Caputo, Harvey Marshall, and Kumares Sinha of Purdue University, the Purdue University-Indiana State Highway Commission Joint Highway Research Project, to the secretaries who labored over the manuscript and to my friends and neighbors who both contributed to the work and gave me encouragement while it was underway.

T. WILLIAM PATTERSON, AICP, M.ASCE

LIST OF FIGURES

LIST OF TABLES

Contents

xvii

LAND USE PLANNING
Techniques of Implementation

1

The context for plan/policy implementation

BACKGROUND

Although cities have been planned—especially new cities—since the times of antiquity, it is only since the end of the last century that planning has emerged as a distinct profession. In England and the United States the industrial revolution in the 19th Century saw a vast growth of cities accompanied by workers' housing developments characterized by deplorable overcrowding, and squalor. Living conditions for workers and the urban poor were protested by various reformers and utopians and their followers and a number of model communities were built in the industrializing countries.

In America the City Beautiful movement sparked by Daniel Burnham, chief architect of the 1893 Chicago World's Columbian Exposition popularized city planning and resulted in a number of cities being replanned in a formal fashion featuring grand avenues connecting monumental building complexes and other focal points. These plans were on a colossal scale reflecting the *beaux arts* esthetic of the times, superficial in relation to solving basic urban problems, and too expensive to be carried out to any great extent.

In England on the other hand, the most important movement was the Garden City movement of Ebeneezer Howard whose book *Tomorrow*, published in 1898 resulted the following year in the formation of the Garden City Association and the subsequent development in 1903 by limited dividend societies of Letchworth and sometime later of Welwyn Garden City. Both were north of London and featured almost complete segregation of land uses. By the beginning of World War II this movement had inspired a number of public and private new towns and garden suburbs elsewhere, including the greenbelt towns and Radburn in the United States. After the war new towns became an integral part of Britain's urban growth policy, influenced Swedish growth policy and more recently and notably the growth policies of France, The Netherlands, Israel, the Soviet Union, Australia, and here in the United States inspired the present private/public new communities program.

Although the City Beautiful movement itself faded and the Garden City movement was slow in gaining influence here, interest in city planning and the regulation of land uses persistently grew. The first National Conference on City Planning was held in 1909 and two years later the National Housing Association was founded. Planning commissions multiplied and in 1913 Massachusetts made these boards mandatory for all cities over 10,000 in population. In 1916 largely as a result of the efforts of New York City attorney Edward M. Bassett, that city adopted the first comprehensive zoning ordinance in the country. The following year saw the organization in Kansas City of the American City Planning Institute (now the American Planning Association), the first professional planning organization in the United States.

Those who declared themselves "professional planners" came from a wide variety of more specialized fields: architecture, landscape architecture, civil engineering, law and a broad assortment of other disciplines, but mostly those concerned with physical development. The formal training of planners, begun in the 1920s, had a physical planning emphasis in most schools until the influx of students with backgrounds in social science and other nondesign fields in the late 1950s and 1960s.

The planning profession, although still small, has been growing steadily and changing its character. The traditional emphasis is continuing to be modified by an increasing concern for social, economic, and environmental problems. The planning profession has come to view its role far more broadly than previously. There has been a parallel increase in the public's concern for these problems which in turn has made itself felt in the urban development process.

Expansion of the planner's role often has not met with ready acceptance by their public employers. Local planning commissions and local governments still see physical planning as the dominant task of the planner except in locations where there is strong and articulate public expression for charging planners with a broader range of tasks. Consequently the planner is often in an advocacy position in regard to redefining his role. Further, both within and without the planning profession long-range comprehensive planning has come under attack as being ineffective, unrealistic, and even irrelevant. As a consequence it is apparent to most planners that not only physical plans and policies but the traditional tools and strategies for carrying them out are either too weak or otherwise defective.

Before describing the various planning tools, their strengths and weaknesses, innovations now being tried, and reforms proposed, it is desirable to describe the context in which they are used. This means examining American urban problems, the roles of the various levels of government, and the nature of the land development market.

AMERICAN URBAN TRENDS AND PROBLEMS

More than two thirds of the population of the United States lives in metropolitan areas (68.6 percent by the 1970 Census). Although there are many significant differences between American cities, their similarities are far more striking. They have grown in many parallel ways and share the same basic problems. The viability of our metropolitan areas is of deep concern as problems mount and the concentration of most of our people in them continues.

Assessments of the urban condition range in point of view from John Reps' critical opinion that[1]

. . . the American urban environment is grossly unsatisfactory. It is inefficient, inconvenient, unattractive, uneconomical, and unloved.

to the more moderate view of Martin Meyerson and Barbara Terrett that the metropolis is a crazy quilt ". . . both haphazard and unplanned . . ." but essentially sound.[2] They go on to argue that the deterioration of housing and community facilities is more rapid than that of purely physical aging; it is in part a product of cultural obsolescence as a result of our high economic and social mobility; that "Urban communities . . . by their very diversity seem to encourage adaptation, birth, growth, transfer, or demise of activities as their importance rises or declines."[3] James Q. Wilson observes that: "Viewed in the historical perspective, and taking American cities as a whole, the conditions of urban life have, by most measures, been getting steadily better, not worse."[4] He goes on to point out that much of what is considered the present urban crisis is a crisis of rising expectations. Urban conditions do not seem to be improving as rapidly as we feel they should. Edward C. Banfield takes the same point of view in *The Unheavenly City*. He points out that: ". . . in many important respects conditions in the large cities have been getting better;" that there is less poverty than ever before; housing is improving rapidly; that more children complete high school; that the treatment of racial and other minority groups is obviously better; but the talk of an urban crisis is based largely on the improvements in performance not keeping pace with rising expectations. He concludes that ". . . although much is seriously wrong with the city, no disaster impends unless it be one that results from public misconceptions that are in the nature of self-fulfilling prophecies."[5]

While there may be no "urban crisis" per se, it is clear that many urban problems are stubbornly persistent and others are growing, especially those attendant on the growth of metropolitan areas in both population and geographic size. It is also clear that with the increasing professionalization of general purpose governments in metropolitan areas the planning process is being more frequently relied upon to help in the solution or management of a widening array of urban problems.

The character of our metropolitan areas has changed markedly in the last half century. Shortly after World War I the great suburban boom began in which for the first time the suburbs grew at a faster rate than the central cities, largely the result of growing wealth, increased automobile ownership, the construction of major arteries and boulevards, and in some cities the introduction of rapid transit. However the central cities and core areas remained strong in spite of the separate

Table 1-1   Population Distribution 1950–1970: Urban/Rural.

	1950	1960	1970
Urban places (all)	64.0%	69.9%	73.5%
Urban places (over 100,000)	—	65.1	68.6
Rural	36.0	30.1	26.5

Source: 1970 Census Vol. 1, Part A, Section 1.

incorporation of the surrounding suburbs and the difficulties of meeting legal requirements which brought most annexation to a halt. The suburbs of this period were still tied tightly to the central city because most of their inhabitants still worked there, did most of their shopping there, went there for much of their entertainment, and relied on central city labor and services.

The next great suburban boom came after World War II. In the decade of the 1950s rural-urban migration was so extensive that more than half of the counties in the United States lost population. This rate of migration slowed down by the late 1960s as the remaining rural farm population was too small to contribute significantly any longer to urban growth (Table 1-1). Around many large cities the rural nonfarm population was and is actually increasing, but this new growth is made up largely of commuters.

The major metropolitan areas continue to gain population at the expense of the smaller cities and towns in rural areas. Within metropolitan areas outer suburbs are gaining population and all except the smaller central cities lost population between 1960 and 1970 after having gained population largely through annexation in the previous decade (Table 1-2).

The most significant aspects of the post World War II migrations both to and within metropolitan areas have been their socio-economic

Table 1-2   Population Distribution 1960–1970: Central City/Urban Fringe.

	1960	1970
Central cities	46.3%	42.8%
Urban fringe	30.2	36.5

Source: 1970 Census Vol. 1, Part A, Section 1.

Table 1-3   1969 Median Income by Race and Location

	All	White	Negro
Metropolitan areas	$10,577	$13,639	$6,863
Central cities	9,545	10,212	6,826
Nonmetropolitan	7,828	8,160	4,071

Source: 1970 Census PC(2)-8A.

character, especially in regard to race. In 1940 less than half the black population of the United States was urban and much of that in small cities. By 1970 about eighty-three percent of America's blacks lived in metropolitan areas and almost two thirds lived in central cities, particularly the older central cities of the larger metropolitan areas. Meanwhile all except the older inner suburbs have remained predominantly white.

The distribution of American incomes has followed this migration pattern. The older city centers are dominated by low income families most but not all of whom are black (Table 1-3). White families remaining in the city tend to be either low income families, the elderly who cannot afford to live elsewhere, or affluent young adults and elderly people who want to be close to the city center's facilities. Middle-class families with children predominate in the suburbs. Clawson observes that, "Sharp differences in life style arose or were accentuated, and some part of the tensions and violence of the postwar period is due to this sorting out of people by race, income, and age."[6]

World War II materials shortages, and recovery from the depression created a pent-up demand for new housing as materials again became available. Long-term, low-interest loans insured by the Federal Housing Administration and Veterans Administration enabled far more suburban residential development than would have been possible with conventional financing. Although it was intended for FHA to take risks, the bankerlike conservative policies of the agency favored the development of middle-income housing in the suburbs. The income tax laws also favored home-owning as opposed to renting and contributed further to suburbanization.

After 1950 the building boom leveled off to a fairly steady rate. With increased wealth there came a steady upgrading of new housing lasting until the mid-1960s when increases in interest rates, the dramatically rising cost of building sites, and construction costs restricted the market for new single family housing (excepting mobile homes). Higher density housing, mostly town houses and garden apartments, has overtaken single family housing in numbers of dwelling units started in most metropolitan areas in the last few years. Lack of central city sites has meant that most of this multifamily housing has been and is being built in the suburbs.

The decline in the quality of life in the central cities particularly as a place to raise children has also been a factor in suburban growth. Concerning this Ranney says: "Noise, dirt, congestion, crime, the growing presence of slums, and a growing concentration of Negroes became forces which pushed those who could afford it to move out of the city."[7]

In this period of suburban expansion the decentralization of living places has been accompanied by a decentralization of economic activities and hence employment opportunities. The growth of suburban retail markets and automobile ownership has resulted in the development of modern, automobile-oriented shopping centers of various sizes, some rivaling the central business district itself. Highway commercial uses have also been proliferating in the suburbs. Consequently the retail functions of many central business districts are either barely maintaining themselves or are declining.

The scarcity of available land for off-street parking and loading, for outdoor storage, and for plant expansion, together with the costs of congestion and the conversion of manufacturing processes from vertical to horizontal has caused industry also to seek suburban locations where more land is available less expensively.

Suburban residential development is on the whole a disorderly patchwork of subdivisions, large and small, multifamily housing in large and small groupings, interspersed with various sizes of shopping centers, straggling strip commercial, industrial areas, community facilities, and skipped-over undeveloped land. But these areas are substantial and have proven to be more to the taste of Americans than their detractors claim.[8]

The long-range impact of low-density sprawl, however, is not so immediately apparent because of the many factors involved. Low densities mean longer, higher cost utility runs, more street length to be paved, longer travel times to work, school, shopping, and community activities and facilities. Low-density development consumes more land, is more expensive to service and cannot support mass transit. As the energy crisis becomes more acute the inefficiency of heating and cooling physically separated units becomes a long-term public concern.[9] In support of these contentions the Real Estate Research authored, federal government sponsored, *The Costs Of Sprawl*, concluded:[10]

> . . . 'planning' to some extent, but higher densities to a much greater extent, result in lower economic costs, environmental costs, natural resource consumption, and some personal costs for a given number of dwelling units.

The proliferating suburbs have most often chosen to incorporate separately from the central city in order better to protect their property values, their way of life, and to avoid responsibility for central city problems. This has led to a pattern of development which is discriminatory to the poor and the minorities. The suburbs have indulged in exclusive and fiscal zoning practices, allowing only low-density housing, and trying to attract light industries for the taxes they will bring in. Low densities mean higher land costs and taken together with current high building costs the lower income groups can afford to live in suburbia only in subsidized housing if it is available. Furthermore the suburbs have resisted efforts to locate low-income housing in them even on a "fair share" basis.

The future of housing subsidies is in doubt. Sections 235 and 236 of the National Housing Act were modified in the 1974 Housing and Community Development Act to limit single-family mortgage, and eliminate multifamily dwelling mortgage insurance for lower-income families, while continuing direct family housing allowances on a limited, experimental basis. Critics of family housing allowances have pointed out that allowance programs may induce higher rental levels without encouraging the building of more housing because they are not tied in directly to new housing production, and they point out that the Kansas City housing allowance trial was largely a failure.[11]

Meanwhile in the central cities deterioration continues at a much faster rate than building and repair. Many residential buildings are abandoned in the face of the high costs of bringing them up to housing code standards, and few cities have adequate programs for coping with this situation although urban homesteading programs are increasing.

The central core areas of many cities are undergoing a boom in the construction of new hotels, office buildings, and convention centers, at the same time making many older structures obsolete. Urban renewal programs are inadequate for the task of stopping the decline of the vast areas of deterioration around the core, even if they were not being held up or stopped because of the inevitable disruption of the social and physical fabric of project areas and the failure to resolve conflicting goals. The disadvantaged in renewal areas have all too seldom been the beneficiaries.

The poor and minorities are increasingly concentrated in central cities and the inner suburbs. The housing supply available to them continues to be both inadequate and overly expensive in proportion to their incomes. Most new jobs are opening in suburban locations difficult to reach for those without cars. The poor cannot afford the city services which they require. The declining financial position of the cities makes the delivery of adequate services ever more tenuous.

Federal general revenue sharing promises some relief for central cities if they decide to use the money to supplement rather than supplant local revenues. The crucial question is whether localities will use these funds as intended by Congress without effective federal strings. The philosophy of the new Federalism of decentralizing decision-making by abolishing categorical grant programs is seen by some as a means of abdicating responsibility. Although there is a need for consolidating programs, increasing flexibility, and simplifying review procedures, there is an equal need for increasing accountability to insure that the most pressing problems are given the attention they deserve.

Although the problems of the suburbs and central cities are clearly interrelated, the fragmentation of government in metropolitan areas leaves them without a sufficiently strong instrumentality to make and carry out plans and policies. Few metropolitan areas have general purpose umbrella governments with plan implementation powers. Although the governments in metropolitan areas are increasingly pressed for solutions to persistent urban problems, they find themselves at cross purposes and unable to make effective inroads toward solutions which are politically acceptable.

The federal and state governments have been promoting the formation of metropolitan and regional councils of government made up largely of elected officials for the purpose of formulating comprehensive plans, coordination of policies, coordination of services, and the review of federal grant applications. Rarely have the states granted these councils more than review and recommending powers and most of them are dependent on their constituent governments for voluntary contributions to their budgets. Minnesota is a significant exception.

THE FEDERAL INVOLVEMENT IN URBAN AFFAIRS

Largely in the absence of any substantial help from the states, the cities have come to look increasingly to the federal government for help in solving their most intractable problems. In this they have met with singular success. The present age has been called the "age of creative federalism." The isolation of the cities from federal concern, symbolized by their not even having been mentioned in the federal constitution, is no longer so. There are no clear-cut lines between the domains of the national government, the states, and the various local governmental entities.

Until just recently, the principal involvement of the federal government in local affairs has been by way of federal grants-in-aid hedged in by numerous requirements of the requesting recipients. In these programs the Congress has taken the reasonable position that if it dispenses funds to the localities it wants to be assured that the money is being thoughtfully and well spent. Accordingly rules have increasingly come into being requiring projects funded to be in accord with comprehensive plans, coordinated, and not in conflict with other projects or plans of neighboring jurisdictions. Further, there is usually a requirement for citizen participation in an effort to insure that those most affected will have a voice in the decision-making.

Often, however, local governmental problems have been compounded. There has been a tendency with each new federal program to develop a new administrative mechanism which is superimposed over the already great proliferation of local entities. The persistent use of semi-independent special districts and authorities tends to result in splintering and reducing the authority of chief executives. The network of working relationships becomes more tangled with each new program.

With the advent of the Nixon administration and what is called the New Federalism there has been some attempt to counter this effect. In

1971, when there were over 530 separate categorical grant programs, integrated grants were introduced as a new way of harmonizing federal assistance with local work programs. Under this new program selected state and local governments were allowed to apply for a number of federal assistance grants by means of a single application. This represented a very considerable simplification over conventional grant administration and has been extended under the 1974 Housing and Community Development Act. In 1973 federal general revenue-sharing began. Under this program for the first time the federal government returned a portion of the federal income tax to the states and localities without the funding being designated for specific programs or any detailed accountability being required. Whether the money will prove to be effectively spent remains to be seen.

Certainly one of the problems in the array of federal grant programs has been the lack of consistent goals for the programs as a whole. In fact, many of the programs have conflicting primary and secondary effects. It has been politically expedient for the Congress to satisfy the conflicting goals of local groups with conflicting programs and leave it to the localities to resolve the resulting differences. Fortunately this is increasingly coming to be seen as a very wasteful process and the pressures for a national urban policy are increasing.

In the Housing and Urban Development Act of 1970 the Domestic Council Committee on National Growth was established "to assist in the development of a national urban growth policy", reporting to the Congress every two years. The first report of this committee in 1972 was very conservative. It recommended congressional passage of the President's government reorganization proposals, especially the consolidation of programs affecting urban areas in a new Department of Community Development; both general and special revenue sharing, expanded rural credit, planning and management assistance, encouraging the states to assume responsibility for dealing with development decisions that have a significant land use impact, state programs for power plan siting, new tax policies for the conservation of natural and cultural values, and welfare reform.[12] Throughout, the report reflected the New Federalism philosophy of the federal government assuming less responsibility for policy decisions in favor of more responsibility being assumed by the states and localities.

The second report in 1974, while still taking note of the difficulties of developing a unified national growth and development plan, is less conservative. It calls for the Domestic Council to take a more active role in policy and program coordination at the national level and for the improvement of communications between all levels of government. [13] Accordingly, it seems unlikely that the Congress and the constituencies benefiting from myriad federal programs will allow the partnership between the federal establishment and the cities to be more than temporarily disarranged. Graham Finney notes that: [14]

> . . . the picture today is characterized by an extensive lobby representing the nation's cities in Washington—among others, the U.S. Conference of Mayors and the National League of Cities, plus individual city representatives alert to the interests back home.

Also there are newer lobbying organizations like the Urban Coalition and its political arm, Common Cause.

THE STATE INVOLVEMENT IN URBAN AFFAIRS

Local governments are entirely dependent on the state governments for the powers which enable them to plan and implement plans and policies. These powers are conferred by means of state planning enabling acts and supplementary legislation. Planning enabling legislation dates back to the 1920s in most states and much of it is modeled on the Standard State Zoning Enabling Act of 1922, and to a lesser degree on the Standard City Planning Enabling Act prepared by the U.S. Department of Commerce in 1926.

Under most of this, state enabling legislation planning is optional rather than mandatory. California and Oregon are among the more notable exceptions. Of course, the federal planning requirements previously noted have had a widespread effect in causing local planning bodies to be formed under the state legislation and have caused states to broaden their enabling legislation in the direction of regional and state planning.

Within states there is often a lack of uniformity of local planning procedures and almost every jurisdiction has differing planning implementation ordinances. The resulting legal jungle has led to recent proposals for some sort of review and appeals mechanism at the state level which would result in establishing uniform statewide standards for legal procedures and the legality of local ordinance content.

The domination of state legislatures by rural and small town representatives resulted in most state governments lacking interest in urban planning and urban problems, especially those of large central cities. For some time their interest has been focused on industrial development and the administration of Federal 701 planning funds in counties and urban places having populations under 50,000. Redistricting mandated by the U.S. Supreme Court has eased this situation somewhat, but with the major population growth in the suburbs and with the central cities losing population the major interest is likely to shift to suburban areas and problems.

Although at present most metropolitan areas receive federal funds directly, there are proposals that these funds be channeled through the states thus strengthening the state role in metropolitan planning and development. State planning has had federal funding available since the 1960s and there are proposals to make more money available for state-wide planning purposes.

The increased interest in state planning has been expressed in the creation in a number of states, of departments of urban affairs. These departments make it possible for these states to better coordinate all state activities which have an effect on urban areas of all sizes. They can give attention to problems of local government such as structure, organization, finance, and planning. Increasingly the states are setting up liaison units to coordinate federal programs within them.

The state legislatures have been more active in the planning area. Both Florida and Massachusetts have new planning legislation. Hawaii is exercising statewide zoning as part of its state planning process. New York has established a State Urban Development Corporation to undertake and assist in urban development throughout the state. These and other innovations are described in later chapters.

States undertaking state planning have found that the division of the state into multicounty planning regions is an efficient tool for administering state programs. The regions are then able to qualify for federal planning funds and to function as coordination review agencies for local federal grant applications as is now required by the federal Office of Management and Budget (A-95 review).

GOVERNMENTS IN METROPOLITAN AREAS

With few exceptions the government in America's metropolitan areas is split between a bewildering number of frequently overlapping units of government. In 1967 these areas were served by 20,703 different local governments or an average of 91 per metropolitan area. For example: the Chicago area had 1,113; Philadelphia had 871; and the Pittsburgh area had 704. Only 20 metropolitan areas had less than 10 local governments each.

In population and physical size most of these local governments in metropolitan areas are extremely small. Two thirds of the units have populations of less than 5,000 and about half occupy less than a single square mile of land. Most metropolitan residents are served by at least a county, a municipality or township, a school district, and one or more special districts such as a sewer district, street improvement district, or fire protection district.[15]

These small units are usually quite weak. They generally lack the population, area, or taxable resources to apply modern methods in solving current and future problems. The overlapping layers are also a source of weakness. They are always in a struggle to obtain revenue from the same land parcels. The division of power among them often leaves no unit with sufficient power to cope with urgent community needs.

In *Modernizing Local Government*, the Committee for Economic Development points out further inadequacies in the local unit. They note that popular control over local governments is ineffective or sporadic, characterized by a low level of interest in local politics. The confusion of the many-layered system with its profusion of elective offices without policy significance together with population mobility, contributes to disinterest. Policy-making mechanisms in many units are weak and inhibit the kind of long-range planning and decision-making essential to effective local government. Antiquated administrative organizations lacking a single executive authority is a common fault causing the quality of administration to suffer. Except in the large cities and some wealthy suburbs there is a lack of technically qualified personnel in positions requiring modern skills. Low pay scales, the spoils system, and the attitudes of influential citizens have contributed to amateurism in local government.[16]

At the same time that metropolitan areas are lacking administrative structures capable of handling overall systems-wide problems, there is at the other end of the scale a lack of responsiveness to the localized problems of neighborhoods, especially in the central cities. Minority groups feel particularly distressed at their lack of control over policy matters local to their individual communities. The desire for a strong sense of local pride and community identity is shared by both the suburbs and the inner city neighborhoods.

These divergent needs in metropolitan areas have led the Committee for Economic Development in its metropolitan government reform proposals to advocate a two-level governmental system:[17]

> The interdependence of activities within metropolitan areas requires area-wide institutions for some functions or parts of functions of government. Just as clear is the need for units of government small enough to enable the recipients of government services to have some voice and control over their quality and quantity.
>
> To gain the advantages of both centralization and decentralization, we recommend as an ultimate solution a governmental system of two levels. Some functions should be assigned in their entirety to the area-wide government, others to the local level, but most will be assigned in part to each level.

The CED proposal, however, conspicuously avoids suggesting which functions should be allocated to which level, a matter of major contention wherever federated metropolitan governments have been formed. In Metropolitan Dade County, for example, the constituent local governments have vigorously fought every attempt of the metro government to take over locally exercised functions, and the second county manager, Irving G. McNayr, after trying to cope with the continuing local entities came to the conclusion that they should be abolished in favor of a single unified government.[18] On the other hand Banfield and Grodzins in criticizing metropolitan consolidation arguments raise a number of significant questions concerning the economic, political, and social benefits of metropolitan reorganization to the population involved.[19] They conclude that no general recommendations can be made either for or against metropolitan reorganization; each situation must be individually evaluated.

Attempts to form area-wide general purpose metropolitan governments have met with only a few qualified successes; Toronto, Miami, Nashville, Jacksonville, and Indianapolis being the most notable examples. More widespread has been the setting up of metropolitan special purpose districts to deal with area-wide problems. These involve such dissimilar purposes as parks and recreation, sewer and water utilities, public transportation, and metropolitan planning.

Where the planning function has been established at the metropolitan level it has very rarely been accorded either the ability to fund itself or to exercise any of the important tools for the implementation of plans and policies. Being merely advisory, these agencies have had relatively little success in getting major plans and policies carried out. Partly as a result of this some areas established councils of governments made up of elected officials from the metropolitan area's local governments for metropolitan planning purposes. It was hoped that these councils would be more effective than purely appointive commissions in coping with the essentially political nature of agreement on metropolitan-wide plans and policies and achievement of their implementation. Sharing this point of view, the federal government for some time has been promoting the formation of councils of government through requiring them in all metropolitan areas to be solely responsible for metropolitan-wide planning. Although these councils are voluntary and essentially weak, there is some hope that they represent a step on the road to the reform of government in metropolitan areas.

At the neighborhood level planning that has failed to take into account citizen reactions, especially transportation planning and urban renewal planning, has run into serious trouble. As a result, metropolitan planning agencies have begun to experiment with different means of obtaining local citizen input more effectively.

THE PLANNING AGENCY

The relationship of the planning function to local government takes a number of forms. There is no uniformly prescribed way in which it can or must take place. Some of these serve particular governmental situations better than others. The three major situations are: (1) the locality with a strong executive form of government; (2) the locality with a weak executive or commission form of government; and (3) the area with geographically related but varying units of government served by a single overall planning agency.

Where the municipality or county has a strong executive form of government the planning agency must be close to the executive and is usually a department of government which may or may not have a lay advisory commission.

Where the municipality or county has a weak executive, or executive responsibilities are divided among the legislative group, the planning agency either reports directly to the legislative group as a whole, or indirectly through a lay advisory commission.

Where the planning agency plans for a varying but geographically related group of governments it usually reports to a lay advisory regional planning commission or is a department reporting to a regional council of governments. If the grouping of governments is within a single county, in some instances a county-wide agency undertakes planning for the county as a whole, reporting to both the county government and to the municipalities within it.

The prevailing form of agency arrangement involves responsibility to an independent or semiautonomous commission. This is in large part a result of requirements spelled out in state planning enabling legislation. Most of this legislation reflects at least in part the proposals in the State Standard Zoning Enabling Act (1922, revised 1926) and/or the Standard City Planning Enabling Act (1927, revised 1928). Most students of government, and an increasing number of planners, feel that the staff departmental form of agency leads to more effective implementation of plans and policies because it brings planners into more direct contact with the politicians responsible for making implementation decisions. In the departmental form an advisory lay planning commission may be retained. As previously noted councils of government made up of elected local officials may have similar advantages over regional planning commissions.

Another organizational form of planning agency in increasing favor is the urban development department which typically combines in one administrative entity: planning, urban renewal, public housing, and code enforcement. This has the virtue of putting most of the planning implementation means under the control of a single director where they can be more effectively coordinated toward comprehensive planning ends.

The administrative planning agency as exemplified by the New York City Plan Commission and the Puerto Rico Planning Board is still another, though infrequent, variation of organizational form in which the planning agency operates essentially as an independent regulatory agency.

Because so few metropolitan areas have consolidated governments, the usual metropolitan planning situation is one in which there are a number of local planning agencies, and regional planning is done by the planning staff of an often just recently formed council of governments. Where regional planning had been already going on it is now being reorganized under such councils. Because councils of government are voluntary agencies lacking statutory powers and made up of representatives of local entities having vastly varying goals and degrees of sophistication in looking at urban problems, it is difficult for these councils to cope with tough problems of resolving value conflicts. Usually the more populous localities are underrepresented on these councils which makes them grossly undemocratic, and the problem of just representation is now an important issue in some metropolitan areas. The most important tool most of these councils now have is their influence as local federal grant request (A-95) review bodies pursuant to U.S. Bureau of Budget and Management requirements. Through helping to direct public investments and federal programs in metropolitan areas they may well come to have a significant role in influencing metropolitan development if they can be strengthened.

PLANNING AND THE URBAN LAND MARKET

Americans traditionally have great faith in the concept of the free enterprise market. The ideal market presumably would result in the most equitable distribution of the goods being traded, at least from an economic point of view. Similarly it is reasoned that a free and unrestrained urban land market should result in each parcel being put to its optimum "highest and best" use. Unfortunately the land market is one of the least perfect markets. Almost none of the requirements for an ideal market are met in dealing with urban land.

Benson and North describe some of the characteristics of that market as follows:[20]

> The market for urban real estate is localized because of the characteristics of real estate. For example, if there is no demand for a particular kind of real estate where it is located, it cannot be transported to where there is demand.

The real estate market is unorganized to the extent that there is no fixed market place, no daily quotations on real estate, and no machinery for short selling. The market is largely an 'over the counter' market, made by brokers.

The market for real estate tends to be thin, sluggish, and erratic. It is thin because a large investment is usually involved, and therefore at times buyers are hard to find for particular properties. It is sluggish because there are technical difficulties involved in passing title and in giving possession. Then, too every transaction involves a careful investigation of the particular property in order to decide what price shall be paid. It appears to be erratic because the market tends to be very active or very inactive. This condition is due to the fact that real estate does not respond quickly to changing economic conditions.

Richard Andrews observes that the land market lacks the characteristics of the buyers and sellers being well informed because of the great variability of physical properties and locations, and the infrequency of most of the participants having market transaction experience. Professionalization of brokers and the growing use of multiple listing mitigates this information gap somewhat. Further there is an inability of the supply to expand and contract quickly in response to increases and decreases of demand. No two pieces of property are identical and this adds to the difficulties of making valid comparisons. The ability to finance purchases may vary sharply with property size and location. Demand effectiveness is heavily dependent on credit availability. Because of tax pressures vacant lots are liable to stay on the market much longer than vacant buildings. The frequent deliberate withholding of land from the market for speculative reasons is a violation of the perfect market requirement that the seller will always sell at the prevailing market price. Moreover, local governments cannot avoid affecting the land market through their tax policies and investments in public facilities such as streets, schools, parks, and utilities.[21]

In the built-up portions of cities it is often assumed that according to succession theory land uses undergo a process of growth, decline, and rebuilding automatically. And in some older parts of cities it is clear that private market conditions make it feasible for obsolete uses and/or structures to be replaced by those more appropriate to current market conditions. At best, however, this is a spotty and time-consuming process which is inefficient and contributes greatly to urban ugliness, especially in transition periods. As obsolescence spreads outwards from the city center it occupies more and more space. The area of obsolescence then frequently exceeds that needed by successor uses or lacks the locational amenities necessary to support these uses. When this occurs the property reaches a low plateau of value marked by such characteristics as dilapidation, abandonment or clearance and land vacancy.

Inner city residential areas are particularly subject to the various aspects of property dereliction. Attempts to maintain them in residential use through building and housing code enforcement often fail because the populations in these areas are already overburdened by disproportionately high rents and cannot afford the extra increments of rent necessary to pay for bringing these properties up to code.

Suburban properties, on the other hand, suffer the inefficiencies of spotty development. Many properties ripe for development are bypassed because they are overpriced or the owners are for one reason or another unwilling to sell. The resulting extra costs of utilities and services are passed on to the community as a whole.

Many planners feel that planning intervention in the land market is necessary to compensate for the distortions in land use patterns which would otherwise occur as a natural result of the characteristics of the market described above. Lloyd Rodwin has said that the planner's position ". . . presupposes in effect the correction, sometimes even the elimination of the market process."[22] In *Nations and Cities* he elaborates on this:[23]

> At present, we have neither accurate tools with which to anticipate urban growth nor the equivalents of thermostatic devices with which to alter its direction and scale. Market mechanisms are supposed to perform these functions. However, when there are sluggish or inflexible adjustments to price signals, differences between private and public costs, and inadequate or wrong information, these market mechanisms work badly. And, for groups living outside the economy or for groups which are unresponsive to economic rewards and penalties, they do not work at all. To make the mechanisms perform better, we would need more relevant information, some effective incentives and controls, and a reasonable concensus on what we want to occur.

Marion Clawson states it this way: "The basic role of urban planning, in economic terms, is to maximize the favorable land use externalities and minimize the adverse ones."[24] The private market does not require the entrepreneur to consider the externalities which his development decisions visit on others. He is free to create conditions which might blight neighboring properties as service stations usually do when located next to residences.

The traditional tools the American planner has at his disposal are for the most part inadequate for effective intervention in the land market for the purpose of carrying out land use plans. A brief discussion of these tools follows after which each will be examined in greater depth.

THE TOOLS FOR IMPLEMENTING PLANS

The tools for carrying out comprehensive plans have not been developed systematically. Zoning and subdivision regulations, two of the most important tools, came into existence to solve specific land development problems independently of the planning process and have frequently been used in the absence of planning. Most of the tools used for carrying out planning have been adapted for planning purposes rather than having been designed for them. Nonetheless there is a recognizable group of instrumentalities and strategies for carrying out plans as part of the planning process which can be described and evaluated for their relative usefulness in solving urban development problems.

Most of the legal tools—controls by code or ordinance—are restricted to the governmental entities to which legislative powers are delegated: the counties and municipalities. In some cases they may be exercised by the state government itself. The noncoercive tools such as the right to plan, to review proposals, and to participate in giving planning advice, have been more broadly delegated.

The legislative tools are established through grants of authority from the state. They consist in delegations of the four basic powers of government: the police power, the power of eminent domain, the taxing power, and the spending power.

The police power is manifested in the enactment of regulatory legislation designed to protect and enhance the public health, safety, morals, and general welfare. Several planning controls used for guiding urban development and carrying out plans are based on this power. The most important of these are: zoning, subdivision regulations, official maps, building codes, housing codes, health codes, fire codes, and business licensing. There are also miscellaneous ordinances controlling such things as signs, esthetics, historic preservation, mobile homes, and flood plains which can be and usually should be made part of the zoning ordinance itself.

Eminent domain is the power to take land for public purposes with just compensation. It is usually exercised in conjunction with the spending power, which is the right of government to spend public monies for public purposes. These two powers are often involved in the condemnation of land for road and utilities rights-of-way and for development sites for such community facilities as civic buildings, schools, parks, fire stations, and other public uses. These powers are also the basis for public housing and urban renewal activities. The use of eminent domain, however, is usually avoided whenever it is possible to negotiate purchasing because its use tends to create adverse public reactions.

The principal use of the taxing power is to raise money for the financing of government spending. A related part of this power is the right to borrow as well. To a lesser degree taxing has been used to redistribute wealth and to encourage or discourage certain kinds of private expenditures and the activities associated with them. Although the property tax remains the principal backbone of local government finance, local sales taxes, local gross income taxes, and federal revenue sharing provide increasing percentages of local tax income. Except for tax incentives to businesses and industries, intended to cause them to locate within localities, and partial exemptions for restrictions placed on historic properties, local taxes and tax policies have been little used directly as a planning tool. There has been an increasing amount of discussion, however, by planners and other professionals concerning more direct use of the taxing power in the guidance of urban development and as a relief to agriculturalists wanting to resist the pressures toward urbanization. The proposed tax reforms include land-only taxes, unearned increment taxes, tax deferral, differential taxation, and tax-base sharing.

The spending power of government can be used to direct growth through public investments and influence economic activities through public expenditure patterns. Spending may be used to create or control access, to attract private investments through the creation of nuclei of public investment, to reserve scenic views and create public open space, to reserve open land for future development and to reduce the cost of overpriced land through "write downs" to marketable levels. Closely related to the spending power are the administrative tools of financial planning and capital budgeting. Through these devices government income and expenditures can be systematically coordinated for carrying out the public portions of the comprehensive plan.

The comprehensive plan itself carries weight as a statement of public intentions, especially if adopted and adhered to, and may be considered an administrative tool for implementation of the plans and policies it contains. As such it is one of the group of tools which Lachlan Blair characterizes as "advice and persuasion."[25] Included in this group are the public information functions of the planning office, the formal and informal working relationships which the planning staff and commissions have with other public agencies at all levels of government, and public relations including citizen participation.

Public authorities are another important category of planning tool. They may be single or multiple purpose in nature established to carry out a wide range of purposes involving planning, housing, transportation, new towns, center city development, industrial development, land acquisition and almost any other aspect of the development process. Public housing and urban renewal are usually undertaken by such authorities. Their severest limitation as a planning tool derives from the high degree of policy-making autonomy which many of these authorities enjoy, but when required and effective interagency coordination can be secured they can be very useful in carrying out planning purposes.

The succeeding chapters examine each of the major planning tools and techniques, evaluate their various aspects, describe reforms that have been experimented with or proposed, and suggest the most hopeful directions for their improvement within the American context.

NOTES AND ACKNOWLEDGMENTS FOR CHAPTER 1

1. Reprinted with permission from "The Future of American Planning—Requiem or Renascence?," by John W. Reps, in *Planning 1967*, p. 47, copyright 1967 by the American Society of Planning Officials.
2. Reprinted from "Metropolis Lost, Metropolis Regained," by Martin Meyerson

and Barbera Terrett in Vol. 314, (November 1957) of *The Annals* of the American Academy of Political and Social Science, pp. 1–3.

3. Meyerson and Terrett, *op. cit.*, pp. 1–3.

4. Wilson, James Q., "The War on Cities," reprinted with the permission of the author from *The Public Interest*, No. 3, (Spring 1966), p. 31. © by National Affairs Inc.

5. Banfield, Edward C., *The Unheavenly City*, (Boston: Little Brown, 1968), pp. 3–22.

6. Clawson, Marion, *Suburban Land Conversion in the United States: An Economic and Governmental Process*, (Baltimore: Johns Hopkins Press, 1971), p. 37. Copyright © 1971 by the Johns Hopkins Press. All rights reserved. Reproduced by permission.

7. Ranney, David C., *Planning and Politics in the Metropolis*, (Columbus: Charles E. Merrill, copyright 1969), p. 89.

8. For a good description of suburban culture the reader is referred to Herbert J. Gans, *People and Plans*, (New York: Basic Books), chapters 10, 25 and 26.

9. "Density Lowers Demand in a Time of Power Shortage," *Planning*, **39**, No. 9, (October 1973), p. 8.

10. Real Estate Research Corporation, *The Costs of Sprawl: Executive Summary*, (Washington: U.S. Government Printing Office, 1974), p. 6.

11. Jacobs, Scott, "The Housing Allowance Program in Kansas City Turns into a Notable Failure," *Planning*, **39**, No. 9, (October 1973), pp. 10–13.

12. Domestic Council Committee on National Growth, *Report on National Growth 1972*, (Washington: U.S. Government Printing Office, 1972), pp. 66–74.

13. ———. *Report on National Growth 1974*, (Washington: U.S. Government Printing Office, 1974), pp. 86–97.

14. From Graham S. Finney, "The Intergovernmental Context of Local Planning" in William I. Goodman, ed., *Principles and Practice of Urban Planning*, (Washington: International City Management Association, copyright 1968 by the Association), p. 37, reproduced by permission of the publisher.

15. Committee for Economic Development. *Reshaping Government in Metropolitan Areas*, (New York: The Committee, 1970), p. 13.

16. ———. *Modernizing Local Government*, (New York: The Committee, 1966), pp. 11–13.

17. ———. *Metro Areas*, pp. 18–19.

18. McNayr, Irving G., "Recommendations for Unified Government in Dade County," in *Government of the Metropolis*. Joseph F. Zimmerman, ed., (New York: Holt Rinehart Winston, 1968), pp. 191–99.

19. Banfield, Edward C., and Grodzins, Morton, "Some Flaws in the Logic of Metropolitan Reorganization," in *Metropolitan Politics*, Michael N. Danielson, ed., (Boston: Little Brown, 1966), pp. 142–52.

20. Benson, Philip A., and North, Nelson L., *Real Estate Practices and Principles*, 3rd ed., (New York: Prentice-Hall, copyright 1922, 1938, 1947), pp. 9–10, reproduced by permission.

21. Andrews, Richard, *Urban Land Economics and Public Policy*, (New York: The Free Press, 1971), pp. 15–22.

22. Rodwin, Lloyd, "Land Economics in the United States," *Town Planning Review*, **21**, No. 2, (July 1950), p. 178. © Liverpool University Press, reproduced by permission.
23. ———. *Nations and Cities*, (Boston: Houghton Mifflin, 1970), pp. 3–4. Copyright © 1970 by Lloyd Rodwin. Reprinted by permission of Houghton Mifflin Company.
24. Clawson, *op. cit.*, p. 180, reproduced by permission.
25. Blair, Lachlin F., "Programming Community Development," in *Principles and Practice of Urban Planning*, William I. Goodman, ed., (Washington: International City Managers' Association, 1968), p. 379. Copyright 1968 by the Association. Reproduced by permission of the publisher.

2

Zoning

Zoning developed in the late 19th and early 20th centuries primarily as a means of controlling nuisances and of protecting property values through the regulation of land uses. It has proven to be a vast improvement over the resolution or prevention of land use conflicts, through nuisance litigation or the enforcement of private restrictive covenants. It provides the benefit of preventing conflicting uses from coming into being through public action, before development takes place, but it is not a very good device for solving existing conflicts or for promoting desired development as envisioned in a land use plan.

Most early regulations dealt only with those uses considered a danger to life itself and they were not retroactive as were actions taken under the law of nuisance. In 1915 the U.S. Supreme Court upheld the use of the police power to eliminate a nuisance by regulation.[1] The first significant modern ordinance in the United States was adopted by New York City a year later in 1916. It provided for the division of the entire city into districts for differing land uses, building heights, and lot coverages. A decade later zoning was firmly established as a constitutional use of the police power in the Euclid, Ohio case.[2]

The U.S. Department of Commerce in 1922 developed the Standard State Zoning Enabling Act (revised 1926) and in 1927 prepared a related Standard City Planning Enabling Act (revised 1928) as models for state planning and zoning enabling legislation. The Planning Act provided for independent city planning commissions with the power to enact zoning ordinances. This act was adopted in some form by a great many state legislatures during the early 1930s. Subsequently many cities established planning commissions and adopted zoning ordinances. At the urging of their city councils these cities frequently moved directly from the level of very general plans to detailed zoning regulations without acquiring any local planning staff or establishing ongoing planning programs.

THE NATURE, PURPOSE, AND LEGAL BASIS OF ZONING

Zoning provides for the division of a local governmental unit into districts by categories of allowed and/or prohibited land uses. Within the districts zoning regulates the height and bulk (cubage) of buildings and other structures (such as walls and fences); minimum lot sizes; the amount of open space (yards); and requirements for such uses as parking and off-street loading.

Most property owners look to zoning for protection from nuisances and preservation of the value of their properties through control over the physical character of the local area. This control is now being extended to include historic preservation and the esthetic aspects of development.

Americans have tended to interpret the right of protection of property to mean protection not only from impingement by government but also from impingement by competing private interests such as speculative developers and unwanted newcomers or the dominance of a private developer over less influential private interests. However, the courts have declared that the use of zoning to accomplish racial segregation or to create private monopolies in opposition to the public interest is clearly unconstitutional and the use of large-lot zoning or other restrictive measures to accomplish exclusion of lower income groups is under severe attack and will be discussed later.

Zoning is an exercise of the police power. As previously mentioned, the other basic powers of government are eminent domain, the taxing power, and the spending power. The police or regulatory power is used to establish laws for protecting the health, safety, morals, and general public welfare. Zoning ordinances must prove to be a reasonable exercise of this power or they risk being in conflict with the state or federal constitutional requirements of "due process."

Regulation based on the Standard Enabling Acts has been upheld in the courts as satisfying constitutional requirements. The creation of large zones governed by prestated regulations segregating conflicting uses from one another satisfies due process. ". . . prohibiting particular uses in particular zones was not viewed as a 'taking' of property rights, but rather as a regulation of externalities—a process the propriety of which was attested to by the nuisance law."[3]

The courts continue to examine individual zoning requirements for their constitutionality although, as previously noted, that of zoning itself is no longer in question. Not only must zoning ordinances meet the test of constitutionality but local units of government must exercise their delegated right to zone in accordance with state enabling legislation. Pursuant to the enabling legislation the local governmental unit may pass a comprehensive zoning ordinance. This ordinance must include the entire jurisdiction. All land within it must fall within some zone designated in the ordinance. But zoning differs from most other kinds of local laws in that the regulations for each district are distinct and different. Within each district, however, the provisions must be uniform for all those uses generally permitted by right. Some uses may be allowed conditionally in certain zones, being permitted only if certain specific criteria are met, possibly including geographical relationships.

Zoning ordinances based on the Standard Act attempt to detail all aspects of regulation and give little scope for discretionary authority. Of this tendency in American controls John Delafons observes:[4]

Since the values conferred or denied by land-use controls are great, their administration affords exceptional opportunities for graft and by the same token exposes them to strong pressures. The result, in America, has been a determination to eliminate the scope for discretion in land-use controls by formalizing them in a set of standard regulations and by laying down in advance the conditions under which, if at all, change may be allowed.

Most of the recent experiments and reforms in land use controls have, however, been in the direction of flexibility and increased delegation of discretionary authority.

THE RELATIONSHIP OF ZONING TO PLANNING

Zoning was not originated as a tool for planning, but planners have tried to use it for implementing plans with mixed results. In fact, many state enabling acts require zoning to be based on a comprehensive plan. Kentucky legislation, for example, even goes so far as to require that the comprehensive plan contain as a minimum certain specified elements and that it shall be based on adequate research.

The courts in reacting to the requirement that zoning be based on a plan have, unfortunately, concentrated on the question of whether *the zoning ordinance itself* constitutes a comprehensive plan rather than on whether the zoning map and ordinance are based on a separate land use plan or planning process.[5] Acceptance by the courts of the zoning map and text as *constituting* a comprehensive land use plan for legal purposes in spite of enabling legislation requiring a separate long range land use plan has weakened the case for zoning based on compre-hensive planning.[6] As a consequence, as Mandelker puts it: "While zoning 'in accordance' with a comprehensive plan has been required by statute in most of the United States, a firm planning foundation for the zoning ordinance has been the exception rather than the rule."[7] In a recent, welcome reversal of this stance the Oregon Supreme Court stated that ". . . zoning must be in accordance with a comprehensive plan."[8] This just possibly may presage more legal support for zoning based on planning in the future.

The attempt to use zoning for implementing comprehensive plan-ning is beset by several kinds of problems. Zoning, generally, is a weak tool for changing already existing uses to those envisioned in the plan.

Even in developing areas the designation of vacant properties for given uses in no way compels them to come into being. Usually unwanted existing uses are classified as nonconforming and subject to limitations intended to discourage their maintenance or expansion. The designation of vacant land for specific uses can only deter its development for nondesignated uses rather than bring into being the planned uses. Zoning creates vested interests and is vulnerable to political pressure.[9]

An often unwanted effect of zoning in developing areas is that through zoning for eventually desirable intensive uses the price of vacant land may be driven up beyond the possibility of any developer being able to afford to develop it later for those intended uses. This is particularly true for shopping center sites. Often the prime corner of such a commercially zoned site will be sold for a service station (an activity which can afford high land prices) which then constitutes a kind of commercial intrusion into the overall site thus making it unattractive to shopping center developers. As a result the rest of the site is likely to remain overpriced and vacant until it eventually is subdivided into smaller plots often sold off piecemeal for strip commercial development. Some attempt to counter this kind of problem has been made by using "floating zones" and "contract zoning" which will be discussed later.

Another kind of problem in relating zoning to planning has to do with the time gap between the present reality of the zoning map and the future orientation of the land use plan. It is simply impractical to zone now for all the uses envisioned in the long-range plan as being ultimately desirable twenty years or so in the future, as this would encourage sprawl and spotty development. The comprehensive plan also tends to be looked at as an end-state document despite the usual existence of machinery for its periodic revision. Reactions to this problem range from one of abandoning the traditional land use plan in favor of having a body of land use policies to one of making the land use plan a continually revised working document of the local legislative body. Another possibility would be the development of stage development plans for shorter intervals of time detailing how land uses should be altered from the present to the time horizon of the long range plan. In this case the zoning ordinance could be tied to the shortest range of these staged plans. For success the short-range plans would have to reflect an intimate understanding of the land conversion process and a better understanding of the political process than do most current plans.

Despite these problems zoning is one of the most powerful tools the planner has for controlling the characteristics of physical development and efforts are continually under way by planners and the legal profession to make zoning into a more effecting planning tool. Some of these innovations and proposals for the reform of zoning will be discussed later in this chapter.

PROPERTY AND TERRITORY SUBJECT TO ZONING

Inasmuch as zoning is primarily intended for the control of private development, all privately owned property is usually subject to zoning control. Some private groups such as utilities may be made exempt from local control. Zoning may extend to include submerged lands within the jurisdiction of the locality. This latter coverage is important for the control of marinas and marine industries.

The zoning ordinance should also be concerned with public uses whether or not state legislation provides for control of such uses. As Robert Leary says:[10]

> Even if this control is not legally required, it is desirable to specify in the zoning ordinance the districts in which recreational facilities, schools, libraries, city garages, land fills, incinerators, fire stations, city halls and other public buildings are permitted, and the regulations controlling them.

The zoning ordinance should also provide for a special review process whereby all public projects are subject to planning review for their conformance to the comprehensive plan. Federal government facilities are generally exempt from local zoning ordinances but it is encouraging that the General Services Administration which is responsible for federal installations has recently adopted a policy of requiring all future projects to be in accord with local land use plans.

Because much of new development takes place outside municipal boundaries it has proven unsatisfactory to limit the power to zone to municipal boundaries. In reaction to this, well over half the states have authorized county zoning to bring controls to the urbanizing but unincorporated areas. Other states have established special planning regions encompassing urbanized and urbanizing areas permitting a single zoning ordinance to serve a group of local governments under a variety of conditions. A third approach adopted by a few states has been for the states to grant the cities extraterritorial zoning powers.

Through enabling legislation, then, the states may confer the power to zone on municipalities, counties, or regional organizations. In fact, some states authorize all three types of zoning. In others the power to zone is restricted to the localities. Zoning at the county level is becoming of increasing importance as understanding spreads of the usefulness of zoning in both urbanizing and rural areas.

Only Hawaii has used state-wide zoning as a tool for carrying out its state plan. All land there is classified into four zones: urban, agricultural, rural, and conservation with regulations for each zone except the urban zones where the counties are delegated the right to control land uses at their own discretion.[11]

In 1969 Oregon passed a law making zoning mandatory for all its cities and counties by the end of 1971, and giving the governor power to adopt plans and zoning regulations for those that failed to do so.[12] Some other states have legislation enabling state control of certain land uses such as industrial location (Maine) or shoreline development (Wisconsin) or in certain critical areas (Florida and New Jersey).[13]

It should be pointed out that extraterritorial zoning has the distinct disadvantage of being undemocratic in that those affected citizens in the extraterritorial areas have no political representation on the council of the zoning locality. And in the case of regional zoning it is usually only the recommendatory power that is conferred upon the regional authority, the final right to zone being limited to the counties and municipalities.

ESTABLISHING A ZONING ORDINANCE: GENERAL CONSIDERATIONS

Standardization

No model zoning ordinance exists which generally fits most localities. The patterns of land use and development differ widely from city to city and region to region. Accordingly each ordinance must be tailored to the needs of the locality, although some zoning standards and procedures may be widely applicable. Many planners and planning lawyers feel that much of the content of zoning ordinances could be standardized throughout the whole of a state so as to make the handling of planning court cases more equitable. More uniformity of planning standards might also contribute to simplifying zoning for large-scale housing development. Nonetheless, there are important idiosyncrasies about each locality which make complete standardization of zoning ordinances impracticable beyond the extent of a metropolitan region. Chief among these obstacles are the historic pattern of older development and the local characteristics of new development.

Drafting the Ordinance

In drafting a zoning ordinance the locality must follow the provisions of its enabling legislation very closely. The prescribed procedures in the relevant enabling legislation must be rigidly followed or the courts may declare the entire ordinance invalid. The substantive requirements must also be met for the ordinance to be legally valid.

Most state planning enabling legislation requires the existence of a planning or zoning commission to be responsible for the task of drafting the zoning ordinance for adoption by local government(s). In the departmental form of planning agency there may be either no commission, an advisory commission or a special commission set up temporarily for the purpose of preparing the zoning ordinance. Close participation by the locality's chief legal officer can help insure conformance to the legal procedural requirements. The use of competent professional planners, either staff or consultant, to do the major drafting of the ordinance helps insure conformance to the substantive planning requirements. The active collaboration of both the legal and planning professionals should be required despite the argument of some members of each profession that they are rightfully the ones to do the whole job.

Interim Zoning

If there is no zoning ordinance in existence in the locality then the question of whether to pass an interim ordinance arises, especially if the local urban growth rate is high and the projected time for the preparation of the intended ordinance is lengthy, as it often is. The courts have invalidated ordinances which cover only part of the community so an interim ordinance must cover the community as a whole. Usually these ordinances do not designate districts on a map but provide for either maintenance of the status quo, or are based on the predominant use in each block.

The use of interim ordinances, however, is usually unwise because they are crude, unfair to many property owners, and give a false impression of the zoning process. The attitude of the courts toward these ordinances has varied. Those decisions in their favor have tended to take into account their overall objectives and consider them as precautionary measures designed to prevent undesirable development while the more permanent ordinance is being written and considered for adoption. Interim ordinances are also less likely to be upheld in court if the enabling legislation makes no provision for them.[14]

Necessary Research

The first task to be undertaken in connection with preparing the ordinance is information gathering. Two principal kinds of information are required: information concerning the community itself and information concerning good zoning ordinance practices based upon responsible professional observations and examples of successful ordinance provisions, especially innovations.

The community information must include a detailed accounting of land use, parcel by parcel, including such information as primary and auxiliary uses, building coverages, building heights, yard sizes, number of occupants, lot dimensions, and street widths. This information must be gathered, mapped, and analyzed to determine the predominant patterns for each kind of data. If there is a zoning ordinance already in effect it is important to compare existing uses with currently allowable uses to determine the extent of nonconformance. The land use information will probably be, or have been, collected in connection with the preparation of the land use plan.

Form and Content

Zoning ordinances are generally made up of two parts: a map showing the boundaries of the various zones or districts within the locality, and written regulations which explain the ways in which property within each district may be developed and used. The map and the regulations have to be prepared in a closely coordinated way. Involved is a careful reconciliation of the intentions of the comprehensive plan with the existing realities of urban development in terms of what is appropriate in the way of controls for each proposed district at the time of instituting the ordinance.

The zoning map must take into account the number of districts, the space to be allocated to each type of district, the suitability of the land for each type of district, the geographical relationships of the districts to one another, and the exact boundary lines of each district.[15]

Considerations of use, height, coverage, density, and other factors are usually combined for each zone into which the locality is divided rather than being separately districted. This simplifies the use of the ordinance by consolidating information.

The number and kinds of districts varies from community to community and is a reflection of the degree of specificity which the drafters think desirable. The tendency in American ordinances is to be very detailed in what is permitted, and the conditions under which it is permitted, rather than to give discretionary authority to the administrators of the ordinance. This often results in unreasonable rigidities which are contrary to the intentions of the comprehensive plan. Part of the root of this problem lies in the usual separation of zoning administration from planning and in the reluctance of American legislative bodies to delegate discretionary power to administrators. In Britain and other European countries there does not seem to be such reluctance and this has allowed considerable flexibility in the administration of planning controls as a result. Where administration of zoning is done within the department of planning or development and where professional competence of the administrators can be assured, it should be possible to write more simple ordinances delegating more case by case discretionary authority within clearly stated guidelines.

The development of use districts also involves compromise between permitting that which exists and adhering to the use standards embodied in the comprehensive plan. Land use plans tend to be very general while zoning ordinances must usually be quite specific. Accordingly many detailed decisions have to be made in translating the land use plan into a zoning map. (Figure 2-1 illustrates inconsistent zoning practices.)

The whole idea of zoning districts is predicated on the notion that

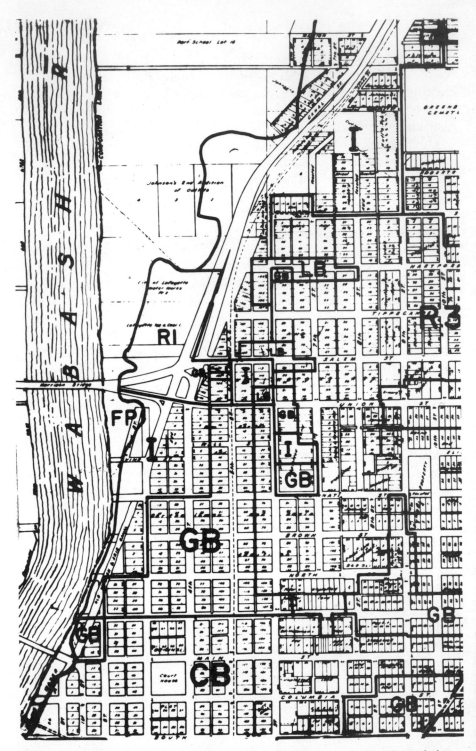

Figure 2-1. Typical Zoning District Map. *Source:* Tippecanoe Area Plan Commission, Lafayette, Indiana, 1978.

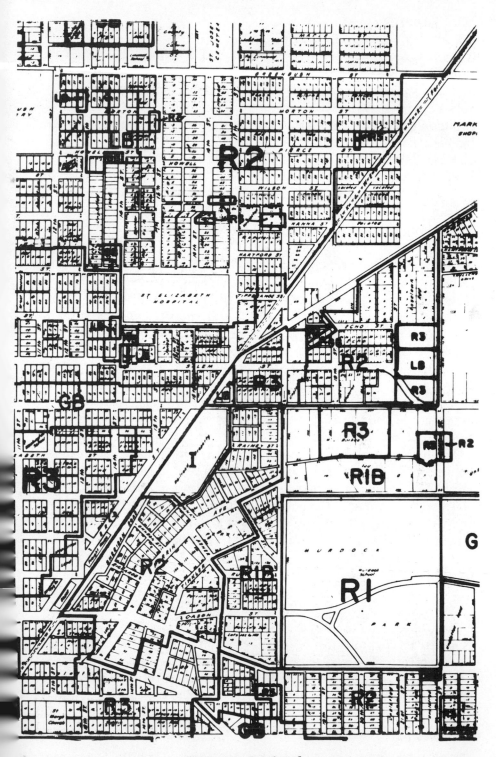

Figure 2-1 (*Continued*)

the segregation of certain uses from others reduces the effect of negative externalities which some uses have on others. Districting provides spacial segregation of conflicting uses but it often does not solve the externality problems where conflicting use districts have common boundaries. Segregation of uses into districts may also have the benefit of increasing positive externalities because many uses find an advantage in being grouped with other similar uses.

Early zoning ordinances developed a hierarchy of zones in which uses allowed were cumulative. Single-family residence was considered the highest use and was placed in a zone allowing that use exclusively. Multifamily housing came next and in zones where it was allowed one could also build single-family houses. Commercial zones came next with all residential uses allowed in them. At the bottom of the list was an industrial zone in which all previous uses were permitted. This system of cumulative use zoning persists to some extent in many present zoning ordinances despite the resultant problems. Experience has shown that single-family residences in an industrial zone, for example, may be as detrimental to industrial development as the introduction of industries into residential zones. Consequently, many recent ordinances attempt to group compatible uses into separate zones. Further, planners are discovering that through architectural and site design requirements many uses not thought to be compatible may be made so.

The form in which the ordinance is put together is important to its being easily understood and accepted. Wherever it can be presented in tabular or graphic form, it should be for ease of use. Carefully worded statements of intent at the beginning of each section may also be used to increase ease of understanding. It is also important to have complete and unambiguous definitions in the ordinance in order to avoid confusion in administration.

Adoption

After the tentative draft of the zoning ordinance has been completed it is necessary to hold formal public hearings. These hearings are in addition to any formal or informal, public or semipublic, meetings with citizen groups which may have been held during the drafting of the ordinance. The procedure for these hearings is usually spelled out in the state enabling legislation and must be rigorously followed. If the hearings result in revision of the proposed ordinance then a second round of hearings on the revised proposal is necessary.

The adoption of the ordinance by the legislative body of the locality follows the same procedure as for any other kind of local ordinance. The ordinance itself usually provides for the mechanism by which it goes into actual effect, describes the procedures for amendment, and spells out certain aspects of enforcement such as: duties of the enforcement officer; right of entry to private premises; stoppage of use orders; and revocation of zoning permits.

Amendments to the zoning ordinance take the form of major amendments which are really a general overhauling of an outdated ordinance, minor revisions of the text to solve problems which have arisen in the use of the ordinance, and revisions in the zoning map. It is revisions in the zoning map which are most frequent and occupy most of the time the planning staff (and commission) spends on zoning. Because of the number of requests these revisions are so time-consuming that they can easily become the principal preoccupation of the planning controls administration staff and the commission. A major problem for planning directors is to achieve a balance of concern for zoning in relation to other planning activities, especially in the smaller agencies.

Because our cities usually develop and change in small increments, and zoning map changes are involved in very many of them, it is extremely important that each of these changes should have the most careful attention that the planning staff can possibly give them. Unfortunately some planners are so disenchanted with zoning that they do not use it as effectively as is possible.

Land Use Districts

The predominant practice in land use districts is to segregate each use or group of compatible and similar uses into separate districts. Some ordinances in recent times have taken the approach of increasing the number of use districts in order to deal with as many specific situations as possible and reduce the need for administrative discretion.

As previously mentioned, another more promising approach is to reduce the number of districts but control the mix of uses through the use of design criteria aimed at eliminating undesirable externalities by controlling glare, noise, ugliness, traffic generation, parking, loading, and landscaping. In this way many uses formerly thought to be incompatible and blighting may be brought into harmonious relationships. Such districting often combines a list of uses-by-right with a list of conditional uses for which the conditions are very specific. This approach requires the careful identification of all factors which determine use compatibility. Extensive utilization of conditional use listings, on the other hand, has often been frowned upon by the courts as granting too much discretionary power.[16]

It is increasingly common for some zones described in the text of the zoning ordinance to appear infrequently or be absent altogether from the zoning map. These have been called "floating zones" and are granted to applicants when the use allowed in them is indicated on the comprehensive plan (often by symbol rather than district), but it is not practical to indicate specific sites on the zoning map in the absence of a bona fide developer. This technique is particularly applicable to such uses as shopping centers where early designation on the zoning map may actually indirectly prevent their coming into being. It is also applicable where a limited area of a particular use is appropriate in a general location, but the designation of the particular site for the use is not necessary in satisfying the policies of the comprehensive plan. This technique is subject to abuse and is less desirable than the conditional use technique when most of the criteria can be specified in advance.

The treatment of certain large projects often containing a mixture of land uses is sometimes handled under special procedures, usually termed *planned unit development*. Large-scale housing projects, shopping centers, office parks, and various combinations of these may be dealt with under these special procedures which involve detailed review of their design and local impact. There have been an increasing number of innovations in this kind of zoning which will be examined later.

Residential Uses

Residential uses continue to be the predominant uses of land in urban areas, and of these single-family housing consumes the most residential land. In the last decade, however, multifamily housing has exceeded single-family in the number of dwelling units started each year in many metropolitan areas. Another trend has been the increase in the number of modular and mobile homes as a proportion of the total single-family units each year. These trends are having an impact on zoning ordinances leading to attempts at accommodation to them on one hand and to attempts at resistance on the other.

The standard practice in zoning ordinances in the past has been to segregate residences by housing type and density simultaneously, grading the districts from low density single-family to high density multifamily, with a number of districts in between. Leary very aptly describes the reasoning behind this approach:[17]

> In general, the arguments made for this classification were that multiple family developments might damage property values in single-family districts, that they tended to cut off light and air of single-family neighbors, that their tenants took up all the curb parking space in the neighborhood, that the increased population density overloaded the street and utility systems, and that rental tenants did not take as good care of their properties as did owner-occupants in single-family residences.

The use-segregation approach to zoning districting is a very crude tool for solving the problems described above. Moreover, it has resulted in the very characteristics of American suburbia most criticized by urbanists. Segregation of housing types has most often resulted in segregation of family types and income groups. A lack of other than superficial visual diversity is also likely to accompany the lack of diversity of uses. Social exclusionary values thrive in these settings and the political expression of them increases the difficulties of implementing more general metropolitan-wide goals in regard to housing and community services. This aspect of zoning is dealt with more fully later in this chapter.

Recently, however, planners have been experimenting with eliminating the adverse features of mixing dwelling types through more detailed control of access, site design, and landscaping with districting based on residential density rather than housing type. Rather than providing a single set of standards for all uses within a zone, the standards for each use are separately tailored to significantly reduce or internalize externalities in relationship to all adjacent uses possible within the zone. The new zoning code for University City, Missouri is an example. It specifies the range of different housing types allowed in each district and the site planning standards for each type. In addition a review of site plans is required for some of the housing types in particular districts.[18]

Most zoning ordinances rely on the space between buildings as a means of increasing privacy and reducing other negative externalities. This often results in unusable sideyards which are an inefficient use of land and not very effective in providing privacy. The newer ordinances require such devices as fences, walls, landscaping screens, provision of off-street parking and loading, density controls, and the control of performance characteristics to insure privacy, adequate light and shade, and to create compatibility between adjacent uses. They may also have certain locational requirements such as permitting the denser uses only where their parking and loading areas can empty onto feeder streets or some higher level of street (with reference to an official street plan classifying the streets) so as to avoid excess traffic on local residential streets or so as not to empty into a major arterial and be detrimental to flow characteristics. When all of these conditions are spelled out in the text these uses become uses by right wherever in the district all the conditions can be met. In some states writing this kind of ordinance may be difficult because of requirement for uniform provisions within districts, but as long as it can be demonstrated that each category of use is being uniformly treated within a district a legal conflict should be avoidable.

Leary notes that it is argued that residential areas composed of mixed dwelling types are more interesting esthetically, more satisfying socially, and have the advantage of offering housing appropriate to the different stages of family needs without the necessity of the family leaving the neighborhood.[19] In addition the mixture of housing types may make possible a wider range of housing costs thereby permitting a better mix of income levels from the point of view of metropolitan housing policies. Further, it should be pointed out that residents in multifamily housing should be able to enjoy the same rights to environmental protection afforded those in single-family housing. Mobile home parks should be allowed only in residential zones subject to special criteria. This will be dealt with further on in this chapter.

A number of nonresidential uses have customarily been associated with and permitted in residential areas. Educational institutions,

religious institutions, social organizations, cultural centers, cemeteries, health facilities, recreational facilities, and agriculture-related
uses are among them. Sometimes these are permitted in residential
zones by right, and in other ordinances they may be permitted only as
conditional uses. Most of them present traffic generation and parking
problems and should be permitted in these zones only where these and
other externality problems can be solved. Some of these uses may no
longer be appropriate in residential zones and should be provided for
in separate zones as will be argued later. Efforts to confine them to
commercial zones may also be inappropriate, and the courts have not
looked on this approach with favor.[20]

Some home occupations have customarily been permitted in residential districts. Professional offices such as those of doctors, den-
tists, architects, beauty parlors, and art studios are examples. While
these uses may in some cases be innocuous, they can often create
severe problems. If they are permitted at all they require exacting restrictions which must be rigidly enforced. Among the items to be
regulated are the size of establishment, number of people permitted
to be employed, hours of operation, amount of traffic generated,
provisions for off-street parking and loading, signs, and visual
appearance.

Commercial Uses

Districting for commercial uses involves some of the most difficult
problems in zoning. In built-up areas old convenience-shopping clusters are shrinking and their fringes becoming derelict, as more and
more organized shopping centers with ample parking come into being.
Increased use of the automobile has also had the impact of decreasing
the density and increasing the quantity of auto-oriented strung-out
commercial strip development along major streets. In both old and
new centers problems of traffic conflict and overloads abound. The
increase in the number of grade-separated freeway interchanges has
also brought new problems in zoning for highway-oriented commercial uses. The proliferation of new commercial service uses of a drive-in
nature has been happening faster than planners have been able to come
to grips with their land use characteristics.

It is quite clear that many commercial uses are incompatible with one another and that finding the means of minimizing undesirable externalities may be far more difficult than simply segregating them as a whole. It is even less clear which uses could feasibly be grouped compatibly or even beneficially, especially among uses not usually found in organized shopping centers.

In an attempt to learn how to deal with existing highway commercial strip development better, the U.S. Department of Housing and Urban Development gave a demonstration grant to Woodbridge, New Jersey in 1967 for an intensive study of 1.9 miles of Route 1. The planning firm of Candeub, Fleissig and Associates undertook the study in cooperation with the Woodbridge Department of Planning and Development. The summary report recommended a many-faceted program using a number of devices beside zoning, but here it is interesting for the zoning proposals. In addition to tightening up all the other provisions of the zoning ordinance it proposed a finer breakdown of the permitted commercial uses. Four commercial subgroups were proposed: an automotive service group, a highway retail group, a highway service group, and a (non highway-oriented) general use group. This regrouping of commercial uses into more mutually compatible groups is a process which should be experimented with and further refined.[21]

At freeway interchanges and at some major arterial crossings it may be appropriate to locate a highway service zone which generally includes service stations, motels, restaurants, travel trailer parks, and other uses catering especially to the traveling public.

The grouping of automobile sales establishments into organized sales centers on large properties with internal circulation has met with some success in Cincinnati, St. Louis, and Riverside.[22]

Scale of development also poses special problems. Large developments such as shopping centers and office parks do not lend themselves well to the usual sort of treatment applied to incremental developments made up of small properties. Furthermore, the use of zoning map districting to locate them in advance of development is rarely workable.

Shopping centers can be economically healthy only if there are not too many of them. Each center must have a partial monopoly of its market area. On the other hand a complete monopoly would result in inconvenience and lack of choice for consumers. An intimate knowledge of shopping center economics is essential to the planner in determining feasible and desirable locations. The precise location of any given center may be of little consequence in carrying out the intentions of the comprehensive plan. What is important is the general spacing of centers of various sizes from the point of view of both economic viability and consumer convenience and the relationship of sites to the transportation network. Designation of sites in the zoning map in advance of a bona fide development proposal is likely to price the land in question out of the market because a locational monopoly has been prematurely accorded.

As a result, Leary says:[23]

> A number of jurisdictions have resolved this dilemma by spelling out in their ordinances the conditions under which an area will be rezoned for shopping center purposes and by placing the burden on the applicant to demonstrate that his tract meets these conditions. The city and county of Denver is one of many jurisdictions, experiencing rapid suburban growth, which reports success with this technique.

This technique is somewhat similar to that of the employment of "floating zones" but has the advantage of spelling out the criteria for establishing shopping center districts. These criteria should tie in with the comprehensive land use plan where shopping center locations are usually shown by a symbol indicating general location.

Although office space is growing in central areas, it is also growing in the suburbs, principally on the fringes of shopping centers and in planned office parks. There is a need for special commercial districts to recognize this trend and accommodate it. Commercial and office parks can often best be dealt with under nonresidential provisions of the planned unit development section of the zoning ordinance. Special enabling legislation such as New Jersey's may be necessary in some states in order to avoid trouble in the courts.

Central business districts are often treated separately from other commercial areas and the larger ones may even be divided into subdistricts according to function. Lively downtowns are likely to have a great mixture of uses, but the intrusion of some uses may produce dead spaces which discourage the pedestrian concentrations necessary for the continued health of these areas. Much downtown redesign and redevelopment has been underway in recent years as downtowns have, through increasing obsolescence, lost many of their functions to outlying organized commercial developments. Studies for downtown redevelopment have often led to the overhaul as well of zoning ordinances as they affect central business districts. Careful control of the mix of downtown uses is important if these areas are to remain in good functioning order. This mix includes vertically related uses as well as horizontally related uses.[24] In order to keep downtown areas alive at night and economically viable, residential uses are now being encouraged in these areas, often in buildings which also include retail business, garage parking, and office space as well.

In older areas unorganized retail areas need to be protected from intrusion by such incompatible commercial uses as filling stations, and nonshopping uses which can produce dead spaces in the district. These less compatible uses can be separately districted in more general commercial areas. Economic and physical compatibility must be carefully determined in drawing up use lists in commercial districting.

Industrial Uses

Most early industrial development occurred along railroads in central locations and was oriented also to workers' housing districts. Factories were frequently multistory and little if any provision was made for off-street parking and loading, or room for expansion. Growing industries met with difficult and often impossible problems when they needed additional land. This usually meant acquisition and demolition of adjacent residential or commercial properties.

Zoning districts for industry were originally the most cumulative in regard to permitted uses and the least restrictive. Industrial zones gave little or no protection to industry and required of it little or no amenity.

As more and more industries adopted the single-floor assembly line type of organization, and as they became more and more dependent on goods coming by truck and workers coming by car, they became larger consumers of land, often no longer able to afford central area development costs or to cope with central area land scarcities. Industry also became more image conscious as it established itself in outlying areas and came to prize the amenities of better architecture and landscaping, in part for their advertising value. Some industrial realtors developed exclusively industrial "parks" and demand for the protection of the new image of industry led to the exclusion of residential and commercial uses from industrially zoned districts and to the establishment of stricter controls, including the introduction of performance standards.

Industrial districts have customarily been divided into classifications of "heavy" or "light." More recently "industrial park" districts have commonly been added which tend to be very restrictive. It is common for some industries, deemed as nuisance or dangerous industries, to be allowed only as conditional or special uses requiring special permission, rather than being allowed by right. Zoning by means of performance standards rather than by use lists obviates the necessity of going through the difficult task of classifying each type of industrial use. Instead, there is substituted the control of such externalities as noise and vibration, smoke and fumes, odor, dust and dirt, glare and heat, fire hazards, industrial wastes, outdoor storage, traffic generation, and appearance. Districts are then established according to the strictness of the imposed standards, those uses unable to meet the stiffer standards being relegated to areas where lower standards are required.

The use of performance standards requires sophisticated techniques of measurement and well-trained personnel in sufficient numbers to insure continuing compliance. This is costly and beyond the capabilities of most smaller cities but is gaining favor in metropolitan areas large enough to afford it. Sometimes the costs are partly transferred to the individual industries concerned in technically complicated situations. With the new state and regional environmental protection programs comes the prospect of the locality relinquishing responsibility for enforcing the air and water quality portions of their performance standards unless they wish to maintain higher standards and are allowed by law to do so.[25]

Public, Quasi-Public, and Institutional Uses

Although, as previously mentioned, government entities have been traditionally exempt from zoning controls, it has become good zoning practice to subject them to the same restrictions as private owners, in the interests of carrying out comprehensive planning. Whether land is publicly or privately owned is not in itself relevant to the purposes of controlling the way in which the land should most appropriately be used. Whether schools, assembly halls, or recreation areas, for example, are publicly or privately owned does not affect the externalities they may visit upon, or have visited upon them, by adjoining development. Furthermore, failure to zone publicly owned lands can result in inappropriate development by the public, or in inappropriate zoning if the land is sold for private development. It is quite clear that government should not be permitted to develop at lower standards than private developers if it is to influence the quality of development in a positive way.

Because of inherent similarities, public uses can conveniently be grouped together with quasi-public and institutional uses, into a larger category which may be called civic activities (as it is in the Oakland, California zoning ordinance). "Civic activities include the performance of utility, educational, recreational, cultural, medical, protective, governmental, and other activities which are strongly vested with public or social importance."[26] Such semipublic uses as churches, clubs, and fraternal organizations should be included.

Once the decision has been made to treat civic uses separately in the zoning ordinance there are three principal ways of handling them: ". . . the conventional or multi-district approach, the special district, and the public use district. These alternatives are not mutually exclusive; a community might choose one of them or all three."[27] Of these approaches there has been least experience with the public use district.

Under the multidistrict approach the civic uses permitted in each district are listed district by district. This is the commonest form of regulating these uses. It is also usual to break up lists of civic uses into a number of subgroupings by similarity of characteristics, and allocate these to the appropriate district or districts by degree of mutual compatibility. Civic uses may be permitted in districts by right or as conditional uses having to meet special criteria. Many of them have unique characteristics requiring special treatment. Because most of them are major traffic generators it is common to restrict them to being on or near arterial streets, particularly in residential zones.

Special zoning districts are often established where functionally related civic uses are clustered or where the comprehensive plan indicates that such clustering should occur. Civic centers, medical centers, and institutional districts adjacent to major shopping centers are examples of groupings which often cluster naturally and can be both encouraged and protected through special districting.[28] Such districts may also include noncivic uses which are compatible, such as related residential and/or commercial uses.

The number and kinds of special zoning districts is a function of local land use patterns and city size. Where the planning policy is to create or strengthen activity nodes within the community the special zoning district can prove to be a useful tool.

The third approach involves putting all public and sometimes quasi-public uses in a separate "Public Use" zone. Unlike special zoning districts no attempt is made to subgroup these uses according to compatibility criteria and the emphasis is on public ownership. This is a cruder tool than special districting and is subject to the accusation of it being spot zoning if used for small parcels of land.[29]

Open Land Zoning

For a number of reasons cities may want to keep certain land areas in a predominantly open state either temporarily or permanently. They may want to keep some land open temporarily which is not yet ripe for development because it is not contiguous with existing development or because it lacks an adequate public service infrastructure and the community is not prepared to provide it. They may want to keep some land open temporarily because it will eventually be, but is not yet, needed for recreational or other public uses. They also may want to keep some land permanently in open land uses as part of a greenbelt or green wedges system (as in the National Capital Planning Commission's Year 2000 Plan), expressing major policies of the comprehensive plan.

Restricting land to agricultural, recreational, and other predominantly open land uses in high land value areas is often looked on by the courts as confiscatory, beyond the proper exercise of the police power, and necessitating compensation. Nevertheless agricultural zoning is common and has won court support where backed up by adequate planning. It is often accompanied by legislation for reduction of tax assessments or tax deferral. In urbanized areas, however, agricultural zoning usually permits very low density residential development on large lots. It can ". . . prohibit conventional subdivisions and other urban uses which (would) encroach upon the preservation of the prime agricultural resource. It is used as a holding zone to contain urban areas and force denser development rather than allowing sprawl and destruction of agricultural areas."[30] Such open land zoning can be used to prevent premature development or, if carefully tied to the comprehensive plan, be used to implement permanent open space where the courts are willing. Otherwise compensation for all or part of the property rights will be necessary for keeping the land in open uses.

Mixed Use Districts

Planners are increasingly concerned with the problem of accommodating complex mixes of land uses at close quarters, especially in central cores and satellite high density nodes.[31] The introduction of multifunctional megastructures such as Chicago's Marina City and John Hancock Building pose the problem of providing for uses mixed vertically as well as horizontally. Older development in a state of changing use mixes also may be amenable to the application of regulations permitting more complex use intermingling in a way which will protect and enhance both old and new.

The use of deed restrictions, particularly in urban renewal areas (and all over Houston) has achieved much in ensuring the compatibility of complex use mixes but there remains the substantial possibility of adapting zoning regulations to the same tasks. In order to do this, much better information is needed concerning the interrelationships of differing land uses at close quarters in regard to how and where compatibility can be established and maintained through regulation. Extensive information is also needed concerning real estate market conditions in the areas where mixed-use zoning is to be applied, so that market conditions can be used to advantage to make possible the intent of the regulations.

The mix of uses must be designed in a way which will encourage the replacement of obsolete uses such as marginal stores while protecting uses which are not obsolete such as low-income housing. The encouragement of redevelopment through overzoning for intensive uses must be avoided because it may drive out healthy existing uses or in some cases absorb the entire existing market for the new uses. Also great care must be taken in mixed-use districts to encourage an increase in levels of amenity at the same time that some increase in use intensity is permitted. Failure to do so may result in premature obsolescence of the new development.

Mixed-use districts may be appropriate, for example, in cities having inner city neighborhoods made up of large, old houses which are ripe for conversion into small apartments or offices. These districts may also have corner groceries and other minor commercial uses which should be retained. The commercial uses could be brought into a state of compatibility through the imposition of design standards providing for adequate off-street parking and loading, screen walls, open space, landscaping, and control of signs and architectural appearance.

SPECIAL USE REGULATIONS

In addition to the use controls embodied in the lists of uses permitted in each district there are other provisions in zoning ordinances affecting uses and dealing with special land use problems. These include: special handling of large development projects under provisions for planned unit development; regulating development in flood plains; review of building and site design for esthetic quality; preservation of historic districts, buildings, and sites; provision for conditional uses; and provision for phasing out nonconforming uses.

Planned Unit Development

The zoning districts previously described were designed primarily for lot-by-lot development. In the urbanizing parts of metropolitan areas, however, most new development now occurs in sizable acreages, each under the control of one development organization. Most of these developments are predominantly residential but may include ancillary commercial, recreational, and institutional uses. Usually a mixture of housing types is part of the proposal.

When these developments are forced to conform to the usual zoning restrictions the result is almost unvaryingly unimaginative, rigid, and lacking in amenity. In order to achieve both greater economy and higher design standards the planned unit development concept has come to be employed. As it is applied to residential development alone this concept is not new. It dates back to a model planning enabling law promoted by the Committee on the Regional Plan of New York in 1925. Only in the last decade or so, however, have large acreage developments become the dominant kind of development and the need for more flexible application of zoning requirements more obvious. Jan Krasnowiecki gives one explanation for the time lag:[32]

> Uniform lot, uniform dwelling type, residential development remained the safest and easiest form of development and there was nothing in the market or in the prevailing competitive conditions that would justify a departure.

Planned unit development involves a review of the proposed development plans and authorizes the review body to modify the district zoning requirements for the proposed development area in accordance with criteria, standards, and limitations set forth in the planned unit development (PUD) section of the ordinance. The planning commission is usually designated as the review body. Less frequently this responsibility is given to the board of adjustment, an unsatisfactory arrangement because of the board's less intimate contact with the planning process.

Concerning planned unit development Mandelker comments:[33]

> To the extent that the planned development method forces large tracts into the zoning process, of course, the chances for implementing the objectives of the comprehensive plan through any one development proposal are increased.

Special state enabling legislation is usually necessary and desirable before local ordinances are enacted although they have been upheld without it.[34] The New Jersey Municipal Planned Unit Development Act is one of the most comprehensive and well-written. It provides for a wide variety of land uses including industrial and enables either the planning board or municipal council to make the final decision on development decisions as provided for in the local ordinance. Where the planning board makes the final decision the courts have determined that this is not an illegal delegation of the power to zone.[35] In some states the designation of a PUD development is looked upon as a zoning change and requires action by the elected local body. This more conservative two-step process is advocated by Daniel Mandelker.[36]

Because most planned unit developments involve the subdivision and sale or lease of land it is necessary for most of them to obtain subdivision approval along with their zoning approval. For this reason the PUD ordinances need to provide for coordination of the zoning and subdivision approval processes. Large projects are usually developed over several years and the regulations should protect developers from changes in what is required of them between initial approval of the overall plan and their submission of the detailed plan for the last stage of a project.

The permit for a PUD involves approval of a precise plan. This plan must indicate in detail all land and building uses, their location, the bulk and height of buildings, and other pertinent information. Often it becomes desirable from the developer's point of view to vary from the plan somewhat as the development proceeds. The ordinance should state very clearly the degree to which the plan may be deviated from without the necessity of securing a new or modified permit.

Most planned unit developments provide for a substantial amount of open space which is separate from the constituent individual properties but is provided primarily for the benefit of the occupants of the development. Except for major parks and community facilities serving large areas the locality cannot be expected to accept dedication of this open space and assume maintenance of it. Accordingly it is necessary to require in the zoning ordinance that the developer of the PUD provide an effective mechanism for the ownership and maintenance of the development's common open space. A frequent solution to this problem involves cooperative or condominium ownership and responsibility for the open space by all property owners or lessees in the development. This is made part of the deed or lease of the individual properties.[37]

Flood Plain Zoning

The regulation of land uses in flood plains has increased rapidly since having such regulations in force became necessary for obtaining subsidized flood insurance under the 1968 Housing and Urban Development Act. Although the TVA and U.S. Army Corps of Engineers had both long advocated enactment of such controls by states and local governments, it required a federal insurance funding incentive to bring them into widespread use. Flood plain management involves coordination of zoning with other regulations often with the construction of dams, reservoirs, levees, and channel improvements, but only zoning of flood plains will be dealt with here.

Despite immense federal, state, and local expenditures on flood prevention measures, flood losses continue at about a billion dollars each year and are increasing. Structural controls alone are unlikely to eliminate the losses even if fundings were unlimited. With the help of regulatory controls, however, there is hope of reducing them substantially.

Standards for regulation generally require that in those parts of the flood plain most susceptible to flood losses land uses such as residences be entirely prohibited, but that in the less susceptible parts a much wider variety of land uses be permitted.[38]

Where the flood plain is free of development, zoning can be effective in preventing future losses but where there is substantial development already in the flood plain, flood-protection structures may be the only feasible means of preventing damage and blighting because it is difficult if not impossible to bring very large numbers of nonconforming uses into conformance.

Some uses are more easily and more extensively damaged by flooding than others. Agricultural, forestry, horticultural, and recreational parkland uses are subject to substantially less flood damage than most residential and some commercial and industrial uses. Water-oriented uses such as many utilities, some warehousing, and some commercial or industrial uses may find it necessary to their effective functioning to be in the flood plain at the cost of undertaking such flood-proofing of their installations as is practicable. Local land shortages may also indicate that it is in the best interests of the locality to make more intensive use of the flood plain than would be justifiable elsewhere.

Flood plain restrictions usually severely limit development and this may lead to problems of their not being upheld by the courts. Because the courts are skittish about restrictions of land use which leave the property owner few economic options holding them to verge on the confiscatory, it is essential in establishing flood plain zones to have adequate information on which to base the levels of restriction. Necessary data for this purpose includes information concerning the kind of flooding, its frequency, depth, velocity, and duration.[39] This information is necessary for establishing the degree of hazard on which the regulations will be based. The reasonableness of the regulations in light of the degree of hazard is an essential consideration to the courts.[40]

Several approaches to flood plain zoning are possible. There is a single-district approach suitable for rural and urban areas where land values are low and accurate data is difficult to obtain. It is not recommended for metropolitan areas. There is a two-district approach which distinguishes between the floodway and flood-fringe zones. This is usually most appropriate for metropolitan areas. Sometimes both approaches are combined using the single district approach only for smaller streams for which there may be inadequate data for distinguishing two districts. In some instances still another district may be added to deal with basement flooding in situations where there are protracted floods affecting basements in buildings outside the flood zone.[41]

In the two-district approach it is usual to prohibit dwellings, fill, and any structures which would seriously affect flood flows in the designated floodway. Permitted uses include agriculture and horticulture; industrial-commercial uses such as parking, loading areas and airstrips; and a wide variety of recreational uses not involving substantial structures. In the flood fringe district all otherwise appropriate uses are permitted subject to the requirement that the lowest habitable floor be above the flood protection elevation either on fill or appropriate structures. Sometimes the appropriateness of structure is controlled by requiring special permits involving planning review.

State action in regard to flood plain zoning is usually either aimed at penalizing localities failing to enact flood plain zoning or at the adoption of regulations on their behalf. California refuses state financial aid for land acquisition in connection with federal flood control projects if there is no flood plain zoning by the locality. Wisconsin, on the other hand, has a state agency authorized to adopt regulations for any governmental unit which fails to adopt them for itself.

Design and Historic Preservation

The control of the appearance of new buildings and sites, sign controls, and the preservation of historic buildings and sites are inextricably related because they are all part of the process of establishing and maintaining the visual and cultural character of the community. They are sometimes considered together in a design section of the comprehensive plan. Although the controls dealing with these aspects of physical development are sometimes embodied in separate ordinances, their being integrated into the zoning ordinances facilitates the coordination of land use implementation policies and plans.

Esthetics.   The regulation of community appearance has had a difficult history. The courts have traditionally held invalid regulations based on esthetics alone. Nonetheless there has been no lack of communities willing to risk passing esthetic regulations of one kind or another.[42] Tomson and Coplan point out that ". . . since the United States Supreme Court ruled in 1954 (Berman v. Parker) that aesthetic objectives may be considered in the exercise of legislative judgement and power, the judicial trend in many states has been to . . . uphold zoning laws which have aesthetic objectives."[43] An example of this is the recent decision of the highest appellate Court of New York. In this case the court stated:[44]

> It is now settled that aesthetics is a valid subject of legislative concern and that reasonable legislation designed to promote the governmental interest in preserving the appearance of the community represents a valid and permissible exercise of the police power . . .

The esthetics provisions in the zoning ordinance can attempt to spell out the requirements in detail, leaving little or nothing to the discretion of the administrator or it can set forth criteria for judgment and place the discretionary authority in the hands of a design review board following recommendations from the planning staff.

Esthetic provisions may control signs (dealt with in the following section), building heights, building appearance, building arrangements on the land, and landscaping. Although the control of signs and building heights are amenable to detailing in the ordinance, the other elements are best handled by a design review board. Such a board should be required to be made up of professionals competent in the design area such as art and architectural historians, architects, landscape architects, and urban designers.

An example is provided in the zoning ordinance for Bratenahl, Ohio. It establishes a Design Review Board made up of experts. They are responsible for reviewing all aspects of design for development proposals submitted to them by the Planning Commission to which they, in turn, make their recommendations.[45]

With reference to the comprehensive plan, different sets of criteria may be formulated for different sections of the city to achieve what is appropriate for each district. These districts may have different boundaries than the zoning districts. For example, in the central business district there may be regulations for entertainment areas much less restrictive than for the retailing and financial areas. Land marks, historic buildings, and historic preservation areas need separate attention. Sound old neighborhoods having a good visual character need protection from intrusion by incongruous structures. New neighborhoods need protection against the worst excesses of eclecticism and poor imitations of earlier styles. Commercial areas need more careful coordination of design and to be protected from gimcrackery and "advertising architecture." New views and vistas need to be established and existing ones protected.

However well they are written and administered, esthetic controls are more effective at preservation of existing beauty and the prevention of new ugliness than they are in guaranteeing new beauty. Nevertheless much of value can be accomplished with esthetic regulations.

Sign Controls.   The control of signs involves concern both for esthetics and visual communication. Some signs give necessary and useful information to those who use the public rights-of-way. Others serve no useful public purpose, may even be safety hazards, and create visual "static" in that they interrupt the view irregularly and unnecessarily. The Chicago Plan Commission stated the situation as follows:[46]

The Plan Commission believes that billboards and signs, especially those whose function is not to advertise the business or service carried out on or furnished from the premises, should be subject to strict regulation beyond the usual interpretation of the police power because:

Outdoor advertising is in fact the use by private interests of public property for commercial gain, since the total value of billboards lies in their ability to be seen from public thoroughfares.

The "right to be seen" from the public ways is not an inherent right in the land and exists solely by sufferance of the public and should be considered as subject to restriction or prohibition.
. . . .
Ugliness which offends the public and which the public cannot readily avoid is a nuisance which ought to be regulated to the same extent as the nuisances of offensive noises and air pollution.

Signs generally fall into three categories by purpose: (1) signs on the premises of a business explaining the name and/or character of the business; (2) off-premises signs which are essentially directional in that they advertise a product or service and direct the viewer to where the product or service may be obtained; and (3) general advertising of a product or service without reference to location.

Sign controls should clearly distinguish these categories, their usefulness to the public, and the character of the district in which they are located. Permitted signs should be regulated as to size, location, amount of information, kind of information, and design. Usually a design review committee is involved as discussed under esthetic zoning. While it may be shown that general advertising signs serve little if any public purpose and are a nuisance in most locations it may be considered that they would serve an esthetic purpose in some downtown entertainment districts where the objective may be to deliberately encourage a lively, vulgar "Times Square" sort of atmosphere.

Sign controls must be very carefully drawn. If they are very restrictive, obtaining political support for their adoption will be very difficult because of the considerable political strength of the advertising industry as evidenced by their success in resisting regulation.

Historic and Cultural Preservation.   Zoning for historic and cultural preservation is a special instance of esthetic zoning which merits separate discussion. Programs for preservation may be aimed at scattered single buildings, small groups of buildings, or entire districts. The degree of preservation sought may involve all elevations, street façades alone, some interior rooms, all interior rooms, landscaping, and open space. Buildings and grounds may be chosen for preserva-

. tion for historic or architectural reasons or because they are significant
local landmarks.[47]

Zoning is only one of the tools used alone or in concert as part of
an historic and cultural preservation program. The others include
outright purchase, scenic easements, urban renewal, federal grants,
and tax incentives. Because historic zoning often restricts the use of
property in parts of a city where densities are high it is frequently
combined with compensatory tax or other incentives. The tax incentives may take the form of tax reductions, tax freezes, temporary
exemptions, and tax rebates. Often the city enters into a contract with
the property owner to insure maintenance in return for the tax con-
cession. It has also been suggested that in high density areas, where
except for historic zoning the properties could be developed at much
higher densities, the square footage which could otherwise be built
should be saleable and transferable to other properties or deposited in
a kind of development rights bank.[48]

Where historic buildings are in a compact area which is easily de-
finable, rather than on scattered sites, it may be sufficient to establish
in the zoning ordinance one type of historic district with provision for
permitted uses, height and bulk, yards, remodeling and renovation
standards, and provisions for a design review board. Where the sites
are scattered or need different degrees of control a more complex and
flexible system of zones, subzones, and supplementary regulations
may be needed. To prevent historic and cultural zones from being
surrounded by incompatible uses it may also in some instances be
necessary to protect them by establishing special regulations for the
transitional areas.[49]

The existence of adequate enabling legislation may be necessary
to forestall adverse court action, especially in regard to historic zoning of small areas or single properties, lest the question of spot zoning
arise. The Norfolk Department of City Planning argued this point as
follows:[50]

> Protection of individual historic buildings and premises by creation of
> small districts is clearly distinguishable from cases branded by the courts
> as illegal spot zoning. Size alone does not determine the appropriateness
> of district boundaries. Where courts have held small zoning districts
> illegal, the opinion usually notes that the action was taken for the benefit
> of an individual owner, that the primary motive was private profit, and

that there was inadequate consideration of, or interest in, the general public welfare, a comprehensive plan, or sound comprehensive planning principles.

The procedure proposed herein permits such zoning only on application by a public body (not a private individual) for a purpose appropriate to comprehensive planning principles, and one which may indeed be a key element in the success of the comprehensive plan for the area. A building may have major historic or cultural significance without being part of a group of similar buildings.

Where an architectural or design review board is provided it is especially important that the ordinance contain clear guidelines concerning esthetic purposes and criteria for making board decisions. The pitfall of restricting architectural styles is a serious one. Historic buildings are not enhanced by being surrounded by fake imitations nor should new buildings contrast in an uncomplementary way with older buildings by attracting undue attention to themselves. Contemporary design should be encouraged but it should be subdued and through careful use of scale and materials complementary to the historic or culturally significant buildings in the area. Careful drafting of the ordinance can help achieve the objectives.

Frederick H. Bair, Jr. has proposed the creation of Special Public Interest Districts as a device for controlling a wide range of special zoning problems including historic and cultural preservation. They would also control such special use areas as river fronts, convention centers, financial districts, old retail districts, and central business districts. These special districts could supplant or overlay existing districts and would have provisions appropriate to the nature of the district.[51]

Conditional Uses

Conditional or special uses are those uses permitted in a given zone or zones only if special criteria or conditions are met, usually in addition to those specified for other uses. If all of the special conditions to be met can be detailed in the ordinance then it is possible to give the zoning administrator the authority to issue the special permit upon receiving sufficient evidence of the conditions being met by the proposed development. More commonly zoning ordinances require review of each individual development proposal by the planning staff and either the planning commission or the board of adjustment depending on the relevant enabling legislation. Such ordinances set forth conditions to be met and/or criteria for judging and the review body may be granted discretionary authority to require such supplementary conditions deemed necessary in the public interest or necessary for conformance to the stated criteria.

The courts have frowned on the use of special or conditional use permits where specification of conditions or criteria to be met are seen as too general, as giving too much discretionary authority to the review body and resulting in arbitrary decisions. If extensive use is to be made of special permits the conditions or criteria to be met must be very carefully and reasonably worked out for the courts to be expected to uphold them. The guidelines for discretionary decision making must be as clearly understandable as possible.

Nonconforming Uses

When a zoning ordinance is adopted or extensively revised there are almost always many existing uses and structures which do not conform to all the provisions of the ordinance. These nonconforming uses consist in nonconforming buildings, conforming uses of nonconforming buildings, nonconforming uses of conforming buildings, and nonconforming uses of land. Such nonconformance may also be created from time to time as the ordinance is amended.

Early zoning ordinances usually allowed such uses to continue because of the financial, political, and judicial problems likely to be involved in forcing their removal or discontinuance. They were restricted, however, in the hope that the restrictions would result in their elimination in the long run. The restrictions usually involved prohibition of: their enlargement or extension, their resumption after a specified period of discontinuance, their conversion to another nonconforming use, and their being rebuilt after a specified amount of damage or destruction.

These provisions have not led to a satisfactory rate of elimination. In fact, Webster says: "The number of nonconforming uses in most cities instead of decreasing with the passage of time as expected, has actually increased, due to the excessive number of variances which have been granted by boards of adjustment."[52] The use of retroactive regulations for the elimination of nonconforming uses, however, has met with many objections by the courts. Of the forms of retroactive regulations those providing periods of time for amortization of the investments in nonconforming uses have met with the most judicial support.

Amortization of nonconforming uses is based on the view that by giving owners of these uses a reasonable time in which to recoup their investments, it is then fair to require the elimination of these uses. Because the amount of investment in these uses varies and the degree of nuisance their continuance causes also varies, the period of time which they are allowed to continue is also varied.

The amortization period can be established in a fixed schedule in the ordinance, or the ordinance may delegate the fixing of the period to an administrator or administrative board within stated guidelines. Robert Scott reports that: "The courts look more favorably upon terminations made by an administrative board or through voluntary agreement which avoids termination of the nonconforming use merely for the sake of homogeneity."[53]

The time period may be set to begin with the passage of the zoning ordinance or may be backdated property by property to the latest date of the transfer of ownership. The latter is more equitable provided there is a minimum period given. Because of the diffusion of termination dates it is also likely to result in less political pressure for wholesale time limit extensions through amending the ordinance.

The Scott report on amortization of nonconforming uses concludes as follows:[54]

The most conclusive finding from our research is that most communities have not adopted amoritization ordinances either (1) because nonconforming uses are not priority problems, or (2) because of a fear of judicial invalidation, or (3) because homogeneous uses were not preferred over an existing pattern. Among those communities having provisions, consistent enforcement is rare for nearly the same reasons. In those instances where enforcement has met with limited success, the success is due to its deterrent effect or because there has been clear community support for elimination of particular uses. The aesthetic and practical objectives of homogeneity must be satisfied in the individual case.

Given these conclusions, then, drafters of zoning ordinances need to rethink how much time, effort, and money should be spent on solving a "problem" about which practitioners and the general public are not particularly concerned. Minor nonconformities do not deserve the attention they have received in the past. What really needs to be done is to identify those nonconforming uses that are in truth harmful and to make efforts to eliminate these.

These conclusions support the contention made previously that compatibility rather than homogeneity of uses should determine what is permitted in each zoning district and consequently which uses would be nonconforming.

SIZE, SITING, AND DENSITY REQUIREMENTS

Minimum Property Size

Minimum property sizes are frequently stipulated in residential districts or for properties to be developed for residential use where allowed in other districts. The specification of a minimum lot size is the most primitive and yet common means of density control. Together with yard regulations, lot size regulations are used as a means of controlling the character of a neighborhood. The establishment of very large minimum lot sizes is sometimes (with decreasing approval of the courts) used to keep land free of conventional subdivisions as was discussed in the section on open-land zoning. Large-lot zoning may also be used where the terrain is very rough and more flexibility is needed for siting residences. Still another use of minimum lot sizes is to ensure enough space for the sanitary use of septic tanks and wells in areas not served by water and sewer but this kind of problem is better handled by way of health and sanitary codes.

Lot sizes are intimately related to development costs and the requiring of large minimum lot sizes is very frequently used by suburbs as a means of preventing an influx of middle- and lower-income groups. Where localities have zoned most or all of their residential land for large lots this is clearly exclusionary zoning and is now more frequently being struck down by the courts. (A discussion of exclusionary zoning appears later in this chapter).

In addition to lot size requirements it is customary in residential areas to specify minimum lot widths or frontages. These provisions lead to problems in lotting out the ends of culs-de-sac and at abrupt turns in streets. In order to ease these problems many ordinances specify that minimum widths be measured at the building line which is usually some distance back from the street. Some ordinances provide for smaller lot widths for lots on culs-de-sac.

Setbacks, Yards, and Coverage

Setbacks and yard requirements are easily confused and are terms often used interchangeably in zoning ordinances. Setback lines are generally imposed to facilitate the subsequent widening of streets. They may be tied in with official map provisions where they exist. The reaction of the courts to setback provisions has been as confused as the use of the term in ordinances, with the result that the use of setback lines is not as legally secure as are yard restrictions.

Yard requirements are imposed for the purpose of providing space, light, fire safety, privacy, usable open space, and for (sometimes dubious) esthetic purposes. They depend on the distance between buildings and the surrounding property lines for achieving these purposes. The ordinance may require front yard setbacks to be measured from the front lot line, the center of the street, as a percentage of lot depth, or as established by the setbacks of existing structures in the block. They usually produce monotonous regularity of building sitings (which should be determined individually through careful study of the relationship of the building being sited to any neighboring buildings). Side yards and backyards are measured from the side and back lot lines, respectively. Most ordinances require side yards too narrow to guarantee effective privacy or serve as usable open space. Yard requirements usually limit buildings to a space in the middle of the lot. This approach to locating buildings on their lots often results in a severe reduction of the potential usable open space.

The requirement for usable open space is usually specified as a percentage of the total lot area. Where there are required off-street parking or loading areas, driveways, or outdoor storage areas, these are usually excluded from being counted as usable open space. In high density residential areas balconies and roofdecks are sometimes allowed to be counted as usable open space.

Other yard requirements include limitations on projections over-hanging required yards, maximum building coverages as a percentage of total lot area, and the construction of walls or fences and the provision of landscaping along lot lines, especially in high density residential areas and along boundary lines between zones.

The lack of flexibility in most yard requirements has led urban designers to propose reforms intended to give developers more freedom in how they locate buildings on the land. Some of these proposals offer the possibility of alternative ways of locating buildings depending on such provisions for maintaining privacy between buildings as the elimination of windows in sidewalls, the use of translucent fixed windows, or providing walls, fences and/or land-scape screening between properties.

Building Height and Bulk

The problems of height, setbacks, and building bulk are closely interrelated. The first two are of immense concern in urban design. The character of the skyline in all the districts of a city is largely determined by building heights and setbacks. Accordingly a primary purpose of height limitations may be esthetic. Setbacks on the other hand, are usually required for reasons of ensuring that an adequate amount of light reaches each window. Bulk is controlled indirectly by height and setback requirements, or directly by bulk control planes, or by floor area ratios.

Heights may be regulated by specifying a maximum number of feet, a maximum number of stories, or a number of feet determined as a multiple of the width of the street on which the building fronts. Height may also be made dependent on the distance back from the lot line in the form of setbacks. This kind of regulation results in the wedding cake profiles characteristic of buildings in central areas of so many cities. Usually ". . . such structures as chimneys, spires, monuments, domes, cooling towers, and elevators towers . . . "[55] are allowed to exceed the height limitations.

As part of its urban design plan San Francisco has recently

(September 1972) adopted height regulations to preserve or enhance the visual character of its various districts. Because of its hilly topography great care was taken to preserve existing views. Although the height district boundries were made to conform with land use district boundaries where possible, they are not entirely congruent.[56]

For urban design reasons some cities have attempted to establish minimum as well as maximum height limits or a cornice line, in some of their denser areas or along particular streets. When tested in the courts in the past these regulations have usually been declared invalid because they were based entirely on esthetics. But since the court decision in Berman vs. Parker[57] concerning esthetics as a legal public concern there has been a stronger possibility of establishing cornice lines where it was felt to be desirable.

A special instance of height limitations are those imposed around airports at the ends of runways. Rather than specifying a particular specific maximum height over an area, these may take the form of a fanshaped height limitation plane starting at the runway ends and getting both wider and higher with distance out from the runway.

Setbacks and bulk are jointly controlled where the regulatory device used is a bulk control plane or angle of light obstruction. This kind of device establishes inwardly inclining planes on one or more sides of the lot beginning at the base on the lot lines or center of the street, and creating a building envelope within which the building is permitted to be built. A more complicated version of this permits averaging the angles of light obstruction to allow compensatory penetration of the building envelope for parts of the building which do not fully fill the envelope.

The most common device for regulating bulk is the "Floor Area Ratio". This ratio is computed by adding the areas of each building floor on or above grade and dividing the total by the lot area. The allowed FAR varies with the district. In residential districts it may be below one and in central business districts it may be as high as sixteen. The FAR is not a substitute for yard, coverage, or height requirements because in any one district it would allow low buildings with high coverage or high buildings with low coverage in the absence of any other regulations.

In 1963 the Federal Housing Administration introduced a new measure of the relationship of land and buildings called Land-Use

Intensity (LUI) for use in their evaluation of multifamily housing projects for mortgage insurance. This measure "correlates the amount of floor area, open space, livability space, recreation space and car storage space of a property with the size of its site, or land area."[58] It is a more sensitive, less variable, but more complicated tool for intensity control. It has not found its way as yet into many zoning ordinances but over time it may prove better than floor area ratios, especially in planned unit developments.

Recently there has been much experimentation with bulk controls which offer developers bonuses of extra floor area if they agree to achieve certain urban design objectives through inclusion in their projects of specific features at a sacrifice of rentable floor space or an addition to building costs. New York and San Francisco are significant among those cities applying the bonus concept in large central business districts and Rosslyn, Virginia near Washington provides an example of the application of this concept to metropolitan subcenters.[59]

New York Theater District.   The value of land in the theater district in recent years had risen too high for theaters alone to remain a tenable investment. The prospect was that they would be torn down and replaced by office space or some other high yielding use. As a result it was decided to offer to the builders of new office buildings, at the discretion of the planning commission, an incentive of up to 20% more floor area than otherwise permitted if they would incorporate legitimate theaters into their structures. So far the ordinance seems to be working well.

Lincoln Center Area (New York).   To encourage development surrounding Lincoln Center which would enhance it, a similar bonus arrangement has been devised. Developers who provide continuous arcading along the streets facing Lincoln Center and who provide for open plazas at ground level and who provide better interior connections to subway stops are granted floor area bonuses.

Greenwich Street Development District (New York).   In the Special Greenwich Street Development District adjoining the World Trade Center in lower Manhattan, which encompasses an area expected to be privately redeveloped over the next 10 to 30 years, by a recent zoning amendment developers are offered FAR bonuses for undertaking to provide parts of below-ground and second-level improvements for pedestrian circulation according to a plan which sets forth some mandatory improvements as well. Also included in the plan are provisions to assure the continuity of street facades and the continuity of retailing along the pedestrian system.[60]

San Francisco.   A large section of the central business district is subject to bonus space provisions. The items for which bonuses are given are as follows: good access to rapid transit and parking, provision of multiple entrances and shortening access between public streets, ground level plazas or setbacks, low coverage at upper floors, and provision of observation decks. The schedule of bonuses was based on the estimated extra cost to the developer of providing the incentive items. (Figure 2-2 on the following two pages illustrates these provisions.)

Rosslyn.   Facing an office boom in the 1960s a plan was prepared for the obsolete commercial center across the river from Washington. The plan featured pedestrian linkages throughout the development and a mixture of residential and commercial uses. The strategy was to zone the area for an intensity of use far below the market demand and offer greater intensity bonuses for developers conforming to the plan. The strategy has been somewhat successful although the desired use mix was only partly achieved and there were holdout problems.[61]

Off-Street Parking and Loading

The provision of space for off-street parking and loading is usually dealt with separately from other yard requirements. It is considered undesirable to permit the usable amenity open space intended for recreation and gardening to be encroached upon by vehicles. Accordingly, separate space must be allocated for off-street parking and loading to suit the needs of the users in each zone.

The necessary space may be provided on the ground or in structure. In the case of parking it may be provided for on separate property owned by the same owner (to avoid the effect of lease cancellations and other problems which might result in diminishing the number of

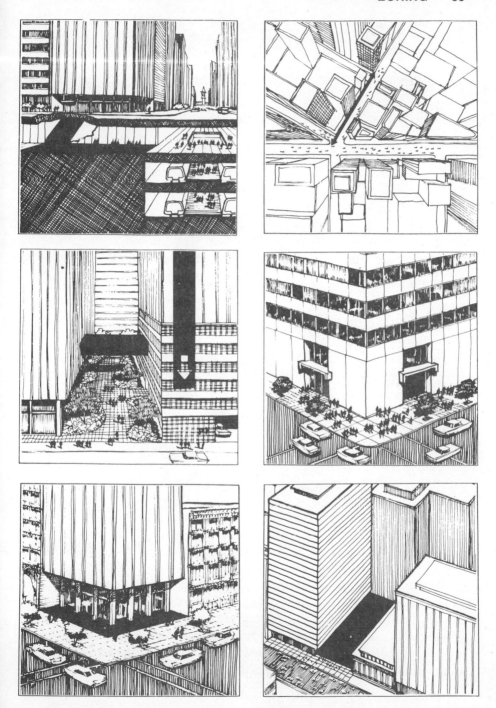

Figure 2-2. Amenities for which San Francisco gives zoning incentive bonuses.
Source: San Francisco Planning Commision, 1978.

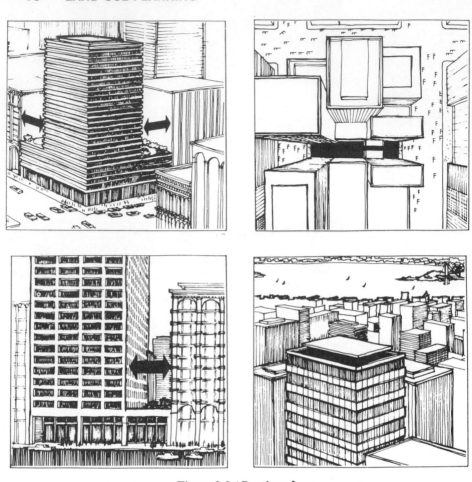

Figure 2-2 (*Continued*)

parking spaces) within a specified maximum distance from the development in question.

The amount of space needed is dependent on the potential allowable uses of the development. In the case of commercial development where several different users may subsequently occupy the property, the parking and loading requirements must be based on the allowable use with the largest requirements. Most noncommercial uses have more stable requirements which can be more easily handled in the ordinance.

In the case of housing for the elderly, lower parking requirements may be allowed.

In central business districts and other older parts of cities, all development except the newest is likely to have insufficiencies of parking and loading space. In these areas zoning can only help with new development and other planning means must be used to upgrade these districts as a whole.

Too few zoning ordinances provide adequately for the landscaping of parking lots—particularly for the planting of trees—and the result is ugly "seas of asphalt". Landscaping should be required as part of the parking area requirements and coordinated with other esthetic provisions as part of the cost of development.

District Size, Spot Zoning, and Floating Zones

Generally district sizes need to exceed the size of a property in one ownership especially if the size is as small as a city lot. There is the danger of very small districts being declared illegal for constituting "spot" zones. Hagman describes the conditions under which the courts may find spot zoning invalid:[62]

> 1. a small parcel of land singled out for special or priveleged treatment; 2. the singling out is not in the public interest but only for the benefit of the landowner; 3. the action is not in accord with a comprehensive plan. . . . If spot zoning is invalid, usually all three elements are present . . .

There are cases where a single property developed in a contrasting or more intensive use than the surrounding property is in accordance with a comprehensive plan and is in the public interest. The most obvious case is that of the neighborhood grocery or small shopping center. If the land is so zoned while it is vacant the price of the land will go up and the proposed development is unlikely to occur. If the use is indicated by a symbol on the plan but not so zoned, a potential developer may have several sites to choose from, and if after making satisfactory arrangements with the owner he applies for and is granted the necessary change of zone, this is in effect a case of the planning commission treating these small centers as floating zones. Unless the zoning category granted has the necessary safeguards, land use conflicts with neighboring uses can result and there is a chance of the change of zoning being declared invalid by the courts.

The development of these small properties can be better handled as conditional uses in a larger zone, with the conditions, including location and spacing, very carefully spelled out with reference to the comprehensive plan. Because of court decisions in regard to spot zoning it is better to keep most districts large.

Districts are usually mutually exclusive but some communities have mapped overlapping zones in which a property may fall in two zones simultaneously. Where this happens usually those regulations apply which are applicable to the district in which the use to which the property owner puts his property is allowed. This practice is of doubtful legality, difficult to administer, and inadvisable.

Another unusual practice is the use of "Q" zones in which the addition of the letter Q to the zone designation indicates that it is temporary. In such a zone if the property owner does not develop the permitted use within a stipulated time period the zoning designation of the property reverts to the previously designated zone. The legality of this practice has not yet been adequately determined in the courts.[63]

ADMINISTRATION OF THE ZONING ORDINANCE

Public confidence in zoning can easily be lost if the ordinance is not carefully enforced and does not reflect the intentions of the comprehensive plan. The enforcement officer, the board of adjustment, the planning commission, and the legislative body may contribute to the erosion of the plan and of zoning through their respective roles, by laxity or indifference of enforcement, too easily awarding variances and special permits, and the too frequent amending of the zoning map contrary to the intent of the comprehensive plan.

The Zoning Administrator

The job of administering and enforcing the zoning ordinance is too frequently divided among several agencies of local government. Most commonly the primary responsibility for zoning administration is vested in the building department. This department administers the building and, often, housing codes and may be a division of the public works department. Because of the complexity of the newer zoning ordinances building permits may be forwarded to the planning department for planning approval in situations where administration is vested in another department.

The administrative division of the planning department provides public information about zoning, processes applications for zoning amendments, and makes recommendations concerning zoning changes to the planning commission. This same staff may, as in Kentucky, process applications for variances and special permits and make recommendations concerning them to the board of adjustment.

With the increasing need for professional competence in dealing with zoning matters, there is a growing tendency to consolidate some or all of the tasks mentioned above in a zoning administrator who is head of a zoning administration division of the planning department or development department where this departmental form is used.

In some cities the zoning administrator is empowered with discretionary authority in the matter of variances and special permits subject to appeal of his decisions to the board of adjustment. Concerning this trend Piero Faraci says:[64]

A major problem in the effective application of land-use controls is the reluctance to recognize the need for the trained technician. Professionalization of the administrative function in zoning, as reflected in the use of zoning administrators who assume certain functions of lay boards, is a sign that the situation is changing for the better.

However, the usual situation is that the zoning administrator, wherever located in the government structure, has the responsibility for carrying out the provisions of the zoning ordinance, literally, without discretionary authority to make any modifications. He may issue zoning permits, handle building inspections, and issue certificates of occupancy when buildings have been built according to the issued permits or the building uses change to other permitted uses. He may administer the provisions of the zoning ordinance concerning nonconforming uses. In the case of violations of the ordinance he may initiate court action.

It is unfortunate that most zoning administrators lack adequate staff to look for violations such as the failure to obtain a building permit. In this situation he is forced to rely for information on citizen complaints and casual observation by other members of the government.

The Board of Adjustment

It is difficult to draft a zoning ordinance and map which is effective but not in some ways arbitrary. All situations in which it is to be applied cannot be foreseen and undue hardship for some property owners avoided. Conditional use permits and variations have to be considered. Only rarely are these duties given to the planning commission. Further, there is sometimes a need for appealing the decisions of the zoning administrator. Accordingly enabling legislation pursuant to the Standard State Zoning Enabling Act provides for a board of adjustment (or appeals). Usually these are five member, citizen boards whose members are appointed by the chief executive(s) for staggered terms. They either serve without pay or are paid a nominal amount plus expenses, for each meeting they attend.

The functions of the board of adjustment are quasi-judicial in nature. They are set forth in the enabling legislation and the zoning ordinance. They have three general areas of responsibility:

1. to correct errors or abuses in the administration of the ordinance by the zoning administrator in interpreting the regulations;
2. to consider applications for conditional use permits ("special use permits" or "special exceptions");
3. to grant relief ("variances") when hardship results from strict application of the terms of the ordinance.

It is most important that the board of adjustment understands the comprehensive plan and the zoning ordinance if they are to act in a manner which will forward the community's planning objectives. Effective liaison must exist between the planning commission, its staff, and the board of adjustment. This may be furthered in several ways: one or more members of the board may also be members of the planning commission; the secretary to the board may be a member of the planning staff; the planning staff may have the responsibility for processing applications to the board and making recommendations to the board. Of these possibilities the last is usually the most effective.

Decisions of the zoning administrator may be appealed to the board of adjustment. When it is alleged that he has misinterpreted the meaning of the ordinance or misapplied its provisions in a particular case the board must judge the meaning of the ordinance, the facts in the case, and the application of the ordinance in the light of the facts. The decisions of the board are subject to appeal in the courts and possible reversal (see Figure 2-3).

Applications for the development of uses which are conditional in the zones where they are requested require conditional use permits from the authorized board. The proposals are examined by the board to see if they meet the criteria listed in the ordinance. If they do the board must issue a permit but the board has broad discretionary power to require additional conditions which are "reasonable" in view of the impact of the requested uses on their surroundings. The board may not waive any of the requirements in the regulations. Any modification of the regulations requires the granting of a variance.

Concerning the granting of variances Leary says: "Probably the major reason for the creation of the board of adjustment is to take care of the special situations that cannot be dealt with in the ordinance without making it unduly complicated. The ordinary workings of the ordinance will produce hardship cases that otherwise would have to go to court for relief."[65]

Most state enabling acts are patterned after the Standard Act, as noted previously, which provides for the granting of variances under special conditions where the ". . . literal enforcement of the requirements of the ordinance would result in unnecessary hardship upon the applicant. Such a variance can only be granted where the general intent and spirit of the ordinance will not be impaired."[66] This is usually construed by the courts as not permitting the granting of use variances and many enabling acts are more specific. For example, the Indiana legislation says:[67]

Neither the board of zoning appeals nor the county board of zoning appeals nor a city board of zoning appeals shall grant a variance from a use district or classification.

The consolidated government of Indianapolis (Unigov) is exempt from this legislation and its special planning legislation permits use

<table>
<tr><td colspan="2">PETITION OF APPEAL
ZONING BOARD OF ADJUSTMENT
CITY OF PHILADELPHIA, CITY HALL ANNEX
(PREPARE IN TRIPLICATE)</td><td>RECEIPT NO.</td><td>LIC. & INSP. APPLIC. NO.</td></tr>
<tr><td></td><td></td><td>APPEAL FEES</td><td>DATE OF APPEAL</td></tr>
</table>

LOCATION OF PROPERTY

SEND NOTICES TO	ADDRESS

ATTORNEY (if any)	ADDRESS

OWNER (Appellant) LESSEE AGENT	ADDRESS

PERSON FILING THIS APPEAL

IF APPELLANT IS NOT OWNER, LESSEE OR AGENT, STATE HIS INTEREST

APPEAL IS TAKEN FROM THE ACTION OF THE DEPARTMENT OF LICENSES IN ☐ REFUSAL ☐ GRANTING OF PERMIT FOR

STATE OBJECTIONS TO ACTION OF DEPARTMENT OF LICENSES & INSPECTIONS

I hereby certify that the statements contained herein are true and correct to the best of my knowledge and belief.
I understand that if I knowingly make any false statement herein I am subject to such penalties as may be prescribed by law or ordinance.

_____
(Signature)

CALENDAR NUMBER _____. The time set for public hearing is 9:30 o'clock A.M., 1:30 o'clock P.M. DST EST

_____ in _____

AVOID UNNECESSARY DELAY BY CAREFUL READING OF THE ATTACHED INSTRUCTIONS.

YOUR ATTENTION IS DIRECTED TO PROVISIONS ON POSTING REQUIREMENTS AND PERSONS ENTITLED TO APPEAR BEFORE THE BOARD.

81-49 (Rev. 8/64)

Figure 2-3. Petition of appeal. From Philadelphia (Pa.) Zoning Board of Adjustment (1964).

variances.[68] As a result, developers can go either to the planning commission or the board of appeals for a change of use depending on their case and which body they feel will be more sympathetic to it. Although it never appears on the zoning map a use variance is in effect a change of zoning classification and often has the same effect as spot zoning.

Where the enabling legislation and/or the zoning ordinance carefully spell out the conditions for proving hardship they usually include the following tests of the owner's situation:

1. If he complies with the ordinance he can make no reasonable use of his property;
2. His hardship is peculiar to his property.
3. His hardship was not self-created.
4. His hardship is not economic.
5. Granting the variance will not adversely affect the neighboring properties nor the public.

Most justifiable hardships involve odd-shaped lots, unique topographic, or soils conditions and the request is for a variance in the dimensional requirements of the ordinance. Many kinds of cases could be avoided by use in the ordinance of the flexible yard requirements discussed previously.

In order to avoid charges of favoritism it is very important that the board of appeals be thoroughly conversant with the zoning ordinance and the comprehensive plan, that they have good rules for processing variances, and that they have good backup staff so each case will be adequately researched and the facts presented in a clear and orderly way. Detailed records should be kept for each case including the reasons for the board's decisions. Lack of adequate information in the record may cause the court on appeal to remand the case for amplification or rehearing.

The means of administering and enforcing the zoning ordinance must be clearly spelled out in the ordinance itself if the risk of having it invalidated by the courts as involving an unlawful delegation of legislative power is to be avoided. The appointment of, and specification of the powers and duties of the zoning administrator and the board of adjustment must be provided unless covered in the enabling act. Also provision for the issuance of building permits and special permits and the handling of nonconforming uses must be covered. Penalty provisions for dealing with violations of the ordinance must also be specified.

Review in the Courts of Zoning and Board of Adjustment Decisions. There are a number of situations in which various parties may wish to resort to seeking court relief in regard to zoning practices:

1. The planning commission or the local governing body may ask the court to terminate a violation.
2. A property owner who has failed to obtain local relief may seek court review.
3. Owners objecting to a rezoning or board of adjustment decision concerning neighboring property which they feel adversely affects their property may seek court review.
4. Property owners adversely affected by a zoning violation may seek court relief.

Not since the case of Euclid v. Ambler sustained the validity of comprehensive zoning have many attempts to have zoning ordinances invalidated been successful. However, there have been many cases where zoning was alleged to be unconstitutional as applied. Also there have been many cases where it was alleged that the statutory procedural requirements had been violated, particularly in regard to adequate notice and the holding of hearings. The importance of good administrative practices in minimizing appeals to the courts cannot be overemphasized.

SPECIAL PROBLEMS IN REGARD TO ZONING

Mobile Home and Travel Trailer Parks

The production and purchase of mobile homes and travel trailers is steadily increasing. Mobile homes are providing permanent housing for more single family home owners, as land and conventional home prices continue to rise. The readjustment of comprehensive plans and zoning ordinances to satisfactorily accommodate them is currently a problem in many metropolitan areas.[69]

Mobile homes are distinguished from travel trailers in their intended use as permanent housing, as opposed to short-term vacation use.

Mobile home parks belong in residential zones with other permanent housing while travel trailer parks belong in highway service zones with other tourist facilities or at recreation sites. To segregate these uses by themselves would be to risk either spot zoning or confiscatory litigation.

Many states, counties, and localities have regulations other than zoning which affect mobile homes and travel trailers. Zoning for mobile homes and travel trailers should take account of other existing regulations and avoid duplication except for the purpose of setting higher standards.[70]

When drafting regulations for mobile home parks it is well to be familiar with the latest edition of FHA's "Minimum Property Standards for Mobile Home Courts" because many developers will want to finance their developments with FHA insured loans and have lots which qualify mobile home purchasers for FHA insured loans. The supplementary regulations permitting mobile homes in the appropriate residential zones may include provisions for location on or access to major streets, minimum size and dimensions of a park and of sites within a park, provisions for internal commercial and recreational facilities, minimum siting and yard dimensions, street and parking provisions, and landscaping and other esthetic provisions.

Most existing mobile home ordinances have been inadequate in regard to their landscaping and esthetic standards especially in view of the generally low standards of exterior design of the models in production. Until this situation improves substantially these parks should be adequately screened from the public rights of way and neighboring properties.

Supplementary regulations for travel trailer parks need not be nearly as restrictive as for mobile home parks. To compensate for the lack of facilities in the trailers the community facilities may have to be more generous but the lots can be smaller. Maximum periods of occupancy must be regulated to prevent use of travel trailers for permanent housing. Landscaping and screening provisions are also needed, especially along the property lines.[71]

Exclusionary Zoning

Exclusionary zoning practices are those which have the effect of preventing the building of housing for people of low and moderate incomes. They are motivated by concern for the population already in the community rather than concern for the overall housing needs of the region of which the community is a part. They are widespread among suburban communities in most of our metropolitan areas.[72]

⬤ Fiscal zoning—zoning for the uses which will produce the most tax revenue for the least cost in community services—is one kind of practice that results in exclusion by preempting land. From racial and economic prejudices and social snobbery other communities set unnecessarily high and expensive development standards. They may severely limit or entirely exclude multifamily housing and mobile home parks from within their boundaries. The setting of unnecessarily high standards involves such requirements as very large minimum dimensions for lot sizes, frontage widths, yard and open space requirements, and floor areas. Limiting the number of bedrooms in multiple-family housing so as to exclude large families is another tactic. As with fiscal zoning, overzoning for industry and agriculture can have the exclusionary effect of limiting the supply of land for low-cost housing.[73]

A different kind of tactic is the use of the referendum to approve or disapprove public housing projects (California), or to reverse legislative rezonings for low cost housing on petition (Michigan and several other states). Opposition to public and public-assisted housing has always been particularly strong and generates political pressure on local governments to use whatever legal devices are at hand to prevent such development.[74]

The attitude of the courts toward suits seeking relief from exclusionary practices is mixed. The U.S. Supreme Court has been inclined to limit its review to cases involving a clear breach of the rights specifically enumerated in the constitution such as cases involving race. This would tend to remove from review cases involving questions of education, welfare, and housing in relation to economic class. It has upheld the right of referendum regardless of motivation.[75] Although upholding the rezoning decision in another referendum case,[76] the Sixth Circuit Court ordered Union City to take steps to house its low-income residents within a specified time limit. The federal courts have also responded favorably in suits involving discrimination by administrative delaying tactics such as refusal to extend utilities,[77] and in 1978 the Supreme Court let stand a lower court decision that communities failing through zoning to provide for low-income housing for blacks and other minorities are in violation of federal law.[78]

Of the state courts only those in Pennsylvania, New Jersey and Michigan have heard enough exclusionary zoning cases to begin to set a pattern, but these cases are important for the precedents they will set for other states. Lauber states that: "The Pennsylvania court decisions have been uniformly hostile to exclusionary zoning practices."[79] The same is generally true of the New Jersey courts. In October 1971 the Superior Court of Middlesex County ". . . struck down the entire zoning ordinance of Madison Township on the ground that it prohibited as much as 90% of the population from obtaining housing in the Township."[80] A similar decision was made the following year in the case of *Southern Burlington County NAACP v. Township of Mount Laurel* by the New Jersey Superior Court.[81] In Michigan the courts have ruled against exclusion of multifamily housing and mobile homes from communities.[82]

Future court decisions are likely to follow this pattern because as Norman Williams, Jr. puts it:[83]

> . . . it has always been recognized that it is an essential part of the judicial function to watch over the parochial and exclusionist attitudes and policies of local governments, and to see to it that these do not run counter to national policy and the general welfare.

Obtaining redress in the courts is a slow process involving case by case decisions. Accordingly approaching the problem through legislation should be a shorter and more satisfactory route. Two options are open: (1) amending the enabling legislation to prohibit exclusionary zoning practices and (2) creating a state agency with power to preempt local zoning authority. The first approach would be the more sweeping, but by mid-1973 no state had taken this route and with the widespread domination of state legislatures by suburban and small town representatives there is small likelihood of this kind of state action.[84] On the other hand several states have, or are considering, the second route. New York has created an Urban Development Corporation with powers to override local zoning but the Corporation has been reluctant to use this authority in the face of considerable local opposition.[85] Attempts by the Corporation to build housing in Westchester County resulted in the legislature stripping it of its override authority in villages and towns.[86] In Florida under the 1972 Land Management Act the ". . . Governor and Cabinet have the power to reverse local rejections of projects and developments of regional impact."[87] In Massachusetts the Housing Appeals Committee of the Massachusetts Department of Community Affairs may issue building permits refused by local governments.[88] Similar legislation has passed or is pending in other states.

The federal government has recently been requiring that metropolitan regional planning bodies have a housing element as part of their comprehensive plans and have generally insisted that the plans include provision of housing for all income groups throughout the metropolitan region as a prerequisite for receiving federal funds. But the cooperation of the federal government in providing housing or rent subsidies is essential to carrying out housing plans for the low- and middle-income groups.

Elimination of exclusionary zoning is likely to be a slow and spotty process but there are some signs that the problems are being recognized, and of corrective action increasingly being taken.

Contract Zoning

Contract zoning involves an agreement between the property owner and the planning commission or the legislative body that the property owner as a condition for approval of having his property rezoned will record certain deed restrictions on it, often making the requesting body a party to them as well as the owners of neighboring properties.[89] The requested restrictions are in addition to those imposed in the zoning district in which the property is to be included. They may involve further restrictions on use, height, bulk, yards, signs, or any other aspect of property development.

The courts have sometimes upheld this kind of extralegal arrangement where it did not involve spot zoning[90] or contract away the government's future right to rezone[91] or conflict with the comprehensive plan; but where the courts have construed the zoning ordinance to be the comprehensive plan contract zoning has been declared invalid as outside the plan. Norman Williams, Jr. states the issue as follows:[92]

Under the enabling acts, zoning regulations must be 'in accordance with a comprehensive plan.' In all the confused litigation over this cryptic language, the clearest (and most valid) principle established has been that such special deals, outside the zoning ordinance, are invalid. If the comprehensive plan does not include the land-use categories inherent in the structure of zoning districts, it is difficult to say what there is left that it can mean. Moreover, such deals are equally obnoxious on practical grounds, for they open up all sorts of possibilities for political pressure, favoritism, and the breakdown of the rule of law.

Further the use of contract zoning indicates deficiencies in the zoning ordinance and in the willingness of official bodies to abide by its provisions. Nevertheless the practice is fairly widespread.

Growth Controls

With the recent weakening of the traditional American growth ethic as the result of increased concern for the environment, increased awareness of rising costs to the community of providing the infrastructure necessary for urban development, growing fear of economic and social change in residential areas, and other factors, a political climate has been created in which some local governments are attempting to slow down or stop further urban development.[93] Land use controls such as zoning and subdivision regulations are being amended to accomplish growth management, sometimes in concert with capital budgeting. Two of the more significant examples are Ramapo, New York and Petaluma, California. Others are described in chapter seven.

Ramapo. In 1965 the town of Ramapo, New York took a different tack. Ramapo amended its zoning ordinance to create a new kind of "Special Permit" use designated "Residential Development Use." No residential development can take place in the community without obtaining this kind of permit. Permits are granted if certain standards are met for minimum services and facilities available to the new development. These include sewerage, drainage, parks (and recreation), schools, access roads, and fire protection. A point system is used to evaluate available services and facilities. Permits require a specified number of development points as a minimum for obtaining a permit.

The Ramapo ordinance was challenged in the courts and finally upheld by the highest New York appeals court. Important in support of this decision was Ramapo's record of taking ". . . great care to provide reasonable procedures, with appeals, variances, and opportunities to developers to speed up the process by putting in improvements on their own, tax relief appeals, and continued use of land at present low density."[94]

The Ramapo ordinance is significant for its establishment of a direct relationship between zoning and capital improvements programming, relating private to public development.

Petaluma.   In 1972 Petaluma chose to try to control development by means of a quota basis under a Residential Development Control System ordinance using a point system similar to Ramapo's for awarding development permits. This ordinance combined aspects of zoning and subdivision controls and was administered by a separate Residential Development Evaluation Board.[95] This ordinance was declared unconstitutional in Federal District Court in early 1974. This decision was reversed on appeal to the Ninth Circuit Court of Appeals on August 13, 1975 and that decision was upheld by refusal in February 1976 of the U.S. Supreme Court to review the case.[96]

Boca Raton.   Feeling that "Rapid, uncontrolled, and mindless population growth . . ." would mean destruction of their highly valued way of life, the citizens of Boca Raton, Florida in 1972 approved a city charter amendment limiting permanently the total number of dwelling units within the city to 40,000 or a population of about 105,000, about two and a half times the 41,000 population estimated for 1973.[97]

To implement this population ceiling, unique to Boca Raton, a series of moratoria were established for all housing construction except duplexes and single-family housing from November 8, 1972 through March 28, 1974 to enable a study to be made of replatting and rezoning designed to reduce the residential densities scheduled for undeveloped land so that when the city is fully developed it will achieve the charter amendment goal. A Moratorium Variance Advisory Board was set up to review all replatting and rezoning in the light of interim densities established in an interim zoning ordinance to control densities while the studies necessary for permanent rezoning could be completed.

Other Uses of Moratoria.   Beside moratoria on building permits as in Boca Raton, local governments have imposed moratoria on water line connections, sewer permits and connections, for the evaluation of environmental impact, and rezoning. Cities and counties that have used various types of moratoria also include: Metro Dade County (Miami), Florida; St. Petersburg and Pinellas County, Florida; Washington, D.C.; Phoenix, Arizona; Albuquerque, New Mexico; Marin County, California; and Prince William County, Virginia.[98] Total moratoria have rarely been upheld in the courts but those of short duration and having a mechanism for allowing some development have more often been upheld.[99]

CONCLUDING OBSERVATIONS

It has been difficult to adapt zoning, an essentially negative tool, to the purposes of carrying out comprehensive plans in both developing and developed areas. In developing areas, for economic reasons, low density development usually occurs even where the plan envisions high density nodal development. In developed areas zoning is a poor tool for altering existing uses to those envisioned in the plan, especially if they are to be lower intensity uses. Even where current enabling legislation requires that zoning be pursuant to comprehensive plans the courts have usually chosen to construe the zoning map *to be* the land use plan.

There are other difficulties in using zoning to carry out land use planning:

1. The long-range comprehensive plans may be too general and give no clues concerning staging of development. Without more detailed intermediate-range plans they are difficult to translate directly into zoning decisions;
2. In undeveloped areas zoning for future intensive uses may be self-defeating, causing land prices to exceed levels conducive to developing the intended uses;
3. In undeveloped areas zoning for low-intensity uses in order to keep the land open, either permanently or as a holding action, is likely to raise a problem of compensation to the owners for so restricting their options;

4. Zoning ordinances generally contain no mechanism enabling or requiring coordination of zoning policies with the other planning implementation tools;

Zoning is also a poor tool for achieving maximum choice in living and working environments in respect to building type, rental or purchase price, site design and general amenity because:

1. Zoning ordinances are essentially restrictive often involving rigid dimensional and area requirements designed primarily for the control of small, incremental developments;
2. Where more flexibility is needed there has been a reluctance to give the appropriate discretionary authority to the zoning administrator;
3. There are localized vested interests in retaining obsolete, pyramidal, and cumulative zoning patterns which perpetuate or promote economic, social, and housing-type segregation.

However, there are recent, scattered efforts to modify zoning and introduce new devices in reaction to these faults such as:

1. The amortization of non-conforming uses;
2. The introduction of performance standards in place of use lists;
3. Substituting density for use as the primary characteristic of zones;
4. Introducing conditional uses which require special permits and review by either the planning commission or the board of appeals;
5. Introducing historic, cultural, and esthetic zoning requiring development review by a panel of experts;
6. Introducing provisions for planned unit development involving review by the planning commission;
7. Introduction into the ordinance of incentives for developers who agree to provide certain amenities.

Some observers feel that zoning is past reform. Others hold out more hope for reform. The American Law Institute has completed a new Model Land Development Code which goes beyond zoning to include other controls. (This will be dealt with more extensively in chapter seven.) The development of better guidance systems for land use is essential and it is unlikely that zoning will be entirely abandoned but rather be incorporated in some modified form into these systems.

NOTES AND ACKNOWLEDGEMENTS FOR CHAPTER 2

1. Hadacheck v. Sebastion, 329 U.S. 394 (1915).
2. Village of Euclid, Ohio v. Ambler Reality Company, 272 U.S. 365, (1926).
3. Heyman, I. Michael, "Innovative Land Regulation and Comprehensive Planning," from *The New Zoning: Legal, Administrative and Economic Concepts and Techniques*, eds. Marcus, Norman and Groves, Marilyn W., a Publication of the Center for New York City Affairs, New School of Social Research. (New York: Praeger, © 1970), p. 24.
4. Delafons, John, *Land-Use Controls in the United States* 2nd ed., (Cambridge, Massachusetts: The M.I.T. Press, 1969), p. 7, reproduced by permission.
5. Haar, Charles M., "In Accordance with a Comprehensive Plan," *Harvard Law Review,* **68**, No. 7, p. 1154.
6. Kent, Jr., T. J., *The Urban General Plan*, (San Francisco: Chandler, 1964), pp. 33–34.
7. Mandelker, Daniel R., *The Zoning Dilemma,* (Indianapolis: Bobbs-Merrill, copyright 1971), p. xii. Reprinted by permission of the publisher, the Bobbs-Merrill Company. All rights reserved. See also p. 58.
8. Hartzer, Timothy J., Comprehensive Plans Edge Zoning Ordinances as Legal Documents for Development," *A.I.P. Newsletter,* **10**, No. 9, (September, 1975), p. 7. Permission to reprint granted by A.I.P., Washington, D.C.
9. For a complete discussion of the politics of zoning the reader is referred to Mandelker, *op. cit.,* and Richard F. Babcock, *The Zoning Game* (Madison: University of Wisconsin Press, 1966).
10. Leary, Robert M., "Zoning", in William I. Goodman, ed., *Principles and Practice of Urban Planning*, (Washington: The International City Management Association, copyright 1968 by the Association), p. 406, reproduced by permission.
11. Marcinkus, Betsy Ross, "Planning for an Island Metropolis," (Washington: American Institute of Planners, 1972), pp. 7–11 (mimeographed).
12. Spicer, Richard B., "Increasing State and Regional Power in the Development Process," *ASPO Planning Advisory Service Report 255,* March 1970), pp. 5–6.
13. ——, *op. cit.,* pp. 1–15.
14. Webster, Donald H., *Urban Planning and Municipal Public Policy*, (New York: Harper & Row, 1958), p. 368, and Norman Williams, Jr., *The Structure of Urban Zoning*, (New York: Buttenheim, 1966), p. 27.
15. Leary, *op. cit.,* p. 409.
16. ——, *op. cit.,* p. 424.
17. ——, *op. cit.,* p. 425, reproduced by permission.

18. Pratter, Jerome, and Ward, Richard, "A New Concept in Residential Zoning," *Urban Law Annual*, 1971:33, pp. 133–41.
19. Leary, *op. cit.*, p. 425.
20. See Webster, *op. cit.*, pp. 381–82 for a less restrictive viewpoint.
21. Candeub, Fleissig, and Associates, *Route 1: A Highway Demonstration Study, Woodbridge, New Jersey*, (Newark: Candeub, Fleissig, and Associates, 1968) pp. 1–172.
22. Ornstein, Gail, "Auto Centers," *ASPO Planning Advisory Service Report 219*, (February, 1967), pp. 1–14.
23. Leary, *op. cit.*, p. 426, reproduced by permission.
24. In conjunction with urban renewal, zoning has been used in central business districts to "clean up" marginal businesses, honky tonks, and skid rows. This may only cause these activities to locate elsewhere in the urban area.
25. For a detailed discussion of the design and administration of industrial performance standards see: Marvin A. Saltzenstein, "Industrial Performance Standards," ASPO *Planning Advisory Service Report 272*, (September 1971), pp. 1–63.
26. "Proposed Zoning Ordinance," *Oakland Tribune*, (August 26, 1965) supplement.
27. Bingham, Charlotte, "Regulating Public Uses," p. 3, Reprinted with permission from PAS Report 228. Copyright 1967 by the American Society of Planning Officials.
28. Bingham, *op. cit.*, pp. 6–7.
29. See the argument concerning spot zoning in the section on historic preservation.
30. Hagman, Donald G., *Urban Planning and Land Development Control Law*, (St. Paul: West, 1961) pp. 108–09, reproduced by permission.
31. Goldschmidt, Leopold A., "Zoning for City Housing Markets," ASPO *Planning Advisory Service Report 279*, (April, 1972), p. 3.
32. Krasnowiecki, Jan, "Planned Unit Residential Development," *Urban Land Institute Technical Bulletin*, No. 52, (May 1965), pp. 11–14, reproduced by permission.
33. Mandelker, *op. cit.*, p. 178. Reprinted by permission of the publisher, the Bobbs-Merrill Company. All rights reserved.
34. Hagman, *op. cit.*, p. 458.
35. Wolfe, Leonard L., "New Zoning Landmarks in Planned Unit Development," *Urban Land Institute Technical Bulletin*, No. 62, (1968), p. 9.
36. Mandelker, *op. cit.*, p. 127.
37. Wolfe, Leonard, describes one such arrangement in detail in *Urban Land Institute Technical Bulletin*, No. 62, (1968), pp. 12–14 and 24–29. For a more detailed discussion of planned unit development with examples see: Robert W. Burchell and James W. Hughes, *Planned Unit Development—New Communities American Style*, (New Brunswick: University Center for Urban Policy Research, 1972) pp. 1–254.
38. Kusler, Jon A., and Lee, Thomas M., "Regulation for Flood Plains," ASPO *Planning Advisory Service Report 277*, (February 1972), p. 1.
39. ——, *op. cit.*, pp. 11–18, *passim*.

40. U.S. Water Resources Council. *Regulation of Flood-Hazard Areas to Reduce Flood Losses,* (Washington: U.S. Government Printing Office, 1972) part III, sec. 323.

41. Kusler and Lee, *op. cit.* pp. 43–44.

42. Fagin, Henry, and Weinberg, Robert C., eds., *Planning and Community Appearance,* (New York: The Regional Plan Association, 1958), Chapters III, IV, and V.

43. Tomson, Bernard, and Coplan, Norman, "It's the Law," Reprinted from the March 1973 issue of *Progressive Architecture,* p. 110. Copyright 1973.

44. People vs. Goodman, 31 N.Y. 2d 262.

45. [Feiss, Carl], *Planning and Zoning Code and Zone Map,* (Village of Bratenahl, Ohio: The Village, July 1962), p. 56.

46. Chicago Plan Commission, *Billboard Regulation,* (Chicago: The Commission 1952), pp. 2–3.

47. For examples of historic preservation programs see: U.S. Department of Housing and Urban Development, *Preserving Historic America,* (Washington: U.S. Government Printing Office, 1966).

48. Miner, Ralph W., "Conservation of Historic and Cultural Resources," ASPO *Planning Advisory Service Report 244,* (March, 1969), pp. 22–34.

49. ———, *op. cit.,* pp. 24–28.

50. Norfolk Department of City Planning, *Preserving Norfolk's Heritage,* (Norfolk, Va.: The Department, (December 1965), p. 22.

51. Bair, Frederick H., Jr., "Special Public Interest Districts," ASPO *Planning Advisory Service Report 287,* (January 1973), *passim.*

52. Webster, *op. cit.,* p. 403, reproduced by permission.

53. Scott, Robert L., "The Effect of Nonconforming Land-Use Amortization," p. 5, reprinted with permission from PAS Report 280. Copyright by the American Society of Planning Officials.

54. Scott, *op. cit.,* p. 21, reprinted by permission.

55. Leary, *op. cit.,* p. 432, reproduced by permission.

56. Svirsky, Peter S., "San Francisco Limits the Buildings to See the Sky," *Planning,* **39,** No. 1, pp. 9–14.

57. Berman vs. Parker, 348 U.S. 26, 75 Sup. Ct. 98, 99 L.Ed. 27 (1954).

58. Federal Housing Administration, *Land Use Intensity,* (Washington: U.S. Government Printing Office, 1966), p. 1.

59. Mandelker, Daniel L., "The Rosslyn Experience," in *The New Zoning: Legal, Administrative, and Economic Concepts and Techniques,* Norman Marcus and Marilyn W. Graves, eds., (New York: Praeger, 1970), pp. 16–17.

60. Marks, Marvin, and West III, John Petit, "Urban Design through Zoning," *Planners Notebook,* **2,** No. 5, (October, 1972), pp. 3–5.

61. For more detailed descriptions and additional examples see: Mary Brooks, "Bonus Provisions in Central City Areas," ASPO *Planning Advisory Service Report 257,* (May 1970), *passim.*

62. Hagman, *op. cit.* (*Urban . . . Law*), p. 169, reproduced by permission.

63. Hagman, Donald G., *Urban Planning and Controls: Problems and Materials, Part II*, (Los Angeles: Institute of Government and Public Affairs, University of California, Los Angeles, 1969), p. N3.

64. Faraci, Piero, "The Authority of the Zoning Administrator," p. 15, Reprinted with permission from PAS Report 226. Copyright 1967 by the American Society of Planning Officials.

65. Leary, *op. cit.*, p. 439.

66. Rody, Martin J., and Smith, Herbert H., *Zoning Primer*, (West Trenton: Chandler-Davis, 1960), p. 27. Reproduced by permission.

67. *Indiana Area Planning Legislation*, (Indianapolis: Division of Planning Department of Commerce, State of Indiana, undated), p. 9.

68. [Unigov Planning Legislation], *Laws of the State of Indiana.* Acts 1955, ch. 283, sec. 68, p. 802.

69. For a more detailed discussion see Frederick H. Bair, Jr., *Local Regulation of Mobile Home Parks, Travel Trailer Parks and Related Facilities*, (Chicago: Mobile Homes Research Foundation, 1965).

70. Bair, *op. cit.,* pp. 23–24.

71. The reader is also referred to: Frederick H. Bair, Jr., "Modular Housing, Including Mobile Homes," ASPO *Planning Advisory Report 265*, (January 1971), entire report.

72. For background see: Mary Brooks, "Exclusionary Zoning," ASPO *Planning Advisory Service Report 254*, (February, 1970).

73. Lauber, Daniel, "Recent Cases in Exclusionary Zoning," p. 3, PAS Report 292, Copyright 1973 by the American Society of Planning Officials.

74. ———, *op. cit.*, pp. 1–2 and for a case study on the problems of locating public housing see: Martin Meyerson, and Edward C. Banfield, *Politics, Planning and the Public Interest*, (Glencoe, Ill.: The Free Press, 1955), pp. 11–353.

75. Ranjel v. the City of Lansing, 417 F. 2nd 321, (Michigan 1969).

76. Southern Alameda Spanish Speaking Organization v. City of Union City, discussed in Lauber, *op. cit.*, p. 9.

77. Lauber, *op. cit.*, p. 27.

78. "Cities Must Change Zoning Laws for Poor," *Lafayette Journal and Courier*, (January 9, 1978), p. A-1.

79. Lauber, *op. cit.*, p. 35, reprinted by permission.

80. Davidoff, Paul, and Rosensweig, Linda, "Entire Township Zoning Ordinance Struck Down as Exclusionary," from *AIP Newsletter*, **6**, No. 11, (November 1971), p. 9, a publication of the American Institute of Planners.

81. Burlington Co., NAACP v. Township of Mount Laurel, 200 A. 2d 465, (New Jersey Super. Ct. 1972).

82. Lauber, *op. cit.*, p. 19; Ed McCahill, "In Mount Laurel, Issues Are Not Black and White," *Planning*, **41**, No. 4, (May, 1975), p. 12–13.

83. Williams, *op. cit.*, p. 77.

84. Lauber, *op. cit.*, p. 70.

85. ———, *op. cit.*, p. 71.

86. "Agency News," *Planning*, **39**, No. 6, (July, 1973), p. 5.

87. Lauber, *op. cit.*, p. 72, reprinted by permission.

88. ——, *op. cit.*, p. 73.

89. Babcock, *Zoning Game*, p. 10.

90. Hagman, *Urban Planning*, p. 174.

91. ——, *op. cit.*, p. 175.

92. Williams, *op. cit.*, p. 33.

93. Scott, Randall W., "Introduction and Summary," *Management and Control of Growth*, Vol. 1, (Washington: The Urban Land Institute, 1975), pp. 5–9.

94. Stollman, Israel, "Ramapo." Reprinted with premission from *Planning*, **38**, No. 6, (July, 1972), pp. 108–09, the magazine of the American Society of Planning Officials, copyright 1972.

95. McGivern, William C., "Putting a Speed Limit on Growth," *Planning*, **38**, No. 10, (November, 1972), pp. 263–65.

96. Scott, Randall, "The Petaluma Decision: Another Sign that Federal Courts Don't Want to Get into Land Use," *AIP Newsletter*, **10**, No. 10, (October 1975), p. 7; see also Jerome G. Rose, "Recent Decisions on Population Growth Control: The Belle Terre, Petaluma and Madison Township Cases," *New Dimensions in Urban Planning: Growth Controls*, Vol. 1, ed. by James W. Hughes, (New Brunswick: Center for Urban Policy Research, The State University of New Jersey, 1974), pp. 180–182.

97. Einsweiler, Robert C.; Gleeson, Michael E.; Ball, Ian Traquair; Morris, Alan; and Sprague, Diane, "Comparative Descriptions of Selected Municipal Growth Guidance Systems, A Preliminary Report," in Scott, *Management of Growth*, (Washington: The Urban Land Institute, 1975), Vol. II, pp. 299–300, reproduced by permission.

98. Carter, Steve; Bert, Kendall; and Nobert, Peter, "Local Government Techniques for Managing Growth," in Scott, *Management of Growth*, (Washington: The Urban Land Institute, 1975), Vol. II, p. 342.

99. Heeter, David, "Interim Zoning Ordinances," ASPO *Planning Advisory Service Report 242*, (January 1969), p. 8.

3

Subdivision regulations

Subdivision regulations, together with zoning, are important in the implementation of land use plans in developing areas. Unlike zoning, the regulation of the subdivision of land into parcels derives from local ordinances used in some of the earliest American colonial cities. However, the concept of making subdivision regulations an integral part of the land use planning process stems largely from the Standard City Planning Enabling Act of 1928.[1]

Whenever a tract of land is subdivided into two or more smaller tracts for the purposes of lease or sale there occur the problems of establishing an adequate legal description of the new boundaries and establishing the quality of the eventual development if the resultant plots are of developable scale. At this point the locality within whose jurisdiction the subdividing takes place has an opportunity to impose development standards and other requirements which will influence the resulting land use pattern. Accordingly, Webster states that: "The primary objective of subdivision control is to assure that the land subdivided will constitute a permanent asset to the community, and will provide the maximum degree of health, comfort, convenience, and beauty consistent with true economy."[2]

Philip Green summarizes the essence of subdivision regulations as:[3]

. . . locally adopted laws governing the process of converting raw land into building sites. They normally accomplish this through plat approval procedures, under which a developer is not permitted to make improvements or to divide and sell his land until the planning commission has approved a plat (map) of the proposed design of his subdivision. The approval or disapproval of the commission is based upon compliance or noncompliance of the proposal with development standards set forth in the subdivision regulations. In the event that the developer attempts to record an unapproved plat in the local registry of deeds (or county recorder's office) or to sell lots by reference to such a plat, he may be subject to various civil and criminal penalties.

A wide range of purposes are served by subdivision regulations affecting many local governmental departments, agencies, and other instrumentalities. They affect public health objectives by insuring that new development will have a safe water supply and an adequate sewage disposal system. For tax officials they are a means of securing records of land titles and alerting them to the need for reassessment. For the city engineer or public works director they are a means of assuring good design and adequate construction of streets, drainage, and utilities. For the fire department they are a means of assuring adequate firefighting water and vehicle access. For education and recreation officials they are a means of reserving or securing the necessary school and park sites to serve the local development. For the local governing body they are a means of assuring quality in the design of the development and the equitable allocation of costs involved between those directly benefited within the development and the tax paying public as a whole. For the ultimate buyer of property in the subdivision they are assurance of adequately served property whose value is more likely to hold up over time. To the developer they are protection against cost cornercutting, substandard adjacent development which might adversely affect the value of his own development.

The question of infrastructure cost allocation in new development will be dealt with more extensively later in this chapter. It is one of the major issues in the establishment of subdivision controls. Because from the local government point of view there is no justifiable reason for the general public to assume the financial burden of capital costs for the infrastructure of streets, public services, schools, and recreational open space which is of primary or even exclusive benefit to the owners and occupants of the subdivision itself, these improvements are usually required to be financed by the subdivider. Where necessary improvements serve a larger area than the subdivision in question some prorating of the costs is usually made between the subdivider and the local government on the basis of shared benefit.

The vast majority of subdivisions are for residential purposes. In recent years, however, there has been an increase in subdivision for industry and a small amount of subdivision for commercial and other land uses.[6]

The legal basis for subdivision regulations, like that for zoning, derives from the regulatory or "police" power. Usually the authority for local governments to exercise this power is established through state enabling legislation. Limitations on the exercise of this power are set by the state and federal constitutions as interpreted by the courts as well as being delimited in the authorizing legislation. Localities operating under "home rule" charters may, however, have more discretionary power than nonhome-rule localities.

Most states exempt minor subdivisions (2–3 lots and sell-offs of part of a parcel to the neighboring owner) from regulation but some states, like Kentucky, even include selloffs of land from one owner to an adjacent owner and subdivision for leasing as well as sale.

Extraterritoriality, allowing communities to control subdivisions for five miles beyond their corporate boundaries, was a feature of the Standard Act which has been embodied to differing degrees in state enabling legislation. Counties are granted subdivision control authority in their unincorporated areas in most states.[4]

Various state agencies such as highway and health departments, usually by way of their county and municipal equivalents, may participate in the approval process. Some states, notably Florida, Hawaii, New York, and Vermont can intervene in the local subdivision process to overrule local subdivision control decisions.

The states vary in regard to whether they require subdivision ordinances to be adopted by the planning commission or by the local governing body on recommendation of the planning commission. They also vary in regard to whether final approval of subdivision plats is granted by the planning commission or the local governing body. The most common arrangement is one in which the regulations are adopted by the legislative body and the approval function is delegated to the planning commission subject to appeal directly to the courts.

Permissible requirements vary from state to state but usually are based on the requirements of the Standard Act:[5]

Such regulations may provide for the proper arrangement of streets in relation to other existing or planned streets and to the master plan, for adequate and convenient open spaces for traffic, utilities, access for fire-fighting apparatus, recreation, light and air, and for the avoidance of congestion of population, including width and area of lots.

Such regulations may include provisions as to the extent to which streets and other ways shall be graded and improved and to which water and sewer and other utility mains, piping, or other facilities shall be installed as a condition precedent to the approval of the plat.

Professor Green describes them as including:[6]

. . . provisions (1) making sale (or negotiation for sale) of land by reference to (or other use of) an unapproved plat unlawful and subject to a civil penalty, (2) authorizing the city to enjoin such a sale, (3) making it unlawful for the county recorder to file or record an unapproved plat, (4) forbidding improvements in or on new streets in unapproved subdivisions, and (5) forbidding issuance of a building permit for a structure on a lot having access only to an unapproved street.

The constitutionality of subdivision regulations has been upheld in court decisions on grounds of the furtherance of public health and safety, conditions simplifying land title transactions, conditions necessary to the local government's acceptance or declining of responsibility for maintaining local streets, ". . . a necessary aid in the maintenance of proper tax records and land titles, and a protection of lot purchases against sharp marketing practices."[7]

Differing sections of subdivision regulations may require differing legal theory for support. Subdivision regulations result in a bargaining process between the developer and the local governmental agency administering them, and as such rarely lead to court action.

COORDINATION WITH OTHER PLANNING IMPLEMENTATION MEASURES

Coordination of subdivision controls with other planning measures is of utmost importance if they are to be used effectively for implementing the plan. Recent attempts to combine subdivision controls with zoning and other planning controls into integrated development controls is symptomatic of the need for coordination. Among the more important planning measures to be coordinated are the land use plan, the community facilities plan, the major street plan, the official map, the capital improvements program, zoning, and the health regulations.

The Land Use, Community Facilities, and Major Street Plans

The land use plan, community facilities plan, and major street plan are commonly elements of the general or comprehensive plan. Examination of them will reveal the appropriateness of the uses for which a prospective subdivision is planned, the possible need for reserving land within the subdivision for community facilities, and the general location within the subdivision of land to be reserved for major streets if any are planned to pass through it. Accordingly many states require that a general plan containing these elements be adopted before a locality can enact subdivision controls. The general plan also provides legal proof that requirements in accordance with it are not arbitrary or capricious.

Coordination of subdivisions with the general plan is an important means of enabling the subdivider to dedicate or reserve land needed for public uses. Through the subdivision approval process agencies of local government have an opportunity to obtain needed land by dedication or purchase.

Official Map

The official map, where one has been adopted, details the specific locations of future streets and other public facilities which are given only generalized locations on the comprehensive plan. It serves to give notice to developers of the public intention to purchase for public use such land as is not required to be dedicated. It also prohibits construction on the indicated sites for a period of time during which the public agencies concerned may arrange to make purchase. The need for coordination of subdivision designs with the provisions of the official map is obvious and legally embodied in the official map ordinance.

Capital Improvement Program

The capital improvement program, described in detail in a later chapter, outlines the locality's intended expenditures for streets, utilities, schools, and other public development expenditures year by year usually over a five- to six-year period. Consequently if there is a lack of public facilities in place, or scheduled to serve a proposed development, it is in the public interest to disapprove the proposed development unless the developer is in a position and willing to supply them himself. However the legal position for refusal is weak except in regard to required utilities.[8] As previously mentioned two notable examples of city experimentation in development timing control are Ramapo, N.Y. and Petaluma, Calif., who chose to limit growth through the zoning ordinance or a separate ordinance limiting the issuance of building permits rather than through subdivision controls. (See chapter seven also.)

Zoning

A number of requirements specified in the zoning ordinance are often also specified in the subdivision regulations; for example: minimum lot sizes and lot dimensions, and setbacks and yard sizes. Accordingly most subdivision regulations require that subdivisions also conform to the relevant provisions of the zoning ordinance.

Often subdivision approval requests require concurrent zoning changes. The planning commission (or department) and its working committees must then arrange for concurrent staff studies and for concurrent consideration of these requests in order to insure proper coordination. Request for variances in connection with proposed development may also need concurrent, coordinated review. These procedures are usually ad hoc in nature and vary from planning agency to planning agency.

Health and Sanitary Regulations

Increasingly health regulations require minimum lot sizes where wells or septic tanks are intended to be used. These requirements are related to local soil and geological conditions. Consequently, in some areas wells and/or septic tanks may be forbidden altogether. Zoning ordinances and subdivision regulations must take cognizance of and be coordinated with such regulations. Because the health agency may be part of a higher level of government, the problems of effective interagency coordination may be more difficult.

Deed Restrictions

In order to make property more saleable developers frequently place restrictions in the deeds of sale which are more restrictive than the provisions of the relevant zoning ordinance or subdivision regulations. These restrictions are not enforceable by exercise of the police power but require recourse to the courts by those made party to the restrictions. The parties named in the deeds are usually limited to the developer and property owners within the subdivision. In some instances an agency of local government such as the planning agency may be made party to the deed restrictions during the bargaining process of getting the subdivision approved. This situation was discussed in the previous chapter in the section on contract zoning.

THE SUBDIVISION APPROVAL PROCESS

Despite differences in enabling legislation from state to state there is a remarkable similarity in locally adopted subdivision regulations. In part this is the result of imitation of other existing local ordinances and in part it is the influence of the HUD-FHA subdivision standards on which federal mortgage insurance commitments are made.[9]

What follows is a description of the most common subdivision regulation procedures. Unsatisfactory aspects of the process in practice will be emphasized and the more important policy issues will be developed further on in the chapter.

Procedures

In jurisdictions where sell-offs and other minor subdivisions are regulated there are often simplified procedures prescribed. These variations from the usual procedures are not important enough to describe here because they have minimal effect on the implementation of the comprehensive plan. It is the more usual subdivisions with which we will be concerned here. The larger-than-average subdivision proposed as a planned unit development will also be dealt with separately.

Preapplication.   Many subdivision regulations either suggest or require that before submitting a preliminary plat the subdivider present to the administering staff a rough sketch of what he intends to do so that he may have advice from the staff which may save him time and money in site planning. The Louisville regulations, for example, specify the following: "The subdivider shall submit for discussion a rough sketch showing generally the boundaries of the proposed subdivision, the proposed street and lot pattern and any other pertinent information then known to the subdivider".[10]

Preliminary Plat or Plan.   After the preapplication conferences the subdivider submits a preliminary plat or plan for approval by the planning commission or other agency charged with administering the subdivision regulations. At this stage the most important decisions are made concerning the acceptability of the subdivision design. The regulations usually describe in detail the information required on this plan. For example, the Louisville regulations detail the required format and materials, legend information, designation of easements and public areas, boundaries, ownership of adjacent property, contours, areas subject to flooding, proposed land use, key map, and title block.

The preliminary plan must be submitted with a sufficient number of copies so that all the interested agencies will have an opportunity to review the plan and comment on it as it affects them. These include the locality's director of public works or engineer, the parks department, school board, public health department, and other relevant agencies. The recommendations of all the reviewing agencies must be sent to the administering agency prior to its hearing.

The administering agency, usually the planning commission, either approves or disapproves the preliminary plan. At this time there may be considerable bargaining between the subdivider and the administering agency. Most often this bargaining takes place in an informal hearing with the subdivision committee of the planning commission prior to the formal public hearing of the planning commission as a whole. This arrangement allows more effective bargaining to take place than would be possible in the formal commission hearing where the primary business is likely to be zoning change applications. Professor Green notes that although unusual, "Some regulations provide for an appeal to the local governing board from the decision made at this time . . . "[11] Usually the planning commission's decision is final with appeal only to the courts.

Construction of Improvements. The developer is required to construct the agreed upon necessary improvements between the approval of the preliminary plan and approval of the final or record plat. Before he begins construction his construction drawings must be approved as at least equivalent to the locality's standards as embodied in the subdivision regulations and/or building code. After construction he must provide "as built" drawings showing accurately what has been built as partial evidence that he has met the regulations as agreed. If the administration is satisfied he can then submit the final plat for approval. However, as Webster comments: "Most regulations . . . permit the subdivider to apply for final approval of only that portion of the approved preliminary plat which he may propose to record and develop at a particular time."[12] This allows the developer to save capital and interest by developing in stages. Further, most jurisdictions allow the subdivider in lieu of actual construction to file a bond guaranteeing performance within a specified time period as a protection to the locality and prospective purchasers.

Recording of the final plat may involve other state legislation pertaining to legal documents as to both form and content. Reference to a plat and lot number is the most convenient way of describing real property in a deed and gives the prospective buyer a better idea of what he may be purchasing than does a written description. The older way of describing property by "metes and bounds" is cumbersome and no longer legally possible in many states.

Fees. It is customary to require the subdivider to help defray the costs of processing his application although there is considerable variation in this practice. Some local governments set a flat fee per application; others base the fee on the area or number of lots involved. The fee may include filing costs, charges for processing and data verification, and expenses for required legal advertising and recording. Fees in lieu of providing for required open space will be dealt with later in this chapter.

Design Standards and Related Requirements

Most subdivision regulations set forth certain general overall requirements in regard to location and type of subdivision, followed by more
specific design standards involving layout, street patterns and widths,
lot shapes and dimensions, utility and access easements, recreational
open space, and provision for community facilities.

The general provisions may specify where in the locality subdivision
is altogether prohibited because of adverse soil, subsoil, or flooding
conditions which are potential health or safety dangers, compliance
with the general land use plan, and provisions for coordination with
adjacent development, especially in regard to streets and utilities.

Streets.   The design of the street system for a subdivision is critical to
the effectiveness of the overall design. Streets provide vehicular access
to all properties and are paralleled by the pedestrian access in most designs. Street rights-of-way also provide space for utilities not otherwise
provided for in separate easements.

The street system is generally classified into a hierarchy of local
streets, collector or feeder streets, and arterial or major streets. The latter are usually shown on the general land use plan and the major street
plan if there is one. Coordination of the differing levels of street design
is important to their effective functioning.

Local streets are low-speed streets designed primarily to give direct
access to individual properties. They should be designed so as to discourage or prevent through-traffic, through the use of loops or culs-de-
sac, or other means of achieving discontinuity because of the safety
hazards of frequent driveways and playing children.

Collector streets should be designed to collect the traffic from local
streets and group parking areas and to provide for minimal access to
single-family lots. Access to the latter should be primarily to local
streets whenever possible.

Arterial streets should be restricted to giving access to collector
streets. Properties along them should front on local or collector streets
or parallel service streets, thus allowing the arterials to carry higher
volumes safely at higher speeds.

The limiting of street access through subdivision ordinances possibly backed by deed restrictions may not be possible in some states
where it is not provided for explicitly in enabling legislation because of
adverse court decisions. Nonetheless it is a worthwhile planning objec-

tive in subdivision design for reasons of safety and increased street capacity.

Overall street design should take proper account of the terrain, avoiding steep slopes, following the contour lines where possible but having sufficient slope for gravity-flow sewerage systems where they are in the street rights-of-way. Multistreet intersections, off-set intersections, and other than right-angle intersections should be avoided. The reader is referred for detailed standards to the latest edition of "Recommended Practices for Subdivision Streets" of the Institute of Transportation Engineers.[13]

An aspect of street design which needs regulation but is often overlooked is that of street naming. Lack of designation controls results in confusing duplication and seriously compounds the difficulties of locating addresses. It may result in needless delay in goods delivery, critical delay in receiving police and fire protection, and irritation to social visitors. A number of schemes are available. One such scheme is illustrated by Green.[14] The numbering or lettering of streets by the quadrant system centered on some important central intersection is the simplest and most direct, but the least esthetically engaging. Among the other systems are the alphabetical systems which by giving names rather than numbers to streets seem less impersonal.

Utility Easements.   Those utilities not in street rights-of-way need to be in dedicated easements which guarantee access for maintenance purposes. Increasingly electrical and telephone lines follow rear lot lines and are placed underground. This practice is required in FHA insured subdivisions except where it can be demonstrated to be economically or physically impractical.[15] Great care should be taken in locating these easements so that building sites are not impaired or the natural landscape needlessly disturbed. Minimum widths of easements should be large enough to accommodate heavy maintenance equipment. Where natural water courses are followed or used for stormwater drainage, care should be taken to avoid damage from construction or flooding so the valley areas will retain their esthetic appeal and recreational value.

Lotting Out.   The depth of lots is dependent on the pattern of street locations and the distance between parallel streets, required minimum lot widths and minimum lot areas. Minimum lot sizes and restrictions on buildable areas are set forth in the zoning ordinance and possibly in the health regulations; accordingly there is no necessity to specify them in the subdivision regulations except by reference.

Compulsory Dedication of Land

There is a long history of requiring developers to provide: ". . . the land needed for streets and for various public areas such as the town common, squares, parks, and public building sites."[16] Colonial town governments, royal charters, and early state charters required such dedications. Accordingly the requirements in modern subdivision regulations that: ". . . developers dedicate street rights-of-way, utilities easements, recreation areas, and school sites are nothing new in our law, but merely a continuation of an old tradition."[17]

The regulations often distinguish between *dedication*, a gift, and *reservation* (the holding of land off the market for a specific period of time in anticipation of purchase of it by a public agency for public uses). A certificate of ownership and dedication is usually required to accompany the final plat and be recorded when the subdivider dedicates land to the public. The ". . . approval of the subdivision plat does not in itself constitute an acceptance of such dedications, because that would make the local governmental unit immediately liable for maintaining the facility in a safe condition", explains Professor Green.[18] The decision to accept dedications is usually made separately. Reserved land is held out of development for the specified period in which the appropriate public agency has the exclusive option to execute a purchase agreement with the subdivider.

In court tests subdivision regulation requirements for the dedication of land for street rights-of-way have usually been upheld, especially when tied in with a master street plan and in situations where the right-of-way dedicated clearly serves the subdivision in question. In the special case of arterial streets or freeways where the amount of right-of-way involved is extensive, and the properties in the subdivision are not the ones primarily served, the public agency concerned may have to purchase all or part of the necessary rights-of-way, depending on the provisions of the subdivision regulations, the relevant court decisions, and the bargaining process involved in getting the subdivision approved.

Subdivision regulation requirements of the dedication of land for schools, parks, and recreational uses have met with mixed reactions in the courts. In order to justify these requirements it would seem to be necessary to demonstrate that the need for the land dedicated is generated primarily by the subdivision in question. At any rate dedication requirements need to be clearly tied to direct benefits to the subdivision involved, and these requirements should be clearly spelled out in the ordinance together with the criteria for applying them. Reservation requirements are not as severe a burden on the subdivider but they also must be clearly related to an official map, adopted land use plan, or clearly set out criteria.

Payments in Lieu of Dedication

There are often problems of equity and suitability in regard to required dedications and reservations. Public uses may serve more than one subdivision and the most appropriate site for public uses serving any given subdivision may lie outside the subdivision entirely. Accordingly it may be impractical to apply dedication or reservation requirements uniformly to all subdivisions under consideration for approval.

As a remedy for these situations many localities permit or require the developer to make monetary payments in lieu of dedication. This alternative is often left to the discretion of the administrators of the ordinance. The amount may be based on the number of lots or the total acreage involved.

Court reactions to this approach have been mixed. The likelihood of a favorable court reaction is increased if there is specific statutory authorization for the requirement, the money so collected is kept in a separate fund for school and park purposes, the regulations require that the money collected be spent in a manner which will benefit the subdivision in connection with which they were collected, and that the amounts collected bear some reasonable relationship to the actual costs of serving that subdivision.[19]

Required Improvements

Effective subdivision control involves more than achieving good standards of design and obtaining adequate dedications and reservations of land needed for public uses. It also requires the installation of an infrastructure of adequate streets and utilities. This infrastructure is of direct economic benefit to the purchasers of lots and affects the costs of providing services and maintenance for the locality.

Standards for improvements must be sufficiently high to insure adequacy of benefits for and reasonable maintenance costs in the subdivision. Unnecessarily high standards in residential subdivisions, on the other hand, may price some income groups out of the market and have the same effect as exclusionary zoning. Standards should vary by land use, intensity of use and location.[20]

Improvements required may include streets, curbs and gutters, sidewalks, street lights, street signs, water and sewer mains, fire plugs, storm drainage facilities, the placing of monuments to mark lot boundaries and street rights-of-way and even planting of street trees. Actual installation of utilities may be done by the utilities themselves, often at the developer's expense. Other improvements may be installed by the developer or his agents. Where a particular required improvement serves more than the subdivision involved—as may occur in the case of sewer and water mains and arterial streets—and costs more to install than necessitated by the subdivision alone, some means of cost sharing with the locality or other areas served is usually provided.

If the matter is one of extending utilities to the boundaries of the subdivision from the nearest terminus, the developer may have his subdivision turned down, delayed until the locality has scheduled the extension, have the option of paying part or all the cost of immediate extension, or have the alternative option of installing and maintaining temporary utilities (package plants) to serve his subdivision until the utilities are extended and he is required to connect to the locality's system.

Timing and Financing of Improvements

The timing of the required improvements must be carefully programmed so that they are installed in the most rational order and are in place when needed. Large subdivisions are usually developed in stages and the programming of improvements must take this stage development adequately into account.

In order to guard against faulty or improperly constructed improvements, or the inability of the developer to finance the required improvements, it is usual for the locality to require the developer to provide a performance bond from an approved bonding company to guarantee completion of improvements to the required standards. If the developer is allowed to install temporary facilities he may be required also to post a maintenance bond to guarantee satisfactory operation of these facilities. These bonds are a safeguard to both the locality and purchasers in the subdivision.

Variances

Where rigid application of the subdivision regulations in unusual circumstances causes unavoidable hardship to the developer the regulations may enable relief by authorizing the administrating agency to grant minor variations on condition that they do not violate the intention of the standards set forth in the ordinance. More rarely this authority is given to the zoning board of adjustment. This authority needs to be exercised with great caution in order to avoid erosion of the effectiveness of the controls by yielding to the subdivider's desire to cut costs and maximize profits by avoiding some of the requirements of the ordinance and therby lowering the quality of the development or shifting costs to the community as a whole. As with zoning only noneconomic hardships arising from specific peculiarities of the property in question should be taken into consideration. Furthermore the courts have ruled that although conditions and requirements may be modified by the administrating agency if authorized, they may not be waived.[21]

SUBDIVISION CONTROL PROBLEMS

Enabling Legislation

Although all states have some kind of subdivision control legislation, some acts are poorly drawn, some are not state-wide in their coverage, and others are inadequate in other ways. These inadequacies are reflected in the requirements of city ordinances indicated in Table 3-1. Yearwood is of the opinion that improvement is needed in many state subdivision control enabling acts if a high level of quality in subdivision development is to be achieved.[22]

TABLE 3-1. Subdivision Improvement Requirements for 692 Cities Over 10,000 in 1958.

Type of Improvement	Cities Requiring Installation at Developer's Expense	
	Number	Percent
Street grading	437	63%
Street grading & surfacing	505	73
Curbs and gutters	454	66
Sidewalks	323	47
Water mains	516	75
Sanitary sewers	539	78
Storm sewers	443	64
Street trees	131	19
No improvements required	77	11

From: Richard M. Yearwood. *Land Subdivision Regulation: Policy and Legal Considerations for Urban Planning* (New York: Praeger, 1971) p. 227. Compiled from data in the *1958 Municipal Year Book*, © copyright 1958 by the International City Manager's Association, reproduced by their permission.

Fragmentation of Controls

Subdivision approval may involve a variety of city, county, and even state agencies. Often a concurrent change of zoning must also be secured. There may be conflicts in the various codes, and delays in securing the various approvals which are needlessly costly to the developer. Integrated land control ordinances with simplified procedures would greatly improve this situation.

Amateur Developers

The development of most large subdivisions is accomplished by experienced developers with the capital and expertise to develop soundly to the benefit of the community, but the most numerous subdividers and developers are small with limited, often sporadic experience, and develop without adequate professional assistance. It is difficult to write regulations detailed enough to induce good development; at best the regulations can prevent substandard design and be flexible enough to enable really inspired design. Often the only means of achieving acceptable design is to have the local government's planning staff virtually redesign the subdivision for the developer. This undoubtedly happens now and then out of sheer desperation on the part of the administering staff, even though that staff is not generally available to offer design services to private developers at public expense.[23]

Limitations of Controls

Subdivision controls are limited by both the adequacy of the state enabling legislation in regard to what is authorized, and by the completeness of the locally enacted ordinances. Inadequacies in either level of legislation may allow evasion of the controls or inappropriateness of the standards for contemplated development.

Evasion of subdivision regulations most frequently takes the form of property being subdivided without an approved plat and sold by metes and bounds descriptions or by reference to an unapproved, unrecorded plat. It is unfortunate that so much enabling legislation has been written in accordance with the Standard Act and provides for approval only as a condition for *recording* a plat. One remedy lies in restricting the issuance of building permits to lots on recorded plats and/or having frontage on dedicated streets.[24]

Another form of evasion is that of leasing the land or developing rental units on a single plot of ground and serving them by means of private streets which may be below standard and whose maintenance is far from assured. Kentucky took this problem into account by having their enabling legislation also cover leased land but most states have not gone this far. The increase of land leasing may encourage such measures.

Unconventional designs like cluster housing and double-tiered lots are rarely provided for.[25] A remedy for this situation lies in tying subdivision approval to the zoning ordinance and having a well-written planned unit development section in the latter.

Hillside subdivisions need special consideration and special development standards. There are often problems of potential earth slides, erosion, and steepness which must be taken into account.[26] The developer may need to be required to provide more detailed information on geology and soils, larger lot sizes may be required, cut and fill operations may need to be closely regulated with maintenance easements provided for cut and fill slopes on the subdivided lots, drainage and sewage disposal systems may need to be designed so as to prevent

accumulations of subsurface liquids, and streets may have to be permitted to be narrower or have steeper slopes than otherwise allowed.
Philip Green observes that "experience shows . . . that if the controls
written for flat lands are not modified for hillside use, subdividers will
simply level the hills."[27] This, of course, destroys potentially esthetically valuable results.

Waterfront subdivisions may also entail special problems and require special provisions. These may include control of pumping and
filling, provision for bulkheads, provisions for the control of flooding
and erosion, special standards for sewage systems placed below the water table, provision for access to the waterfront from inside lots, reservation of appropriate shoreline areas for public recreational use and
attendant parking, and limitation of the use which can be made of bodies of water within the subdivision.[28]

Subdivision for Other Than Conventional Single-Family Development

Where land in mobile home parks is subdivided for sale there may need
to be provisions (beyond those in the zoning ordinance) for special
standards for required improvements adapted to the scale of mobile
home developments. There may also need to be provisions for shared
ownership and maintenance of common facilities.[29]

Commercial and industrial subdivisions need different standards
from those applied to residential subdivisions. Higher standards of
street construction are needed because of the heavier vehicles using the
street system. Larger water requirements and amounts of liquid wastes
in turn need larger water and sewerage systems. In addition, lotting out
is usually incremental and tailor-made to the needs of the purchaser so
the provisions for processing these subdivisions must be modified to
take this into account. Accordingly industrial subdivision blocks are
usually platted without lots. Also the requirements for land to be set
aside for public use may be quite different because there is no need for
schools or parks in these subdivisions.

The Timing and Guidance of Development

Another significant failure of subdivision regulations lies in their inability to control the timing, balance of uses, and location of new de-

velopment. Although development can be banned from flood plains and dangerous slopes, as Yearwood indicates, the ". . . courts have ruled unfavorably on attempts to prevent, through zoning amendments or subdivision regulations, subdivisions that would burden municipal facilities, services, and/or finances."[30] (Note: Some of the more recent court decisions in regard to the guidance systems described in chapter seven show a reversal in this trend.)

It has been very difficult through subdivision regulations alone to accomplish this. Yearwood suggests that the best approach lies in basing control on a comprehensive plan, in having a sound policy for extension of street and utility infrastructure which is reflected in an adopted capital improvements program, and in zoning land not yet scheduled for development for agriculture or industry.[31] An increasing number of regulations now base subdivision permission on the availability of off-site facilities. Chapter seven deals more extensively with the problems of growth guidance.

Administrative and Political Difficulties

Poor enforcement is also a problem in subdivision regulation as with other land use controls. There is a reluctance by some administrators to apply the regulations rigorously enough; enforcement is subject to erosion by political pressure from developers and their cohorts; and there are special difficulties attendant on administering regulations which apply extraterritorially. These problems can be overcome only through having professionally competent administrators who have the strong support of their superiors, the governing body, and the full cooperation of related public agencies.

CONCLUDING OBSERVATIONS

For subdivision regulations to be effective in guiding the pattern and quality of development, they must be backed up by adequate enabling legislation, supported both in the courts and by local government, well-drafted both in the legal sense and in the sense of requiring a high level of design, and they must be well administered.

They are most effective in regard to large subdivisions because of the problems involved in coordinating small-scale development. Anthony Downs, for example, in discussing this problem suggests that 1500 acres should be the minimum size of development[32] but this would probably require land banking which is discussed further on. Because most subdivisions are small this limits the use of subdivision regulations as a tool for carrying out land use plans.

The principal weaknesses in subdivision regulations lie in inadequate enabling legislation, the concentration on single-family residential development to the exclusion of other uses for which land may be subdivided, the lack of procedural coordination with other related control devices, and the concentration of concern by the courts on private property rights rather than on the general public good.[33]

NOTES AND ACKNOWLEDGMENTS FOR CHAPTER 3

1. Green, Jr., Philip P., in *Principles and Practice of Urban Planning*, William I. Goodman, ed., (Washington: The International City Management Association, copyright 1968 by the Association), pp. 443–44.
2. Webster, Donald H., *Urban Planning and Municipal Public Policy*, (New York: Harper and Row, 1958), p. 437, reproduced by permission.
3. Green, *op. cit.*, p. 445, reproduced by permission.
4. ———, *op. cit.*, p. 446.
5. As quoted by Green, *op. cit.*, p. 447, reproduced by permission.
6. Green, *op. cit.*, p. 447, reproduced by permission.
7. ———, *op. cit.*, p. 447, reproduced by permission.
8. Yearwood, Richard M., *Land Subdivision Regulation: Policy and Legal Considerations for Urban Planning*, (New York: Praeger, copyright 1971 by Praeger Publishers, Inc.) pp. 183–84.
9. Green, *op. cit.*, p. 449.
10. *Metropolitan Subdivisions*, (Louisville: Louisville and Jefferson County Planning Commission, 1969), p. 5.
11. Green, *op. cit.*, p. 452, reproduced by permission.
12. Webster, *op. cit.*, p. 480, reproduced by permission.
13. *Traffic Engineering*, **37**, No. 4, (January 1967), pp. 15–29.
14. Green, *op. cit.*, p. 459.
15. U.S. Department of Housing and Urban Development. *Subdivision Analysis and Procedures*, (Washington: U.S. Government Printing Office, January 1973), pp. 1–18.
16. Green, *op. cit.*, p. 460, reproduced by permission.
17. ———, *op. cit.*, p. 461, reproduced by permission.
18. ———, *op. cit.*, p. 461, reproduced by permission.
19. ———, *op. cit.*, p. 463.
20. Kaufman, Jerome L., "Varying Improvement Requirements," *ASPO Planning Advisory Service Report 174*, (1963), pp. 11–12.
21. Yearwood, *op. cit.*, p. 237.

22. ———, *op. cit.*, p. 279.
23. From the author's personal experience in Louisville in the 1960s there were several subdividers the staff really hated to see coming in with plans because they would have to rework them so extensively before achieving an acceptable plan.
24. Yearwood, *op. cit.*, p. 281.
25. For a good discussion of cluster subdivisions see John Rosenthal, "Cluster Subdivisions," *ASPO Planning Advisory Service Report 135*, (June 1960).
26. The Los Angeles area has had particularly serious problems with earthslides.
27. Green, *op. cit.*, p. 467, reproduced by permission.
28. Green, *op. cit.*, p. 447, "Public Open Space in Subdivisions," *ASPO Planning Advisory Service Report 45*, (January 1953); "Waterfronts: Planning for Resort and Residential Uses," *ASPO Planning Advisory Service Report 118*, (January 1959); and Rick, William B., "Planning and Developing Waterfront Property," *Urban Land Institute Technical Bulletin 49*, (June 1964).
29. "Regulation of Mobile Home Subdivisions," *ASPO Planning Advisory Service Report*, No. 145, (April 1961), pp. 1-36, *passim*.
30. Yearwood, *op. cit.*, p. 281, reproduced by permission of Praeger Publishers, Inc., a Division of Holt, Rinehart and Winston.
31. ———, *op. cit.*, p. 281.
32. Downs, Anthony, *Urban Problems and Prospects*, (Chicago: Markham, 1970), p. 21.
33. Yearwood, *op. cit.*, p. 289.

4

Supplemental regulations and tax policies

Although zoning and subdivision controls are the most important of the controls currently available for implementing land use plans, there are other regulatory controls and governmental policies which affect the pattern and quality of urban development. This chapter will explore a miscellany of regulatory devices which may directly or indirectly support or otherwise affect the implementation of land use plans and policies, although not necessarily designed to be planning implementation tools. It will also explore the effects of various tax policies on urban development, especially in urbanizing areas.

The regulatory devices to be examined here are building codes, hosing codes, health and sanitary regulations, and the licensing of businesses and professions. The real property tax is the principal tax to be examined, but the influence of other forms of taxation will be commented on.

BUILDING CODES

Building codes are designed primarily to insure that buildings will be safe and healthy for human occupation. They are applied mainly at the time of construction; they also may be applied to derelict or unsafe structures needing to be condemned. Usually they are adopted and administered by local government. Less usually they are adopted by the state and administered locally. As Webster states: "The primary function of such codes is to ensure that within the community the design and construction of all structures and the installation of all utilities and fixtures shall be in accordance with established principles and practices in the interest of public safety."[1]

To the degree that building codes insure sound development they are an instrumentality for deterring physical blight and accomplishing some of the general goals of comprehensive land use planning. As with other regulations, if they are to be effective they must be well-written and well-administered. Building codes are tied in with zoning in that building permits may be issued only if the proposed construction meets the zoning requirements discussed in chapter two. In Philadelphia a Zoning Permit is required as a prerequisite to obtaining a Building Permit as a means of insuring coordination (see Figure 4-1). They should also be coordinated with housing codes so that completed construction will meet compatible standards.

Building codes are based on the police power of government. They are administered through review of construction and site plans for conformance with the code as a condition for issuing the building permits required before any construction can take place legally, thorough inspection of construction at critical points when it is underway to insure that it conforms to the approved plans, and through the issuance of occupancy permits when the construction is satisfactorily completed.

The most exhaustive research into building codes and their effects on urban development was undertaken by the staff of the Advisory Commission on Intergovernmental Relations in the mid-1960s. The summary of the Commission's findings was as follows:[2]

The Commission finds that:

1. Obsolete code requirements, unnecessary diversity of such requirements among local jurisdictions, and inadequate administration and enforce-

C APPLICATION FOR ZONING PERMIT AND/OR USE REGISTRATION PERMIT
CITY OF PHILADELPHIA
DEPARTMENT OF LICENSES & INSPECTIONS

NOTE: The requirements for this permit are in addition to all others required by law or regulation. The issuance of this permit does not imply that a building permit or other permits will be issued if the specifications do not conform with the Building Code, Plumbing Code, Housing Code, Fire Code and all other pertinent laws or regulations.

Application is hereby made for the permit or permits required by the Philadelphia Zoning Ordinance before commencing the use or the work described herein, and as shown on accompanying plan.

LOCATION OF PROPERTY *(Street and House Number)*

situated on _____ side of _____ Street
at the distance of _____ feet _____ Inches ____ from _____ side
of _____ Street _____
Front _____ feet _____ Inches. Depth _____ feet _____ Inches.
If lot is irregular in shape, give deed description below:

APPLICATION NO.
DISTRICT DESIGNATION
ZONING MAP NO.   SUB.
F. A. VOL. PL.   WARD
PREVIOUS APPLICATION
CALENDAR NO.
ZONING REFUSED
USE REFUSED
APPEAL
APP. GRANTED·   CERT.
APP. REFUSED   CERT.
REF. TO B. OF A.
REF. GRANTED   CERT.
REF. REFUSED   CERT.

EXPLAIN ANY ALTERATIONS OR PROPOSED CONSTRUCTION

THIS SPACE FOR OFFICIAL STAMP
(Do not write in this space)

STORIES AND HEIGHTS FROM GROUND TO ROOF

HEIGHT	EXISTING BUILDING			PROPOSED ADDITION, ALTERATION OR NEW BUILDING		
	FRONT	SIDE	REAR	FRONT	SIDE	REAR
In Feet						
In Stories						

TABULATION OF USES

FLOOR NO.	PRESENT USE	LAST PREVIOUS USE	DATE LAST USED

FLOOR NO.	PROPOSED USE OF PRESENT BUILDING	PROPOSED USE OF ADDITION OR NEW BUILDING

Additional use information, if required _____

OWNER	ADDRESS	PHONE
ARCHITECT OR ENGINEER	ADDRESS	PHONE
CONTRACTOR	ADDRESS	PHONE
APPLICANT	ADDRESS	PHONE

81-16 A (Rev. 12/63)

Figure 4-1. Application for zoning permit. From Philadelphia (Pa.) Department of Licenses & Inspection (1963).

ment, taken together tend to place unjustified burdens on the technology and economics of building.

2. Too many building codes contain unnecessarily high standards, prevent the use of economical methods and materials in building, and include provisions extraneous to the basic purposes and objectives of building controls. Local governments in the exercise of their building regulatory powers often include provisions that go beyond establishment of minimum requirements for public health, safety, and welfare. The cost of adhering to excessive requirements bearing only superficial relation to health and safety limits the economic range of housing that can be made available within a community.[3]

3. The full benefits of a comprehensive building construction code cannot be realized unless the construction aspects of mechanical (i.e., plumbing, electrical, elevator), fire and special-use (factories, hospitals, hotels, theaters, etc.) codes are integrated within the requirements of a single building construction code.

4. Approval procedures for building materials, components, and systems by a myriad of public and private groups has made the development and acceptance of new products a difficult process.

5. Many States have adopted mechanical codes that apply uniformly throughout the State but to date only a handful of States have provided for adoption of statewide general building construction codes.

6. Intergovernmental problems of code uniformity are greatest in metropolitan areas. Current efforts in a number of metropolitan areas to achieve a common building code hold considerable promise in reducing diversity. But even if successful, these efforts have the inherent limitations of differing from the codes in other parts of the State and independence upon a variety of inspection practices among the localities adopting the code.

7. Although the Federal Government is involved in building code uniformity and modernization through direct construction, specifications for housing, housing guarantees, support of research, testing activities, and administration of anti-trust laws, it has followed no consistent path or objective toward modernization and uniformity codes.

8. Resistance by various interests to the Federal Government playing a major role in the field of building techniques and methods because of fear of Federal involvement in product approvals has been accompanied by fragmented and disparate approaches to building research in the United States.

9. Insufficient knowledge is available at the present time for the writing of full and complete "performance codes" (i.e., codes based upon perfor-

mance such as load-bearing requirements, in contrast to specification of type and thickness of material). The availability of knowledge to establish performance criteria would go far toward encouraging development of new and improved building materials and reduction of restrictive building code practices.

The Commission concludes that a widely adopted uniform building code would go far toward eliminating arbitrary restrictions adding to the cost of new construction materials and techniques by making possible a prompt, wide market for such products; it would eliminate the conflict arising from responsibility for both issuance and enforcement of codes; and it would reduce the cost of research, testing, maintenance, and servicing of building codes.

Finally, the Commission concludes that even if the building industry continues to increase its efficiency and economy, the continuance of obsolete and diverse building codes will remain a formidable obstacle to the fullest exploitation of new technology. Remedial action is needed by local, State and Federal governments . . . .

These findings need some elaboration:

Obsolete code requirements exist where there is no institutionalized way of updating the codes. Several of the national model codes have research organizations which test new materials and construction methods and send updated amendments to their subscribing localities for an annual fee. The updated standards vary from code organization to code organization resulting in bewildering differences from code to code. These differences result in increased building costs for builders who build in several different jurisdictions.

Inadequate or unevenly administered and enforced codes contribute further to costly uncertainty in the construction process because if the provisions of a code are not clear, or the interpretations of it by the building department are arbitrary or in doubt, there may have to be costly revisions of construction plans before a building permit can be obtained, and/or delays on the job caused by the building inspector.

The problem of "unnecessarily high standards" is often the result of code obsolescence. This, in turn, is often the result of mistrust of new or relatively untried materials and methods together with inability of the locality to get reliable information. There is a lack of nationally recognized, up-to-date building research. In some cases the problem is complicated by political pressure from materials suppliers and/or construction unions. Materials suppliers may pressure for codes to require more expensive materials, those on which they make the largest percentage of profit, or those for which they have an exclusive dealership—all in the interest of maximizing their income. The unions similarly want to maximize income for their members through pressuring for codes to require labor-intensive construction techniques and require materials which must be site-fabricated or otherwise take more labor to assemble.

Where the building regulations involve a collection of codes applicable to various aspects of construction rather than a single integrated code there is likely to be overlapping and conflicting requirements causing confusion and inefficiency in administration.

The lack of state-wide building codes in most states together with the multiplicity of varying local codes, limits the possible economies to be obtained through factory manufactured housing by limiting the possible market areas. It is obviously uneconomical to modify a factory product to meet requirements varying from local jurisdiction to local jurisdiction. There is also a problem of under-construction inspection of factory models produced outside the code area of jurisdiction.

Architects who design for, and builders who build in, several different jurisdictions having a wide diversity of building codes are discouraged from introducing new methods for building better and at lower cost. Similarly code diversity and the time and difficulty involved in getting code clearance discourages materials manufacturers from introducing product innovations which would reduce construction costs.

The nature of building codes is changing and most commentators feel that building codes based on the "performance characteristics" of building materials and methods of construction are preferable to "listing" allowable materials and methods but even the most advanced performance codes do not cover every item or method and must rely in part on "listing." In fact, Sanderson in discussing specifications and performance standards observes that:[4]

As a practical matter, a pure *performance code* would be impossible to enforce because the only proof of inadequate design or poor construction would be the failure of the building. What is important about a *performance code* is that where specifications are used, provisions are made for the substitution of alternative systems and materials that can be proved adequate by tests or engineering calculations.

To remedy the problems in regard to building codes the Advisory Commission on Intergovernmental Affairs Recommended:[5]

1. A Federal program coordinating public and private efforts ". . . *designed to develop national performance criteria and standards and testing procedures for building construction.*" This recommendation aimed at improving performance and other technological information together with elimination of duplication of research. As noted further on this recommendation is now in the process of being implemented.

2. Establishment of ". . . *a continuing national program of building research . . .*" involving identification of problem areas, gaps in knowledge, integration of knowledge, provision for demonstration projects, and coordination of the related work in Federal agencies. This program would be aimed at stimulating building research.

3. The establishment ". . . *by appropriate State agencies and institutions of higher education . . .*" of programs in building construction research. This proposal is aimed at encouraging research at the local level—especially research adapted to peculiarly local conditions of climate, topography, soils, and geology.

4. *"Development of a Model Code by a National Commission."* This recommendation aims at reducing the unnecessary differences in building codes from locality to locality. The Commission goes on to say:

The benefits resulting from a widely adopted uniform model building code may be summarized as follows:

(a) Elimination of arbitrary restrictions which add unnecessarily to the cost of construction and the price to the buyer.

(b) Stimulation of initiative and innovation on the part of material suppliers and builders by reducing the cost and delay involved in securing wide approval.

(c) Improvement of the legal climate for codes by relieving enforcement agencies of conflicting responsibility for the promulgation as well as the enforcement of codes.

(d) Assistance to code-promulgation bodies having limited access to technical guidance in resisting the prejudicial influence of self-serving voluntary advisors by making available the benefits of technically sound conclusions embodied in a uniform code.

(e) Assist in combining and harmonizing standards originating in different industry groups. These would be brought into proper relationship in a uniform code.

(f) Reduction in the cost and the local technical requirements for maintaining and servicing a code which would be kept abreast of the demands of a modern building industry by the promulgating agency.

(g) Assist in the training and in establishing qualifications of local inspectors needed for rational, as distinct from arbitrary, interpretation of a code.

It also urges the development of "... appropriate permanent machinery for keeping the code revised and up-to-date."

5. *"Uniform Standards for Federal Construction."* By adopting uniform standards for Federal construction the Federal Government would be both setting an example and encouraging widespread adoption of the National Code.

6. *"Development of a State Model Building Code."* These state codes would be based on the national code except as affected by the peculiar needs of the state concerned. Local codes would be superceded by the state codes. Such direct action by the state would advance the adoption of modern and uniform codes by localities throughout the state without disturbing the traditional authority of the localities in regard to the administration and enforcement of building codes.

7. *"Establishment of a State Construction Review Agency to Develop Statewide Standards Through an Appeals Procedure."* This would help ensure uniform administration of the code throughout the state, especially in regard to the application of standards. Because building codes would be written more in terms of performance standards, it would be likely that the technical findings of the local appeals board would be as useful as the legal findings.

8. *"Enabling Legislation for Local Adoption by Reference of Model Codes."* Where states do not preempt code adoption at the state level this would encourage localities to adopt future code changes by administrative rather than legislative action. This means that as the model code adopted by the locality is revised by the organization promulgating it to take into account new materials and the most recent research findings, that the local code would be automatically revised through administrative action by the local government rather than having to be revised through enacting amendments to the code by ordinance. This procedure would avoid destroying the uniformity of the code through local legislative tinkering and take some of the pressure off local officials to modify the code requirements.

9. *"State Licensing of Building Inspectors."* This should encourage the professionalization of building inspectors, improve the quality of code administration and consequent evenhanded treatment of developers.

The state licensing program would establish minimum training standards for building inspectors, examine candidates for their competency in this field and certify those who have passed.

10. *"Training Programs for Building Inspectors."* This is a recommendation in support of the previous one.

11. *"Provision of Local Building Inspection Services."* Under this recommendation the states would establish minimum staffing requirements for localities and be enabled to supply services on a reimbursable basis where localities requested them or wished to share services with adjoining localities. This provision would be especially useful in metropolitan areas with many small jurisdictions.

Two years after the Advisory Commission on Intergovernmental Affairs made its recommendations, another commission studying the same problem, the National Commission on Urban Problems, duplicating much of the earlier study, made substantially similar recommendations.[6]

Quite a few of the recommendations of these two commissions have been or are in the process of being put into effect by the Federal Government and the states. In 1967 in response to the ACIR recommendations the National Conference of States on Building Codes and Standards was created to act as:[7]

... a forum for the states to discuss problems relating to the administration and enforcement of building codes and standards. . . . Program activities undertaken by NCSBCS have directly related to several of the ACIR recommendations (No. 6 through No. 11). For example, NCSBCS in cooperation with the Department of Commerce and others have recently developed several pieces of model legislation. . . . (the) State Building Code Act, Mobile Home Act, and Manufactured Building Act.

In regard to the other recommendations in the ACIR report, very little has been done to establish *new national programs* for performance standards development, building construction research and the development of a model code by a national commission. . . .

A Center for Building Technology has been created in the National Bureau of Standards[8] and pursuant to the recommendations of the National Commission on Urban Problems the 1974 Omnibus Housing Bill provided for a National Institute of Building Sciences.[9]

There has also been progress at the state level. According to the March, 1972 "State Building Code Profile"[10] at that time there were 13 state-wide building codes, many of which were preemptive, and most of which excluded 1–3 family site-built housing. Also at that time 21 states had building codes covering factory-built housing. And mobile homes were covered by state codes in 28 states. Indiana is an example of a state having a statewide building code which supercedes local codes and has special provisions for mobile homes and factory-built housing.[11]

HOUSING CODES

Housing codes differ from building codes in that they are designed to be applied to housing already built for as long as it can be occupied. They are intended to insure the continued safety and healthfulness of buildings for human occupation. Unlike building codes they are customarily applied only to places of residence.

Also based on the police power, they prescribe the minimum conditions under which a building or dwelling unit may be legally occupied. The conditions usually include the condition of the structure, the adequacy of plumbing and heating, the level of building maintenance, and the size of rooms in relation to the number of persons occupying them. All housing within the locality's jurisdiction is subject to an adopted housing code. The code is enforced through periodic inspections by housing inspectors. On the discovery of failures of a building to meet code requirements the owner is notified by being issued a notice of nonconformance indicating what he must do and the penalties for his failure within a reasonable time to bring the building into conformance. Buildings meeting the code are granted occupancy permits indicating conformance.

Housing codes are one of the tools used in urban renewal areas to upgrade existing substandard housing or to determine deterioration. Code administration is subject to severe erosion and abuses. It is also responsible for unwanted side effects such as housing abandonment where upgrading may be uneconomic or the necessary financial resources are not available. As a consequence housing codes and their application are often involved in controversy and code enforcement programs need to be carefully coordinated with other related programs such as urban homesteading if they are to be successful.

The first housing code in America was enacted in Baltimore in 1941. It required "'. . . that dwellings be kept clean and free from dirt, filth, rubbish, garbage and similar matter, and from vermin and rodent infestation and in good repair fit for human habitation, and authorizes the Commissioner of Health of Baltimore City to issue orders compelling the compliance with said provisions, or to correct the condition, at the expense of the property owner, and charge the property with a lien to the extent of the necessary expenses.'"[12]

Generally housing codes cover three main areas according to an in-depth report of the National Commission on Urban Problems:[13]

(1) The supplied facilities in the structure, that is, toilet, bath, sink, etc. supplied by the owner;
(2) The level of maintenance, which includes both structural and sanitary maintenance, leaks in the roof, broken banisters, cracks in the wall, etc;
(3) Occupancy, which concerns the size of dwelling units and rooms of different types, the number of people who can occupy them, and other issues concerned on the whole with the usability and amenity of interior space.

This commission found that the ". . . provisions established in the codes for 'minimum' standards of health, safety and welfare are often inadequate to provide even a 'minimum' level of performance for the bulk of the population. A house can meet the legal standards set in a local code, pass a housing code inspection, and still be unfit for human habitation by the personal standards of most middle-class Americans."[14]

Contending that current housing standards lack an adequate research base, Eric Mood says:[15]

A critical examination of the existing data upon which housing codes and standards are based will reveal that little is known about the requirements for family life. A majority of present housing code provisions are usually a combination of rule-of-thumb, personal experience, and professional judgement with limited supportive scientific data.

The impact of a housing environment on public health is hard to measure partly because housing environments are composites of many components capable of influencing health in many different, often unrelated ways.[16]

The process of developing housing code standards involves the development of criteria and then the promulgation of standards. The standards must be feasible and practical if they are to be useful and there is a great need for developing a satisfactory definition of *substandard housing* which is usually loosely defined as *housing substantially failing to meet accepted minimum housing code provisions.*[17]

Even if the codes contained sounder standards, as Lieberman points out, ". . . the weakest link in the process is their administration and enforcement."[18] Part of the problem lies in the ambiguities in the administrative provisions of the national and model codes but much of it lies with the local governments themselves. Often there is no organized program of inspection and inspection is made on complaint alone. This is clearly unsatisfactory as well as unfair. There are wide variations in notice of violation and compliance provisions and usually the only course of action lies in bringing criminal rather than civil court action thus making the owner rather than the building the principal issue.

A study by Lieberman made in 1965–66 covering 39 selected municipalities made the following findings in regard to housing code administration:[19]

Organizational status. The following chart shows the status of the code agency in the various size cities covered by the report. (For the purpose of analyzing the organizational status, a "department" under a mayor or city manager was considered as the "top or first level," a "division" or a "bureau" within a department as "second level," and a "section" or a "unit" within a division of bureau as third level).

Population of Municipality	Organizational Level		
	First (%)	Second (%)	Third (%)
Under 100,000	None	50	50
100,000–249,000	None	38	62
250,000–499,000	14	43	43
500,000–999,000	13	25	62
Over 1,000,000	60	None	40

Planned Program of Code Enforcement. The codes officials in 18 percent of the municipalities covered frankly admitted they made inspections *only* upon complaint. Most of these involved municipalities under 100,000 population. Although the code officials in the remaining municipalities stated they also made house-to-house inspections in prior selected areas, it was clear from their description of these area programs that they could not be considered "systematic" or "planned" inspection programs under a strict interpretation of the Workable Program requirements.

Administrative Initiative. It was found that the individuals engaged in the direction of housing inspections in the cities covered by the study were of surprisingly high quality. These men were anxious to do a good job. However, they were being hampered by a lack of resources, by lack of status in the local municipal organizational structure, unsympathetic superiors in many cases, and the lack of understanding by the community of their role in the total urban development picture. Obviously, under these conditions there is little motivation to exercise administrative initiative.

Coordination. It was generally found that an area was selected for house-to-house inspections in the following manner:

(1) Use of the 1960 report on housing to determine substandard areas,
(2) The code official's personal knowledge of bad areas in his municipality.
(3) Organized citizen pressures to clean up a slum area.

In only 28 percent of the localities did the planning agency play some part in selecting the areas for code enforcement. Only 20 percent of the municipalities mentioned that Community Renewal Program studies were under way in their communities. Many of the completed CRP studies failed adequately to discuss plans for the use of code enforcement in the city program. Fifty-four percent of the municipalities stated that the "tie-in or coordination" with the local urban renewal agency was "minimal." Thirty-four percent of the code officials answered "none" to the question: "To what extent is code enforcement tied in or coordinated with the urban renewal or the public housing programs?" It was significant that no code official mentioned the Local Public Agency as playing any part in the selection of code inspection areas. Only 10 percent of the code officials described the relationship between their local urban renewal agency and the code agency as "close."

Development of Compliance Policies. Not more than six code officials had any definite policies to be applied or methods to be used. Only two of the 39 code officials involved in the study had given any thought to compliance policies. For instance, in one of the largest cities a deficiency point system was developed and different procedures were followed based on the

seriousness of the housing conditions. Properties with more than 59 deficiency points were presumed to be in serious condition. If the first notice to
make the necessary repairs was not complied with, the policy was immediately to hold a hearing to declare the property unfit for human habitation.
In cases where the deficiency points did not exceed 20, two notices to
comply were issued and then if compliance was not obtained the non-
complying property owner was "Summoned" to appear before a representative of the code agency to show cause why he should not be prosecuted.
This had a good psychological effect and in two-thirds of these cases compliance was obtained without the necessity of legal proceedings.

Sixty percent of the municipalities did not require full compliance with the
minimum standards of the housing code in the worst areas of the city even
when the areas had not been scheduled for clearance and redevelopment.
Action in these bad areas was taken only upon complaint and then the
requirement to comply applied only to the serious items of safety and
health. It appeared that the code officials stopped code enforcement in
these exceedingly bad areas as soon as an area became "an urban renewal
gleam in the eyes of the planners."

The lack of conscious enforcement policies was due to the failure of top city
officials to give some direction to the code official and the low status of the
code agency requiring the code official frequently to pass on his ideas
through two and three intermediaries in the line of authority before they
could reach the city policymakers. Frequently the code official's superiors
were unsympathetic to code enforcement. Further, the record-keeping of
the code agency was usually inadequate so that the code official, even if he
wanted to, did not have sufficient information on which to base enforcement policies and procedures.

Factors Hampering Code Enforcement. Two-thirds of the officials listed
the chief obstacles to improved code enforcement in the following order:
lack of resources, lack of political leadership and political support, lack of
public interest, and lack of planning. Some of the other obstacles most frequently mentioned were lack of better trained personnel and adequate
salaries for the personnel, need for better coordination with other urban
renewal efforts, need for housing maintenance training for owner-occupied
houses, the increase in tax assessments after rehabilitation is completed,
racial antagonism, need for greater tenant education and easier financing
for owners who want to fix up their properties.

In *New Approaches to Housing Code Administration*, Slavet and
Levin make a number of practical proposals for the improvement of

housing code administration. First they set forth a series of principles on which housing code programs should be based:[20]

1. The programs focus on people rather than on building alone and on the needs of all families and individuals in the community for housing at costs they can afford; high standards of housing maintenance depend on people and how they live.
2. The programs emphasize services and incentives designed to encourage high standards of housing maintenance and voluntary rehabilitation rather than the enforcement of a legal code: services and incentives to tenants, to property owners, to community and neighborhood groups.
3. The programs accent the positive not the negative; they stress the rehabilitation and conservation of neighborhoods and housing instead of the narrow exercise of police power and law enforcement.
4. The programs lean heavily on techniques of prevention in recognition of their logic, lower cost and more permanent benefits as compared with corrective and treatment techniques.
5. The programs give priority to persuasion and to voluntary compliance, legal compulsion being reserved as a measure of last resort where it can be fairly, consistently and successfully applied.
6. The programs encourage and support efforts to expand the numbers of owner occupants, including cooperatives and condominiums, since owner occupancy stimulates continuing high-quality maintenance of housing and since maintenance rather than the provision of mechanical facilities is emerging as a major problem of housing code administration.
7. The programs promote the development of a constituency of tenants, property owners and community groups dedicated to housing code administration and neighborhood improvement and allied closely with code administration agencies.
8. The programs evolve from and are designed to be subjected to continuing planning and evaluation; they also reflect a comprehensive thrust and systematic analysis and application.
9. The programs complement, supplement and are closely coordinated with public and private activities designed to develop, improve and conserve the physical environment and human resources of a community.
10. The programs are oriented toward entire neighborhoods rather than individual structures and their operations are decentralized and neighborhood-based.

11. The programs incorporate activities and/or are allied with actions which generate clearly visible neighborhood improvements, thereby producing a constructive image for housing code administration.
12. The programs reflect adaptability to changing patterns of housing supply and demand for different groups of people and give consideration to the housing needs and choices of persons for whom government has become a special advocate: low-income families, especially large families; the elderly; and minority group families.
13. The programs provide for the constructive participation in program planning and execution of tenants, property owners and representatives of neighborhood and community groups concerned with housing.
14. The programs make adequate provision for relocation of families and persons displaced as a result of code compliance activities into decent, safe and sanitary housing.

Subsequently they describe program differences based on the character of the neighborhoods involved. In the worst areas the program would be designed for stop-gap holding action pending the application of urban renewal treatment. For declining gray areas they propose a combination of code enforcement with local public and private rehabilitation and improvement. For good areas a three-year inspection schedule is proposed to keep these areas from deteriorating. They further recommend that programs be planned consisting of services and incentives, making use of a complete range of inspectional devices, involving substantial citizen participation, recognizing and emphasizing the need for tenant education, and incorporating a full measure of administrative remedies and workable court remedies.[21]

Frank Grad in *Legal Remedies for Housing Code Violations* discusses the legal problems involved in housing code administration. He suggests that the building rather than the owner be the focus of attention, that through administrative tribunals repair schedules be set up and that violations be handled through special housing courts capable of levying cumulative per diem penalties.[22]

HEALTH AND SANITARY REGULATIONS

Health and sanitary codes are another form of regulatory device having some influence on urban development patterns though less than building and housing codes. Health and sanitary regulations are usually adopted at the state rather than local level and administered by the state or a local governmental unit acting as an agent of the state These codes vary greatly in scope and content from state to state.

Subjects covered by these regulations may include air pollution, sewage disposal, water supply, public and private swimming pools, restaurants and food service, and certain classes of housing such as hotels, motels, rooming houses, and mobile home parks. Zoning regulations need to take these codes into account in order to avoid conflicting standards and unnecessary duplication.

These codes may affect the geographic location of certain uses (for example: where septic tanks and wells may be used and how they must be related) or construction standards (for example: required screening of outdoor eating areas or required fencing around swimming pools).

MISCELLANEOUS OTHER REGULATIONS

States and localities sometimes enact other supplementary regulations affecting land use patterns and hence the implementation of land use plans. Most of those locally enacted would better serve their intended purposes if they were incorporated into the zoning or subdivision controls where appropriate as previously suggested. These regulations may pertain to such things as architectural, sign, or esthetic controls, historic preservation, mobile home parks, flood plain controls, and the licensing of businesses. Business licensing is the only one of these not previously discussed.

The licensing of businesses may have a number of different purposes. Where it is *persons* who are being licensed, the licensing is usually directed at ensuring in the public interest that those licensed are competent to perform the services in which they are engaged. The licensing of *premises*, on the other hand, may have more diverse purposes and affect land uses in regard to number, location, distribution and operating conditions. For example, the licensing of restaurants, bars, and stores for the sale of alcoholic beverages may affect neighborhood planning goals. On the whole, however, the general effect of licensing regulations on the implementation of land use plans is minimal and licensing has rarely been considered important as a planning tool.

THE INFLUENCE OF TAX POLICIES ON URBAN DEVELOPMENT

Like the supplementary regulations of the various levels of government just examined, the tax policies of governments influence directly or indirectly the patterns of urban development and may have some potential for aiding the implementation of land use plans. Although tax policies are primarily designed to raise revenue for funding public expenditures, it may be possible to design them to serve planning purposes as well. The forms of taxation to be examined here are income taxes and real property taxes because these are the most pervasive and potentially influential.

Income Taxes

Individual federal income taxes and state income taxes modeled on the federal tax have had a great role in shaping land use configurations and affecting the timing of development. Consideration of the effects of income taxes is essential to any discussion of land development.[23]

Federal and some state income tax policies encourage the purchase of homes as opposed to renting and speculation in land. The consequent result is the fragmentation of land tracts, rising land prices, and the promotion of sprawl. The encouragement of home ownership, according to Clawson, takes three forms:[24]

1. The imputed rent of the owner's dwelling does not have to be included as part of his income for federal income tax purposes.
2. Payments for real estate taxes may be deducted from gross income.
3. Interest on home mortgages may also be deducted.

Speculation in land is encouraged because (with some exceptions) income from land sales qualifies as capital gains which are taxed at a lower rate than ordinary income. The encouragement of home ownership affects the market for single-family houses, town houses, condominiums, and mobile homes. This, in turn, affects various income groups as illustrated in Table 4-1.

Although, beginning in 1946, the countervailing policy of accelerating the rate at which commercial and rental housing could be depreciated for tax purposes, stimulated the development of apartments and

TABLE 4-1. The Extent to Which Federal Income Tax Provisions Assist Home Ownership.

	Annual salary before taxes					
	$15,000	$20,000	$25,000	$30,000	$35,000	$40,000
Tax exemption plus deductions[1]	4,500	5,000	5,500	6,000	6,500	7,000
Taxable income	10,500	15,000	19,500	24,000	28,500	33,000
Income tax, 1978 rates (joint return)	1,105	1,877	3,171	4,464	5,777	7,632
Marginal rate of tax[2]	27%	31%	36%	40%	45%	50%
Net income, after tax	13,895	18,123	21,829	25,536	29,223	32,368
Price of house[3]	27,800	36,300	43,700	51,700	58,500	64,800
Annual payment to lender[4]	3,330	4,349	5,235	6,194	7,008	7,763
Interest payment first year[4]	3,024	3,858	4,753	5,624	6,363	7,049
Annual real estate taxes[4]	417	545	656	776	876	972
Interest and taxes paid, first year	3,441	4,403	5,409	6,400	7,239	8,021
Reduction in income tax[5]	929	1,365	1,947	2,560	3,258	4,011
As percent of net income	7	8	9	10	11	12
As percent of income tax	84	73	61	57	56	53
As percent of payments to lender	28	31	37	41	46	52

[1]Assuming 4 dependents at $750 each, plus 10 percent for miscellaneous deductions.
[2]Rate applicable to last income earned.
[3]Assuming double net income after taxes, rounded upward to nearest $100.
[4]Assuming 10.5 percent interest, 1 percent for amortization and mortgage insurance, for 90 percent 20 year loan plus local real estate taxes at $1.50 per $100 full value.
[5]On assumption interest and taxes are net additions to deductions and that marginal rate applies.
From: 1978 Income tax information and conversation with local bank officials.

shopping centers, the scales were tipped heavily in favor of home purchases. Consumer preferences led to space-consuming single-family housing being the predominant housing type, contributing heavily to suburban sprawl until the rising cost of land, construction labor, and building mateials in the mid-1960s led multifamily housing and mobile homes to comprise a steadily increasing share of the housing market in many metropolitan areas.[25]

Another undesirable effect of present federal income tax policy is that because of the ability to write off depreciation under the laws, owners of deteriorating rental housing make more profit by not rehabilitating it, thus furthering the decline of blighted areas. All in all, present federal income tax policy is not only not lending itself to the purposes of carrying out land use plans but is interfering with their implementation. The National Commission on Urban Problems summarized the questionable or undesirable features of federal tax laws as they affect housing as follows:[26]

(1) Tax provisions make no distinction between investment in rental housing and in other income-producing real estate, despite the special public concern for housing.
(2) They provide little or no effective preference of tax treatment for investment that actually enlarges the stock of usable housing (through new construction or renovation), as compared with investment that merely involves ownership of existing structures.
(3) They stimulate relatively frequent changes in the ownership of rental housing, and thereby in at least some instances would work against acceptable standards of maintenance of such housing.
(4) They tend to reinforce, rather than to offset, the unfortunate economic and social conditions that inhibit adequate maintenance and renovation of rental housing in deteriorating city neighborhoods.
(5) They include no preferential treatment for investment in low and moderate income housing, relative to other rental housing.

While there is considerable agreement about the effects of federal income tax policy on urban development among planners, housers, and land economists there is no clear consensus on how it should be modified. In early 1972 Representative Keogh of New York recommended modification of the capital gains tax to apply only to the sale of properties held for seven years or more as a means of curbing speculation in real property. Clawson had previously raised the question that if the tax laws were changed to allow housing rental payments to be deductable would this not reduce the advantage of single-family housing over other forms of housing where rental is the predominant form of tenure and consequently support the higher densities envisioned in most metropolitan land use plans. After a study of a wide variety of proposals the National Commission on Urban Problems made a series of proposals as follows:[27]

Recommendation No. 1—U.S. Treasury Study. The Commission recommends that the President direct the Treasury Department to make an intensive analysis and submit explicit findings and recommendations concerning tax law changes best suited to provide materially more favorable treatment for investment in new residential construction (including major rehabilitation) than for other forms of real estate investment.

Recommendation No. 2—Tax incentives for upkeep of older rental housing. The Commission recommends that the Internal Revenue Code be amended to provide specific incentives for adequate maintenance and rehabilitation of rental residential property by allowing, within appropriate limits, for especially generous tax treatment of investor-owners' expenditures for these purposes with respect to structures of more than some specified age, such as 30 or 40 years.

Recommendation No. 3—Tax incentives for low and moderate income housing investment. The Commission recommends prompt revision of the Federal income tax laws to provide increased incentives for investment in low and moderate income housing, relative to other real estate investment, where such housing is governmentally subsidized and involves a legal limit upon the allowable return on investors' equity capital. Specifically, we propose that the Internal Revenue Code be amended to provide especially favorable treatment (whether through preferential depreciation allowances or through investment credits) for investments made under governmentally aided limited-profit programs for the construction and rehabilitation of low and moderate income housing.

Nevertheless the Commission qualified its recommendations with the conclusion that ". . . governmental efforts to encourage the construction and rehabilitation of housing for low and moderate income families should rely primarily on direct subsidy programs rather than upon special tax benefits."[28]

Of the tax policy recommendations cited here all have somewhat different objectives. Keogh is concerned with curbing land speculation and its impact on land prices and patterns of development (sprawl and leapfrogging). Clawson is concerned with rental vs. ownership of housing and its consequences in regard to the mix of housing produced (variety, density, and sprawl). The Commission is concerned with increasing housing production, rehabilitation of older rental housing, and increasing investment in lower-income housing. These objectives are all compatible with the objectives of comprehensive plans in most of our metropolitan areas, though they may not accord with the planning objectives of smaller cities and suburban communities. No one set of income tax policies at the state or federal levels is likely to further the planning interests of all localities. National and state goals can be furthered by their respective income tax policies but these policies are rarely available for use as a tool for local land planning purposes and those tax policies in effect are often at odds with local planning purposes.

Most local income taxes are in the form of gross income taxes or a surcharge on state income taxes where they are permitted at all. Consequently the localities have very little opportunity to design local income taxes in support of local land use planning. On the other hand, real property taxes, as will be seen in the balance of this chapter, offer somewhat more opportunity for adaptation to local objectives.

Real Property Taxes

Both the equity and developmental effects of real property taxes have been a subject of discussion since the 18th Century, if not before, in regard to urban development. Consideration of the real property tax is also important because it is the largest single source of revenue for local governments. As such it will be dealt with in the next chapter in connection with financial planning.

USING THE PROPERTY TAX FOR LAND USE OBJECTIVES

It has been suggested that although the main purpose of the property tax is to raise revenues, it may also be viewed as a means for the promotion of sound urban development.[29] Charles Abrams went so far as to contend that: "The taxation of land is a more effective method of controlling its use than regulation is."[30] Accordingly here the effect of real property taxes on urban development, and proposals for using this tax for achieving land use planning objectives will be examined. (The term "property tax" as used hereinafter in this chapter will refer only to the tax on real property).

The property tax has two distinct components: the tax on the land and the tax on the improvements on the land. The effects of these taxes may be conflicting because heavy taxes on improvements may discourage development and light taxes on land may discourage development and encourage speculation. Furthermore, tax policies may have quite different effects in the central city than in the urbanizing fringe, effects counter to plans which generally seek to promote urban renewal in central areas and seek to discourage suburban sprawl and the leap-frogging of development caused by speculation and other problems.

Pickford and Shannon contend that tax and land use policy objectives should be coordinated in a way which would:[31]

(1) encourage the rehabilitation of slum property,
(2) ensure the timely fill-in of vacant land in areas that are largely built up, and
(3) prevent the premature development of open space on the outer fringes of suburbia.

They further suggest that preconditions for this coordination include an efficient uniform assessment system, an adequate land use control system, and effective capital budgeting for community facilities. Other objectives include incentives for new development of various land uses in accordance with land use plans and policies, the preservation of open space, and the preservation of historically or esthetically valuable areas and structures.

The devices to be discussed here are the land tax, differential taxation on land and buildings, tax deferral, tax subsidies, taxation of unearned increments, selective taxation, and tax-base sharing. Issues of equity and developmental effect arise differently in each of these, but the stress here will be put on the latter.

The Land Tax

Henry George, one of the most avid advocates of a single tax on land alone was interested primarily in questions of equity and argued that the increase in the value of property is not the result of action by the owner but instead is created by the community and therefore should be shared by the community. He also felt that the American system of taxation of land and improvements was inconsistent with the best use of land.[32] Others who have argued for the land tax on the basis of equity are Lindholm, Heilbrun, Brown and Netzer.[33]

The question of greater interest for planning purposes is that of the developmental effect of taxing the land alone or at a heavier rate than the tax on improvements (differential taxation). The argument in favor of the land tax is that by taxing the land alone the tax would fall as heavily on undeveloped land as on developed land so that it would be too expensive to keep land vacant for speculation and this would encourage in-filling and development or redevelopment in areas ripe for development.

In a study of taxation in British Columbia for the Urban Land Institute Mary Rawson observed:[34]

> One may say then that the components of the property tax work at cross-purposes as far as the development of the city is concerned. The tax on improvements evidently contributes to the shortage of housing and to the deterioration of our cities by its inhibiting effect on building and capital investment. The tax on land, through its tendency to lower land prices, lowers the real cost of housing. By providing a stimulus to the efficient use of land, it encourages rebuilding in central areas and it checks the practice of holding land in a vacant or ill-used state.

In 1969 a blue ribbon panel representing a wide variety of interests from government, industry and the universities advocated a shift to the land tax and in doing so quoted an Urban Land Institute Study as outlining the expected results of a shift to the land tax as: (1) increasing the tax take on idle land, parking lots, gas stations, deteriorating or obsolescent structures and ill-suited land uses in a way which would make it almost prohibitively unprofitable to keep developable or redevelopable close-in land idle or misused; (2) shifting the tax burden away from sound development; (3) reducing the need for subsidizing redevelopment; (4) stimulating new construction; (5) making good urban planning more necessary and effective; (6) increasing the profitability of good development; (7) stimulating more intensive use of land in close-in areas; (8) reducing land values and development pressures in outlying areas; reducing transportation costs by encouraging more compact development; (9) simplifying the task of assessment and increasing its accuracy; and (10) reducing the tax burden on most owner-occupied homes. The panel goes on to say that some of their contentions have been borne out in Southfield, Michigan after a partial shift in the tax burden from improvements to land.[35]

Walker[36] and Gaffney[37] advocate the land tax as a stimulant for urban development. They present closely reasoned, persuasive arguments but without supporting evidence. Similar arguments were made in an anonymous article in the *Yale Law Journal*[38] and by Larsen in a paper on Arden, Delaware.[39]

A number of empirical studies have been made of the effects of the land tax and the differential tax. Hutchinson made a study of Australian taxes;[40] Williams examined differential taxation in Pittsburgh where the tax on land is at a rate twice that on improvements;[41] Rawson made a study of land taxation in British Columbia[42] and a broader study was made by Brown.[43] One of the latest studies was made by Clark and concentrated on cities in New Zealand.[44] Using eyewitness rather than statistical evidence, Cowan[45] and Woodward with Ecker-Racz[46] made still other studies.

Most of these studies conclude that the use of the land tax does not result in significant differences in land use patterns. Clark suggests that the complex causes of blight and fringe-area sprawl are unlikely to be affected very significantly by a switch to land or differential taxation.[47] Nonetheless it is strongly advocated by many planners and economists in spite of no firm evidence being available.[48] Hopefully further research will reveal the land tax to be useful in the implementation of land use plans because the arguments for it are so very persuasive.

Preferential Tax Incentives

In order to encourage certain kinds of development, to discourage premature development, or to compensate for regulations preventing change of use, some states have permitted local governments to establish various preferential tax incentives.

The most widespread form of tax incentives now in use are those directed to the purpose of preserving open space and keeping land in forest, agricultural or horticultural uses, especially in urban fringe areas where development pressures are most severe. In previous chapters the use of agricultural zoning and restrictive agreements to preserve open space have been discussed but the use of tax incentives has not. The two most prevalent tax incentives are preferential assessment and tax deferral.[49]

Preferential assessment, the more common approach to the problem, provides that land actively farmed or predominantly open shall be assessed only for its agricultural use value not taking into account alternative development values. This approach is simple and direct but

TABLE 4-2. State Preferential Assessment Programs.

State	Eligibility Criteria					Conversion Controls	
	Agriculture	Forest	General Open Space	Special	Pre-Designation	Rollback Penalty	Other Penalty
Alaska	X					X	
Arkansas	X	X					
California	X		X		X	X	
Colorado	X						
Connecticut	X	X	X		X		X
Delaware	X	X					
Florida	X		X				
Hawaii	X	X	X			X	X
Illinois	X			X		X	X
Indiana	X						
Iowa	X				X		
Kentucky	X	X				X	X
Maine	X	X	X		X	X	X
Maryland	X	X		X	X	X	
Massachusetts		X					
Minnesota	X		X	X		X	
Montana	X					X	
New Hampshire	X	X	X		X		X

State						
New Jersey	X				X	
New Mexico	X	X				
New York	X				X	X
North Carolina	X	X			X	X
North Dakota	X			X		
Oregon	X				X	X
Pennsylvania	X	X	X	X	X	X
Rhode Island	X	X	X		X	X
South Dakota	X			X	X	
Texas	X				X	
Utah	X				X	X
Vermont	X					
Virginia	X	X		X	X	X
Washington	X	X	X		X	X
Wyoming	X					

From: Economic Research Service, U.S. Department of Agriculture, State Programs for the Differential Assessment of Farm and Open Space Land (1974).

it raises problems of defining which land should qualify and of arriving at true farm values in urbanizing areas (See Table 4-2).

Tax deferral is a variation on the preferential assessment approach. The deferral method involves two assessments on each agricultural property: one of the land's value for agricultural uses and another of its value for more intensive urban uses. The land owner pays only the tax on the lower agricultural value until the land is developed and then he pays part of the back taxes at the higher level. Usually the back taxes are collected for the last three to five years, and some states charge interest on the deferred taxes. The same definitional problems exist as for preferential assessment.

The states using preferential assessment by 1969 were Arizona, California, Colorado, Connecticut, Delaware, Florida, Indiana, Iowa, New Hampshire, New Mexico, and Utah. The states using tax deferral schemes by 1969 were Maryland, Minnesota, New Jersey, Ohio, Oregon, Rhode Island, and Texas. Table 4-2 shows the status in 1974.

Preferential taxation has been applied as well to other than open space, forest or agricultural land uses by dividing uses into classes, each of which is assessed at differing percentages of market value according to current use or according to uses permitted in the zoning district in which the land falls. A number of states singled out historic sites, historic buildings and conservation areas for special tax treatment. Some of the more extensive approaches in effect in 1969 were in Arizona, Connecticut, Hawaii, Minnesota and New Hampshire. New York City is an example of a municipality which has a program of granting exemptions and abatement of property taxes for the purpose of encouraging specific types of improvements or rehabilitation. In rehabilitation areas the abatement of taxes is used as an incentive for owners to bring their buildings into compliance with building and housing codes.[50] Boston, on the other hand, negotiates assessed valuation with developers before construction, a practice which would run into legal difficulties in most communities because of uniform assessment requirements.

Tax abatement has been used to encourage home ownership, (e.g. homestead exemption in Florida) relieve the tax burdens on the elderly, and to attract industry but Netzer points out that these selective measures are ". . . clumsy and inefficient . . ." and often benefit others than those for whom they were intended and tend to shift the tax burden unfairly to those who remain taxed.[51] Nonetheless they are still being experimentally used.

Preferential taxation and tax deferral on open land have not been in use long enough for empirical studies of their effect on fringe development to have been made, or their effect on the preservation of open space to be conclusive, but the obvious intent of these practices is to reduce urban sprawl by enabling owners of agricultural land in urbanizing areas to resist development pressures until the land is ripe for development. Of the two methods it is reasonable to suppose that tax deferral will prove to be the more effective because of its rollback feature.

Taxing Unearned Increment

Real property values may rise because of population growth and public expenditures on expressways, mass transit, or community facilities. Because this kind of value increase is not the result of anything the property owner has done, it is termed *unearned increment*. Most arguments for taxing unearned increments on real property are made on the grounds of equity: that increases in values resulting from the community rather than the owner should be returned to the community. However, it can also be argued that the lack of such taxation encourages speculation and discourages development and is counter to the purpose of discouraging sprawl and carrying out the land use plan. Hagman has made a persuasive argument in favor of such a tax[52] but this author has been able to unearth only one example, the City of San Jose, California, which has a city real property sales tax,[53] and no empirical studies concerning the land use implications of such a tax. Because of the lack of examples and studies of land use effects it remains unclear what benefits the taxing of unearned increments in real property would have for implementing land use plans.

Selective Taxation

In an article in *Planning* Pickford and Shannon suggest that ". . . a highly selective or pinpoint approach to the meshing of tax and planning objectives might be the most feasible way of making sure that the property tax promotes rather than undercuts . . . the orderly development of the urban landscape."[54]

They argue for a series of coordinated measures: shielding abnormally low-income families from the full impact of property taxes, creating partial tax abatement districts in built-up districts having abnormally low building to land value ratios, imposing special assessments against owners of vacant land being held speculatively out of development where development or redevelopment is the intent of the land use plan, and protecting land for future development through tax deferrments until it is intended to be developed.

Their arguments are convincing and such selective measures should be beneficial when coordinated with land use planning, but they raise serious legal questions, especially where state constitutions require uniform taxation, and practical questions of coordination where local governmental units are fragmented. Placing these selective powers in the hands of planning agencies would be very difficult if not impossible to achieve given present day political and legal obstacles.

Tax Base-Sharing

In urbanized areas having many local governments it is often impossible to implement rational land-use plans because of the competition between these governments for development yielding the highest property tax revenues. Tax base-sharing is a scheme for the reallocation between local governments of property taxes raised by them. Lyall says that it is designed to ". . . strengthen the fiscal capacity of local governments to respond to local public service demands *including* those for more rational land development, open space, and environmental preservation."[55] Base-sharing legislation has been adopted in New Jersey for the Hackensack Meadows reclamation area, and in Minnesota for the Twin Cities area. In Maryland in 1975 a state-wide base-sharing bill was under consideration.[56]

Lyall contends that by incorporating in the formula for local property taxation links with the pattern and pace of land development in adjacent jurisdictions, local autonomy is strengthened and this rearrangement of market incentives would favor more rational land use planning. Some of the advantages Lyall lists as being claimed for base-sharing as affects land use patterns are as follows:[57]

1. Base-sharing would reduce competition among jurisdictions for commercial and industrial development to help relieve the property tax burden on residential property by granting special assessment, depreciation, and tax privileges.
2. Base-sharing would reduce the incentives for "fiscal zoning" which has created barriers between the central cities and their suburbs, locking into the cities low-income population unable to contribute in taxes enough to carry the existing average share of suburban public services at current levels of provision and spending.
3. Base-sharing would aid environmental preservation and rational long-term economic and land use planning by partially "compensating" localities that voluntarily, or in compliance with a land use plan, provide open space and recreational resources for the region and by reducing the pressures to locate public investment as political spoils.

The Twin Cities plan, enacted in 1970, encompasses Minneapolis, St. Paul, and seven adjacent counties including some 300 independent taxing units. Under it 40 percent of the net growth of commercial-industrial valuation since 1971 has gone to the Twin Cities Metropolitan Council for redistribution among member governments according to population and need.[58] In the Hackensack Meadowlands Reclamation program in New Jersey the redistribution of taxes serves to compensate localities whose land is withdrawn from potential industrial use for reasons of environmental conservation. In Maryland the statewide base-sharing plan would have established a "growth pool" to which would have been assigned 60 percent of all increases in the assessed value of commercial and industrial properties occurring after a specified date. The average tax rate of all 24 counties would have been applied to this assessed value and the resulting revenue would have been redistributed to them on the basis of population and per capita residential wealth.

Although there is little empirical evidence, base-sharing may prove to be a useful instrument in the kit of tools for implementation of land use plans and one that should not be overlooked.[59]

CONCLUSIONS

Because this chapter dealt with a miscellany of legal devices affecting development, each somewhat differently, no generalization about them is appropriate as a whole in regard to their usefulness in the implementation of land use plans. However, as was pointed out in discussing them individually, some of them have promise and should be seriously considered in developing land use implementation programs.

NOTES AND ACKNOWLEDGMENTS FOR CHAPTER 4

1. Webster, Donald H., *Urban Planning and Municipal Public Policy*, (New York: Harper and Row, 1958), p. 293, reproduced by permission.
2. Advisory Commission on Intergovernmental Relations (ACIR), *Building Codes: A Program for Intergovernmental Reform*, (Washington: U.S. Government Printing Office, 1966), p. 8.
3. Many local governments, especially suburban governments embody excessive requirements in their building codes to discourage the construction of low-cost housing and therefore the migration of low-income families into their communities. Only through court action or state intervention can these exclusionary tactics be thwarted as is the case with exclusionary zoning which was discussed in Chapter Two. Also see ACIR, *Building Codes*, p. 7.
4. BOCA International, *Codes and Code Administration*, (Chicago: Building Officials and Code Administrators International, 1969), p. 15, reproduced by permission.
5. ACIR, *op.cit.*, p. 84.
6. National Commission on Urban Problems (NCUP), *Building the American City*, (Washington: U.S. Government Printing Office, 1968), pp. 254–72.
7. Letter from Gene A. Rowland, Chief, Office of Building Standards, Center for Building Technology (Washington, D.C.), August 8, 1974.
8. Rowland letter and letter from Robert Wehrli, Chief, Architectural Research Section, National Bureau of Standards (Washington, D.C.), July 15, 1974.
9. Public Law 93-383, Title VIII, Sec. 809 (1974), pp. 96–101.
10. "State Building Code Profile," *Construction Review*, (March 1972).
11. Letter from Dale R. Gatlin, Director of Code Research, Indiana Administrative Building Council, Indianapolis, May 28, 1974.
12. As cited by Eric W. Mood, "The Development, Objective, and Adequacy of Current Housing Code Standards," in *Housing Code Standards: Three Critical Studies, Research Report No. 19*, (Washington: The National Commission on Urban Problems, 1969), p. 3.
13. NCUP. *op.cit.*, p. 274.
14. ———. *op.cit.*, p. 174.
15. Mood. *op.cit.*, p. 13.
16. ———. *op.cit.*, p. 18.
17. ———. *op.cit.*, pp. 28–31.
18. Lieberman, Barnet, "Administrative Provisions of Housing Codes," in *Housing Code Standards: Three Critical Studies, Research Report No. 19*, (Washington: The National Commission on Urban Problems, 1969), p. 61.

19. ———. *op.cit.*, pp. 62–64.
20. Slavet, Joseph S., and Levin, Melvin R., *New Approaches to Housing Code Administration, Research Report No. 17*, (Washington: The National Commission on Urban Problems, 1969), pp. 24–26.
21. ———. *op.cit.*, pp. 28–33.
22. Grad, Frank P., *Legal Remedies for Housing Code Violations, Research Report No. 14*, (Washington: The National Commission on Urban Problems, 1968), pp. 149–53.
23. Wolfe, Myer R., "Land Use Economics and General Taxation Policy," in *Urban Land Use Policy*, ed. by Richard B. Andrews, (New York: The Free Press, 1972), p. 231.
24. Clawson, Marion, *Suburban Land Conversion in the United States: An Economic and Governmental Process*, (Baltimore and London: The Johns Hopkins University Press, published for Resources for the Future, 1971), pp. 42–43. Copyright © 1971 by The Johns Hopkins University Press, all rights reserved, reproduced by permission.
25. U.S. Department of Housing and Urban Development, *Housing in the Seventies*, (Washington: U.S. Government Printing Office, 1974), p. 171.
26. NCUP, *op.cit.*, p. 405.
27. ———. *op.cit.*, pp. 406–07.
28. ———. *op.cit.*, p. 405.
29. Rawson, Mary, *Property Taxation and Urban Development*, Research Monograph 4, (Washington: The Urban Land Institute, 1961), p. 8.
30. Abrams, Charles, "The Uses of Land in Cities," *Scientific American*, **213**, No. 3, (September 1965), p. 155, reproduced by permission.
31. Pickford, James H., and Shannon, John, "Harnessing Property Taxes and Land-Use Planning," reprinted with permission from *Planning*, the magazine of the American Society of Planning Officials, **38**, No. 11, (December 1972), p. 304, copyright 1972.
32. George, Henry, *Progress and Poverty*, (New York: Henry George, 1888), pp. 357–61 and 367–78.
33. Clark, W. A. V., *The Impact of Property Taxes on Urban Spacial Development*, (Los Angeles: The Institute of Government and Public Affairs, The University of California, Los Angeles, 1974), pp. 6–10.
34. Rawson, *op.cit.*, p. 11.
35. Prentice, Perry, ed., "Financing Our Urban Needs," *Nation's Cities*, reprint (March 1969), pp. 40–42.
36. Walker, Mabel, "Tax Responsibility for the Slum," *Tax Policy*, Vol. 26 (1959)
37. Gaffney, Mason, "Property Taxes and the Frequency of Urban Renewal," *National Tax Association Proceedings*, (Harrisburg: The Association, 1964), p. 282 and Gaffney, "Land Planning and the Property Tax," *Journal of the American Institute of Planners*, Vol. XXXV, No. 3, (May 1969), pp. 178–83.
38. "Municipal Real Estate Taxation," *Yale Law Journal*, **57** (1947), pp. 219–242.
39. Larsen, Peter A., "Arden, Delaware—Utopian Experiment in Single Tax and Success as a Planned Community," unpublished paper presented at the 1973 Confer-In of the American Institute of Planners in Atlanta, pp. 1–13 (mimeographed).

40. Hutchinson, A. R., *Public Charges Upon Land Values in Australia* (Melbourne: no publisher given, 1961).
41. Williams, P. R., "Pittsburgh Pioneering in Scientific Taxation," *American Journal of Economics and Sociology*, **21** (1962).
42. Rawson, *op.cit.*, entire article.
43. Brown, H. G., and others, *Land Value Taxation Around the World*, (New York: Robert Schalkanback Foundation, 1955).
44. Clark, *op.cit.*, entire publication.
45. Cowan, H. B., *Municipal Improvement and Finance*, (New York: Harper and Brothers, 1958).
46. Woodruff, A. M., and Ecker-Racz, L. L., "Property Taxes and Land Use in Australia and New Zealand," *Tax Executive*, **18** (1960), p. 47.
47. Clark, *op.cit.*, pp. 113–14.
48. Legler, John B., *Some Critical Comments on Property Taxation as an Alternative to Site Planning*, (St. Louis: Institute for Urban and Regional Studies, Washington University, 1970), p. 20 (mimeographed).
49. Friday, Richard E., *Summaries of State Legislation Dealing with the Preservation of Farmland*, (Ithaca: Department of Agricultural Economics, Cornell University, October 1969), pp. 1–5.
50. Price, Waterhouse & Co., *A Study of the Effects of Real Estate Tax Incentives Upon Property Rehabilitation and New Construction: Summary*, (Washington: U.S. Department of Housing and Urban Development, 1973), p. 4.
51. Netzer, Dick, *Impact of the Property Tax: Its Economic Implications for Ubran Problems*, (Washington: The National Commission on Urban Affairs, 1968), pp. 45–46.
52. Hagman, Donald G., "A New Deal: Trading Windfalls for Wipeouts," *Planning*, **40**, No. 8, (September 1974), pp. 9–13.
53. City of San Jose, *Ordinance No. 16251*.
54. Pickford and Shannon, *op.cit.*, p. 305, reprinted with permission.
55. Lyall, Katherine C., "Tax Base-Sharing: A Fiscal Aid Towards More Rational Land Use Planning," *Journal of the American Institute of Planners*, **41**, No. 2, (March 1975), p. 90, reprinted by permission of the author and journal.
56. Lyall, *op.cit.*, p. 90.
57. ———. *op.cit.*, p. 92.
58. "Fiscal Disparities Bill," *Planning and Development Newsletter*, Dakota County Planning Advisory Commission, Vol. 1, No. 4, (August 1971), unpaged.
59. ———. *op.cit.*, pp. 98–99.

5

Financial planning and capital improvement programming

Planning agencies are interested in the financial aspects of municipal and local governments for a number of different reasons. They are interested in planning for local government income in order to insure that there will be enough money for financing operational and capital budgets. Their concern about operational budgets includes the financing of the planning process and the economic and social programs which are part of the comprehensive plan. They are concerned about public improvement programs because they determine capital expenditures in support of community facilities plans and in turn influence the timing and location of private development in support of land use plans.[1]

The extent to which planning agencies can intervene in financial planning and public improvement programs as a means of implementing land use plans is the principal concern of this chapter. Participation by

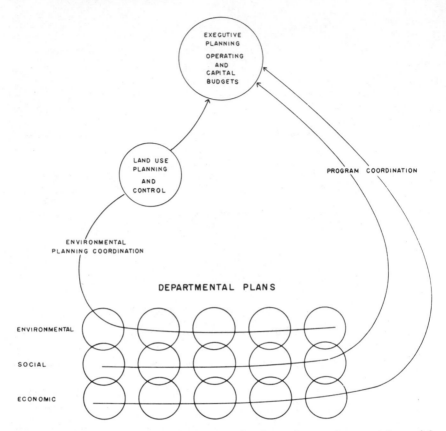

Figure 5-1. Coordination of departmental plans for environmental, social, and economic development through land use and executive planning.

From Joseph M. Heikoff, *Planning and Budgeting in Municipal Administration*, copyright 1965 by the International City Management Association. Reproduced by permission.

planning agencies in financial planning and public improvement programming is an important way of influencing political decision makers in aid of the coordinated implementation of physical plans and policies. In discussing operating and public improvement programs, Heikoff asserts that they should ". . . have as their main purpose the statement of the community's development objectives and of the financial program by which these objectives are to be achieved."[2] He observes further that:[3]

Although much has been written about municipal planning and municipal budgeting, comparatively little has been said about the relationship between these two important governmental activities. Planning is not even an organized activity in many municipal governments . . . Neither is formalized budgeting a universal practice in municipal management . . .

Planning may be conceived of . . . as one approach to management . . . It is . . . a method by which the efficiency of management in meeting its responsibilities may be improved.

Except for the determination of the operational needs of the planning agency itself, planners have traditionally been excluded from the operational budget-making process, this being the province of the locality's chief executive and his finance department. Planning for the locality's financial income has also until recently been the province of finance departments and the executives and councils to whom they are responsible. Increasingly, however, planning agencies are being consulted for their advice concerning income, especially that which is to be assigned to capital items and for physical development programs related to planning. For a much longer time assembling capital improvements programs and budgets has been a task for planning agencies where permitted or required under state enabling legislation. Figure 5-1 is an illustration of how Heikoff proposes that planning be related to other agencies and departments and to the executive in the budgeting process.

LONG-RANGE FINANCIAL PLANNING

Only a few cities have undertaken long-range financial planning closely related to comprehensive planning but this is a process essential for attaining maximization of benefits for the largest number of people within the limit of available resources. Long-term financial plans may cover periods up to 20–25 years and set forth estimates and objectives for both public services and public improvements together with the means of financing them.[4]

The financial plan serves a number of important purposes in the allocation of governmental monies in light of the usual condition in which the demand for public services and capital expenditures far exceeds available revenues. As an economic document the financial plan identifies and allocates budget resources. As a political document it serves to hold decision makers accountable for their constituencies.

And as a decision-making document it serves to support the policy decisions financially.

Major general considerations in drawing up the financial plan are the decisions concerning the allocation of funds between capital and operating budgets, the choice between borrowing and pay-as-you-go, and the choice between regressive and progressive forms of taxation. Also involved is the consideration of the allocation of funds in regard to need, equity, and geographic distribution[5]

The elements which make up a long-range financial plan are: the public services program, the public improvement program, the long-term revenue program, the capital budget, and the annual operating budget. The public services program is a long-range plan for all public services such as public safety, recreation, welfare, planning, etc. It represents a projection of the annual operating budget. The public improvement program lists comprehensively all the capital investments in community facilities necessary to carry out the agreed upon program of public services. The long-term revenue program details the funding of the public services and public improvement programs. The capital budget relates on a shorter term (5–6 years) the highest priority public improvements in a schedule of intended expenditures, and the annual budget allocates revenues and expenditures for regular and recurring operations of the local government and is the primary instrument of planning and financial control.[6]

Responsibilities for Long-Range Financial Planning

The chief executive of the local government is responsible for the preparation and maintenance of the long-term financial plan and for the submission of the annual operating and capital budgets to the governing body of the local government. Much of the preparatory work is done, however, by the finance or budget officer, the planning agency and other local government department and agency heads both individually and working together. The chief executive, however, is the focal point of the endeavor.

THE PUBLIC SERVICES PROGRAM

This program is an extension of the annual operating budget in that current local government services and activities budgets, together with budget needs for anticipated new services and activities, are projected over the long term as related to program goals and anticipated revenue.

One reason for preparing the public services program in conjunction with the other financial planning activities is to make clear to all concerned, in and out of government that:[7]

> . . . there is a fundamental difference between expenditures for continuing operating requirements and expenditures for capital improvements which are nonrecurring and of enduring value . . . A second reason for a long-term operating budget is the practical problem of keeping total costs of regular operations and capital improvements within the limits of sound financing and a reasonably uniform tax rate. This can hardly be accomplished unless an estimate is made of future operating costs including the additional costs of operation of contemplated capital improvements.

Costs of substantially increasing services of one kind can be incurred only by decreasing other services, reducing capital expenditures, raising more revenue or developing new sources of funding. Failure to anticipate the operational costs of capital improvements can result in such anomalies as inoperable or undermanned facilities (parks, playgrounds, schools, libraries, etc.). Operational costs are relatively inflexible and are likely to increase from year to year because of inflation, population growth, staff seniority, and neighborhood deterioration.

In programming municipal services the objectives of each department or agency must first be determined and then the need for these services must be projected in relation to the locality's expected growth and development. The statements must be comprehensive and will inevitably set forth both concrete and intangible objectives. Standards of adequacy for the services to be provided must be determined and related both to cost and citizen demand.

Heikoff cites three approaches to the evaluation and synthesis of budgetary information:[8]

> The 'accounting' approach has the objective of good housekeeping. Its criteria are economy and efficiency. The 'economic' approach seeks objective economic criteria, such as marginal analysis, for allocating resources among government programs. The third approach might be called the 'policy' approach because its criteria for resource allocation are based upon policies developed by the interaction of executive judgement and political action. . . . It is likely that all three approaches contribute to budget-

making in most communities. Overemphasis on any one approach, with consequent neglect of the information and insights provided by the others, may lead to budget decisions that appear irrational in relation to community development objectives.

These approaches are applicable to all aspects of financial planning as is the Planning-Programming-Budgeting System (PPBS) developed in the U.S. Department of Defense in the 1960s. The latter is an elaborate process whose supporters assert that it results in a better, more rational allocation of scarce resources among local governmental contenders. It is probable that this system will be useful only to the larger units of government because of the expertise required and the inflexibility involved in properly applying it.

THE PUBLIC IMPROVEMENT PROGRAM

This program is based on the general land use plan and in particular on the community facilities and transportation sections of the plan. It consists of: ". . . broad evaluation and establishment of priorities for capital projects essential for future development."[9] The capital budget, which is usually only the first five or six years of the longer-range program, is much more detailed and immediately applicable.

The public improvement program and the capital budget, through the control of public spending for the infrastructure necessary to private development, influence the timing and location of that private development toward the implementation of the land use plan. Further, the public projects may be complexly interrelated and the public improvement program together with the capital budget are a means of properly coordinating the capital expenditures of the diverse departments and agencies in the area covered by the process. We are all familiar with the waste involved in such an instance as that of street resurfacing done in one year only to be torn up the next for the replacement of utility lines. Such unnecessary costs and inconveniences could be minimized through careful coordination of public improvement programming in accordance with land use stage development plans. Webster points out that public improvement programming ". . . offers a better prospect for getting first things first. . ." and ". . . it establishes a sounder basis for long range decisions . . ."[10]

The often extensive fragmentation of government at the local level complicates the problem of coordinating public improvement programming and makes it more important that a planning agency with jurisdiction over the entire urbanized and urbanizing area concerned should be given the task of putting the program together and analyzing it.

Before the public improvement program can be drawn up an immense amount of information must be collected. This responsibility may lie in the planning agency or a budget department, or be shared. Each agency or department making capital expenditures must submit to the program-assembling agency an itemized list of proposed expenditures for each year of the years of the public improvement program, together with the suggested priority and written justification for each item. An indication of possible sources of funding for each item should also be included.

The function of the planning agency is both coordinative and evaluative. Although capital budgets and public improvement programs are sometimes prepared without reference to long-range comprehensive plans it is poor practice for the planning agency not to take maximum advantage of the capital budgeting process for plan implementation, especially in view of the tendency of other government departments and agencies to accord the comprehensive plan lower status. If there are mid-range or stage development plans in existence the task is made much easier.[11]

As part of the review process the planning agency often prepares a procedures manual for the use of those from whom capital items are solicited. The procedures manual explains the budgeting process and how to fill out the required forms. On the forms each expenditure is described by name, type, location, and purpose. The need must be explained with reference to the comprehensive plan where applicable. The relationship of the expenditure to other projects or expenditures, if any, must be explained. Costs must be broken down into their logical components and if they can be scheduled over several years, estimates for each year must be provided. Expenditures for additional staff, operational costs, and maintenance resulting from the capital items must also be estimated. This enables coordination of the public improvement program with the public service program.

The listed items of all departments are reviewed for their practicality, their interrelationships in time, the validity of the priority suggested for them, their conformance with short- and longer-range plans, and the availability of funds to support them. The assembled requests together with planning staff recommendations are then forwarded (with the approval of the planning commission if there is one) to the chief executive for his review and subsequent legislative adoption.

THE LONG-TERM REVENUE PROGRAM

If the public services program and the public improvement program are to be carried out there must be sufficient money to fund them. The long-term revenue program must be set up to establish fiscal policies to enable the funding of these programs. The first step in this process of developing a revenue program is to project the revenue which will be available if the locality's present fiscal policies are continued. Next, alternative fiscal policies are explored. The possibilities of obtaining a higher yield from present sources are examined, together with the possibilities of developing new sources of revenue. Various borrowing policies are also analyzed. Then a mutual adjustment between the revenue program, the public services program and the public improvement program must be made.

Urban governments are limited in their ability to choose between revenue sources because of constraints put upon them by state constitutions, state and federal laws, and by state and federal administrative policies and regulations. The principal sources of revenue at the local level considered in developing the revenue program are property taxes, income taxes, sales taxes, special tax assessments, user surcharges or service charges for utilities and government services, licenses, fees, and intergovernmental aids and revenue sharing. Borrowing is also an important source of funds, especially for public improvement projects.

Real Property Taxes

Historically the tax on real property has been the primary source of revenue for local government. It is criticized as placing an inequitable burden on the owners of real property, especially in today's industrialized world where the ownership of real property does not fairly represent ability to pay. The administration of tax assessments and collection presents other problems such as lack of uniform assessments, failure to assess at market value, and failure to collect delinquent taxes. If they constitute a large proportion of the jurisdictional area tax exempt properties such as those owned by governmental, educational, religious and charitable institutions, and cemeteries, shift the real property tax burden to a disproportionally small number of land owners.

Despite the inequities in the real property tax the Institute for Training in Municipal Administration concludes that it ". . . provides an equitable method for spreading the cost of services that benefit property owners . . . but the administration of the tax . . . should be improved, especially with regard to the method of assessment and collection . . . , reducing the amount of exempt property, abolishing arbitrary tax limits, and eliminating overlapping governmental units."[12]

Personal Property Taxes

Personal property, as opposed to real property, is considered to be movable and is classified in two categories: tangible and intangible. Tangible personal property consists of such things as automobiles, household furnishings, and the merchandise in stores. Intangible personal property, on the other hand, consists of such things as money in cash or bank deposits, stocks, and bonds.

Because personal property is easily moved or hidden, taxes on personal property are subject to a high degree of avoidance and evasion, especially if the tax rates are high. And because of the difficulties in the administration of these taxes, the tendency is to place the burden on those classes of property less easily hidden, such as automobiles, machinery, store inventories, and other tangibles. As a consequence of the problems of fairly administering this easily evadable tax, local governments cannot and do not rely on it for much of their revenue.

Income Taxes

Income taxes are increasingly being permitted to be levied by localities. These may take the form of a surcharge on the state's income tax[13] or of a direct gross income tax levied at the place of employment. The latter has the advantage of capturing income at the source which might otherwise be exported to other jurisdictions.

The most common form of local income tax is the gross income tax on salaries and wages, often combined with a net income tax on businesses and corporations. Where the local income tax has been used it has often produced a significant portion of the locality's revenue. It is also the most productive of any of the nonproperty taxes and may lessen the pressure to raise real property tax rates.[14]

The disadvantages of the local gross income tax are its regressiveness, the extra costs of administering it for both businesses and local government, and possible problems of double taxation when home and work place are in different jurisdictions. It also fails to tax income derived from intangible personal property and, usually, from rentals of real property when it is not operated as a regular business.

Sales and Excise Taxes

Sales and excise taxes provide high yields even in adverse economic conditions but have the disadvantage of being regressive, especially when items of necessity are not exempted from taxation. Excise taxes such as those on cigarettes and alcoholic beverages may raise objections that they are really designed to modify human behavior rather than simply to raise revenue, and therefore are an invasion of personal liberty. Other special taxes such as those on hotel rooms, entertainment admissions, and airport landings, although raising some revenue, are subject to various objections because of their selectivity, unless earmarked for direct benefits to those being taxed. Further, many such taxes can be evaded through the purchasing of the taxed items in neighboring jurisdictions which do not levy them; however, this kind of evasion is not frequent if the rates are kept low.

Special Tax Assessments, User Surcharges, and Service Charges

A form of the real property tax is the special assessment which may be levied where specific public improvements benefit identifiable properties. The use of special assessments and the creation of assessment districts is enabled by state legislation or, more rarely, embodied in local government charters. This mechanism is most commonly used for street, sidewalk, and utility improvements, and more recently, for funding improvements in central business districts such as pedestrian malls and attendant parking facilities.

The drawbacks to the use of special assessments lie in the danger of default, the high cost of special assessment borrowing, and the difficulties of administration and accounting involved. The advantages lie in that those not benefitting do not have to share the cost, that properties exempt from general property taxes can be reached, and in some states they are not restricted by constitutional or statutory debt or tax limits.[15]

Licenses, Fees, and Fines

Licenses, permits, fees, and fines are also sources of local revenue although in many cases the primary purpose of them is regulatory or punitive. The amounts involved are often established or restricted by state legislation, thus limiting the freedom of localities to use them as sources of revenue.

There is no clear distinction between licenses, permits, and fees, but some generalizations about them can be made. Where it appears essential to public health or welfare, licenses may be required as a means of controlling and regulating occupations and businesses for stipulated intervals. Permits, such as building, vending, and parade permits may be required as a means of regulating specific activities usually over a limited period of time. Fees, such as those related to filing applications of various sorts, are usually a means of recouping the costs of processing.

Fines and penalties, ranging from library fines and traffic fines to penalties for late payment of taxes, are all clearly punitive and designed to encourage conformance to the law.

Income from Public Services

The income from public services is varied. User surcharges and service charges by utilities and public enterprises may include revenue from gas, electric and water supply as well as surcharges for sewage collection and processing (usually based on water consumption because of the difficulty of metering sewage). Garbage collection is usually charged for on a flat rate basis according to the land use classification. Other revenues from user charges may come from such sources as parking charges, airport landing charges, port facilities charges and rental of space in public-owned buildings or leases of public lands.

Service districts levying property or other taxes combine aspects of previously discussed taxing methods. They differ from utility surcharges and service charges in that the districts are rarely conterminous with the boundaries of local governments and may include parts of more than one jurisdiction.

School districts, fire protection districts, utility districts, and mass-transit districts are among the differing kinds of service districts. The revenue from these varied sources is not insignificant and must be taken into account in developing the long-term revenue program.

Intergovernmental Aids

Intergovernmental aids are an important source of money to be considered in the financial plan. Federal aids take the form of categorical grant programs, general revenue sharing, and special revenue sharing. They are predictable only to the degree that legislation continuing them in effect and funding them is predictable. How these funds are permitted to be used will determine the flexibility of their allocation in the financial plan. State aid programs have similar characteristics and problems of predictability.

Next to real property taxes, intergovernmental aids are the largest single source of income for local governments.[16] Most of these funds come from the federal government either directly or by way of the states. The amount of general revenue sharing (unearmarked) as opposed to special revenue sharing (earmarked for a limited number of purposes) and categorical grant programs (earmarked for specific use) has been on the increase in recent years.[17]

Of special interest to planners in regard to the implementation of physical development plans is the block grant program established by the Housing and Community Development Act of 1974 which consolidates in one programmatic grant the funding of urban renewal, model cities, neighborhood facilities, open space acquisition and development (including historic preservation and beautification), water and sewer facilities, and also includes public facility loans.

Except for federal general revenue sharing, most intergovernmental aids are accompanied by conditions, restrictions, and obligations. These are generally aimed at encouraging administrative and financial responsibility on the part of the recipient governments. To the extent that intergovernmental aids can be projected into the future with confidence they must be taken into account in the long-term revenue plan.

Borrowing

Many major public improvements are financed by borrowing. The power to borrow is both enabled and limited by the state. Usually bonds are issued and sold as the principal method of borrowing. Bonds are promises to repay the amount borrowed at a stipulated time with a stipulated amount of interest. The amount issued is often limited to a certain percentage of the locality's total assessed valuation of real property. Bonds may be backed by income from the improvements they finance (revenue bonds) or backed by the locality's general tax and revenue income (general obligation bonds).

The formulation of the locality's debt policy within the limits set by law must be very carefully done. Borrowing is fraught with risks and hazards (e.g. New York City recently). Certain kinds of capital expenditures may be reasonably and safely financed through long-term borrowing. Self-supporting public utilities are an example. In general, very expensive projects which have a long life and do not frequently recur are legitimate subjects for bond issues. Care must be taken that the debt will be amortized before the bond-financed improvement needs to be replaced. Equipment with a short life and operating expenses should never be financed by borrowing.

A sound debt structure is crucial to the formation of a sound debt policy. The locality's borrowings for tax-supported purposes, according to Funk:[18]

> . . . should be arranged so that there will be no pronounced irregularities in debt service from year to year to cause erratic gyrations in the tax levy, and that there will be a downward trend in annual requirements which will make room for new borrowings without pyramiding debt service costs. When new borrowing is undertaken it should be so fitted into the existing structure that no irregularities, actual or potential, will result.

The long-term revenue program must carefully coordinate all of the various revenue resources in support of the long-term public services and public improvement programs.

THE CAPITAL BUDGET

The capital budget is adopted each year for the projected budget period of five to six years. It represents in greater detail the early part of the long-term public improvement program. Also it is usual that only the first year is binding as part of the locality's annual budget.

Customarily the budget is projected forward each year for another year and the first year of the revised budget is again reviewed and adopted. This procedure allows the budget to be flexible enough to take into account changing circumstances and yet be firm enough to be an effective instrumentality for carrying out early programmed parts of the transportation, community facilities, and open space portions of the long-range land use plan. In addition the capital budget may contain unearmarked contingency funds for unforeseeable needs that may occur during each budget year.

Each agency or department of local government must submit an itemized list of proposed capital expenditures for each of the budget years together with an indication of their priority of importance, a written justification for each item and a suggested source of funding in a more detailed way than was necessary for the long-term public improvement program, as previously indicated (See Figures 5-2, and 5-3). As Frank So suggests, it is also important that: "The planning agency should strive to be in a position whereby it is consulted when projects are in the idea stage and in generalized form prior to the development of detailed plans."[19]

There must be careful coordination between the capital budget and the operating budget in relation to the available revenue. The preparation of both operating and capital budgets provides information, in turn, for revising the long-term financial plan.

When all of the requested information is in, the planning agency reviews each item proposed for the capital budget in the light of development plans for the budget period, the available funds, and the interrelationships between items in order to assign a revised set of priorities. This process may involve extensive conferences with all of

ESTIMATES FOR FIVE-YEAR CAPITAL IMPROVEMENT PROGRAM

JULY 1, 1968 - JUNE 30, 1973

INDIVIDUAL PROJECT DATA SHEET

CITY OF LOUISVILLE ☐

JEFFERSON COUNTY ☐

JOINT AGENCIES ☐

1. Department, Board or Commission _____

2. Submitted by _____ Title _____ 3. Date _____

---

4. Description of Project

  a. Project Number _____

  b. Project Name _____

  c. Physical Description _____

    _____

    _____

    _____

  d. Location _____

  e. New_____ Addition_____ Replacement_____

    Other _____

  f. Date Begun _____

5. Need for Project (use separate sheet if necessary)

  a. Why requested _____

    _____

  b. Department's priority _____

6. Relation to Other Projects in this Department _____

7. Relation to Other Department's Programs _____

8. Total Estimated Five-Year Costs, 1968-69 - 1972-73

        . Amount . Subtotals

  a. Planning (1) + (2) $ _____

    (1) Architects services $ _____

    (2) Engineering $ _____

  b. Land $ _____

    (1) Site is secured $ _____

    (2) Site to be secured $ _____

  c. Construction (1) + (2) $ _____

    (1) Labor $ _____

    (2) Non-Labor $ _____

  d. Miscellaneous (1) + (2) $ _____

    (1) Equipment $ _____

    (2) Furniture $ _____

  e. Other $ _____

  f. TOTAL FIVE-YEAR COST

    OF PROJECT $ _____

  g. Who prepared the estimate _____

    _____

  h. Date _____

9. Summary Total Estimated Cost

  a. Estimated Five year cost of project (8f) $ _____

  b. Estimated cost beyond five years $ _____

  c. Subtotal (a + b) $ _____

  d. Cost prior to July 1, 1968 $ _____

  e. TOTAL COST OF PROJECT $ _____

10. Future Costs (Savings) Resulting from Project

  a. Annual Cost: maintenance, repair and operation $ _____

  b. Annual Estimated Cost of new staff required $ _____

  c. Future Expenditures For Additional Equip-
    ment not Included in Project Cost $ _____

    TOTAL $ _____

Form CB-a 4.1M 3/68
Planning Commission

---

11. Estimated Annual Income from Project $ _____

12. a. Estimated Construction

    Time _____ months

  b. Estimated Life of

    Project _____ years

  c. Estimated Completion

    Date _____ years

13. Status of plans and specifications –

  (Place check mark opposite proper status)

  _____ 0 Plans not needed

  _____ 1 Nothing done except this report

  _____ 2 Preliminary estimate received

  _____ 3 Surveys completed

  _____ 4 Work on plans scheduled

  _____ 5 Sketch plans in preparation

  _____ 6 Sketch plans completed

  _____ 7 Detail plans in preparation

  _____ 8 Detail plans and specifications completed

  _____ 9 Construction begun

14. Proposed Manner of Construction

  By Contract _____

  Other (specify) _____

15. Total Funds Authorized $ _____

  Source _____

16. Project Estimated Expenditures by Years

  a. Expenditures prior to July 1, 1968 (9d) $ _____

  b. 1968 - 69 $ _____

  c. 1969 - 70 $ _____

  d. 1970 - 71 $ _____

  e. 1971 - 72 $ _____

  f. 1972 - 73 $ _____

  g. Expenditures beyond 1972-73 (9b) $ _____

  h. TOTAL COST OF PROJECT (9e) $ _____

17. REMARKS: (Use separate sheet if necessary)

_____

_____

_____

_____

_____

_____

_____

_____

FOR USE BY FINANCE or AUDIT DEPARTMENT

18. Specific Expenditure Ledger No. or Account No.

Figure 5-2. Capital budget request form.

From the Louisville & Jefferson County Planning Commission, 1968.

SUMMARY OF A FIVE-YEAR CAPITAL IMPROVEMENTS PROGRAM

SHOWING METHODS OF FINANCING

METHODS OF FINANCING

CITY
a. Bond Fund
b. Special Capital Fund
c. Public Works Cumulative Reserve Fund

COUNTY
d. General Fund
e. Bond Fund

f. STATE

g. FEDERAL

CITY OF LOUISVILLE

JEFFERSON COUNTY

JOINT AGENCIES

1	2	3			4	5	6	7	8	9						10	11	12	13
		Priorities								Expenditures by Years and Methods of Financing									
Dept.	Dept. Project Number	Dept.	Planning Comm.	Final	Project Name and Description	Date Begun	Estim. Compl. Date	Cost Prior to July 1, 1968	Cost of Five-Year Program	1968 - 69	1969 - 70	1970 -71	1971 - 72	1972 - 73	Cost Beyond June 30, 1973	Total Cost	Status When Submitted	Future Costs (Savings) Resulting From Project

Form CB-c
1.5M 3/68
Planning Commission

Figure 5-3. Capital budget request summary form.

From the Louisville & Jefferson County Planning Commission, 1968.

the parties concerned to clarify the meaning of the written materials and obtain necessary additional information. The budget is then assembled and submitted to the planning commission at a public hearing for their approval, or where there is no commission, directly to the legislative body through its executive officer. If the budget passes through the hands of a "strong" executive he is likely to add another somewhat differing set of item priorities before placing the budget in the hands of the legislative body for final adoption, possibly with further modifications.

CONCLUSIONS

A major determinant in the location and timing of development is the availability of community facilities and urban services. The provision of new or additional facilities and expanded services is, in turn, dependent on the availability of the necessary funds and the decisions of local government concerning where and how to spend them. Financial planning and capital improvement programming are orderly methods for determining both short term and long term local government income and expenditures. They provide a mechanism for coordinating the funding and expenditures of interrelated programs of the participant government agencies and departments and for organizing the relevant expenditures in support of the land use planning implementation program.

The linkage of capital budgets to other planning implementation elements in growth guidance systems was mentioned in chapter two in regard to Ramapo, New York and is an important feature of several of the guidance systems described in chapter seven. It is clear that the value of financial planning and capital improvement programming undertaken as an integral component of land use planning implementation programs is increasingly being recognized by local governments.

NOTES AND ACKNOWLEDGEMENTS FOR CHAPTER 5

1. Heikoff, Joseph M., *Planning and Budgeting in Municipal Management* (Chicago: The International City Managers' Association, copyright 1965 by the Association), p. 36; also Lachlan F. Blair, "Programming Community Devel-

opment" in *Principles and Practice of Urban Planning*, ed. by William I. Goodman and Eric C. Freund, (Washington: The International City Managers' Association, 1968), p. 388.

2. Heikoff, *op. cit.*, p. 37, reproduced by permission.
3. ———. *op. cit.*, p. 1, reproduced by permission.
4. Funk, Robert L., ed., *Municipal Finance Administration*, (Chicago: Copyright 1962 by the International City Managers' Association), p. 337.
5. Levy, Frank, Meltsner, Arnold J., and Wildavsky, Aaron, *Urban Outcomes—Schools, Streets, and Libraries*, (Berkeley, Los Angeles, and London: University of California Press, 1974), pp. 2–3.
6. Funk, *op. cit.*, pp. 338–39.
7. Rogers, William B., "Clinic: Fiscal Planning and Capital Budgeting," reprinted with permission from, *Planning 1954*, (Chicago: Copyright 1954 by the American Society of Planning Officials), p. 94.
8. Heikoff, *op. cit.*, p. 9, reproduced by permission. See pp. 9–14 for a detailed discussion of each of these approaches.
9. From Funk, *op. cit.*, p. 343, reproduced by permission.
10. Webster, Donald H., *Urban Planning and Municipal Public Policy*, (New York: Harper and Row, 1958), p. 315, reproduced by permission.
11. Meyerson, Martin, "Building the Middle-Range Bridge for Comprehensive Planning," *Journal of the American Institute of Planners*, Vol. XXII, No. 2, (Spring 1956), pp. 58–64.
12. From Funk, *op. cit.*, p. 42, reproduced by permission.
13. The Indiana optional local government surcharge on the state income tax is an example.
14. Buehler, Alfred G., "Revenue Improvements under Present Laws and Government Structure," in *Financing Metropolitan Government*, (Princeton: Tax Institute, Incorporated, 1955), p. 208.
15. Funk, *op. cit.*, p. 112.
16. Webster, *op. cit.*, p. 338.
17. Subcommittee on the Planning Process and Urban Development of the Advisory Committee to the Department of Housing and Urban Development, *Revenue Sharing and the Planning Process—Shifting the Locus of Responsibility for Domestic Problem Solving*, (Washington: National Academy of Sciences, 1974), pp. 5–7.
18. From Funk, *op. cit.*, p. 311, reproduced by permission.
19. "Capital Improvement Programming," p. 16, reprinted by permission from PAS Report 151. Copyright 1961 by the American Society of Planning Officials.

6

Special districts and public authorities

GENERAL CHARACTERISTICS

In the previous chapter special assessment and service districts were mentioned in connection with financial planning and capital programming as devices for funding public or public-assisted development and services. This chapter will address itself to describing those characteristics of these governmental entities which are of special interest in regard to their usefulness in the implementation of land use plans and policies.

Definition

The terms "special district" and "public authority" are not easily distinguishable; in this chapter the term "special district" will usually be the term used, and it will usually be construed to include most governmental entities called "public authorities." They are defined by the Bureau of the Census as being organized governmental entities having substantial autonomy.[1] Because there are so many variations among them they are difficult to define. For example, public housing agencies increasingly occur as departments of local government and therefore no longer meet the criteria of "substantial autonomy." Special districts may be wholly public or quasi-public; independent, partly dependent, or wholly dependent in relation to local general-purpose governments; they may be single-purpose or multipurpose; they may undertake land acquisition and/or construction of facilities and/or operate facilities and/or deliver services or any combination of these things; they also may be temporary or permanent in nature. The broadest interpretation of the Census definition will be employed here in order to avoid excluding forms of special districts meaningful for the planning implementation process.

Reasons for Creating Special Districts

The Committee for Economic Development summarized some of the reasons as follows:[2]

> Most special districts were formed to provide urban services in unincorporated areas. Some were created to solve problems extending over several political jurisdictions. Others were established coterminously with an existing unit, where legal or financial restrictions prevented performance of a particular function by that unit. Almost half of these special districts have taxing powers and many have the right to issue bonds, but most of their revenues come from service charges, sales, rents, and tolls.

> The advantages of special districts in overcoming political and financial limitations are generally offset by each district's preoccupation with a single function. Resulting fragmentation complicates coordinated development of the entire area. Other obvious weaknesses are absence of broad legal authority and lack of political responsiveness due to appointment or ex officio composition of many governing bodies.

> Not typical are such examples as The Port of New York Authority or The Delaware River Port Authority, ranging across state boundaries to solve regional problems. These and some others within a single state—e.g., San

Francisco's Bay Area Rapid Transit District—are ingenious and creditable efforts to rise above or bypass the inherent weaknesses of the prevailing patterns of local government. They provide useful services on a cost-benefit basis. But a revitalized and reconstituted system of local governments would afford alternative approaches to the desired ends, without the inherent disadvantages of the special district device.

They also describe the proliferation of special districts as ". . . stimulated by the failure of existing units to meet basic needs . . ." and as resulting ". . . in unprecedented overlapping among local governments."[3] Urban service districts are created for such functions as providing for fire protection, water supply, public housing, urban renewal, sewage disposal, parks and recreation, gas and electricity, and construction and/or operation of water ports and airports. Examples of districts created for performing mixed urban and nonurban functions are health and hospital districts, library districts, and highway and street lighting districts. Other districts are created to deal with natural resource functions such as soil conservation, drainage, irrigation and water conservation, flood control, and similar functions. Still others may be created to serve some combination of such functions.

Bollens asserts that there have also been political reasons for assigning certain functions to special districts such as a feeling that independent districts would be more responsive to those they serve, a general preference for small government entities as opposed to larger governments, a desire for taking a given function "out of politics," and a widespread mistrust of general governments. Another reason for creating special districts is that it is claimed they are more effective and expeditious in performing their functions than are general purpose governments because they attract better comunity leadership to serve on their boards, attract better professional personnel by paying higher salaries, and are relatively free from traditional local government personnel restrictions. There is empirical evidence giving some support to this claim.[4] Also national legislation has led to the formation of such entities as housing authorities, urban renewal authorities, mass transit authorities, and councils of governments.

Metropolitan and regional special districts are often a substitute for politically impractical governmental reorganization. They have the advantage of having extensive precedents, ease of establishment, maintenance of the status quo, and general practicability. In this regard the Commission on Intergovernmental relations quotes Professor Zimmerman as commenting that:[5]

> . . . The creation of multipurpose State authorities to perform what are considered by some to be "local" functions may appear to be a violation of "home rule" and less democratic than the creation of popularly controlled metropolitan government. Nevertheless, political realities must be faced— metropolitan governments will not be created by local initiative in most areas.

Allen Manvel similarly observes:[6]

> Much of the growth of special districts is a response to the outward thrust of today's 'spread city', which often, at first, involves a scattered and patch-work urbanization. In most parts of the country, traditional general-purpose governments have not kept pace with the needs arising from such development. In only a very few metropolitan areas has there been a basic reordering of local government arrangements reflecting 20th century conditions.

The Formation of Special Districts

The formation of special districts generally requires state enabling legislation. Such legislation may be ". . . general legislation authorizing a wide range of functional responsibilities; general legislation authorizing only one function; special legislation authorizing multi-functions; and special legislation for one function."[7] Such enabling legislation together with state restrictions on local general purpose governments encourage the creation of special districts. Also pressing local problems may lead to local initiative in securing and using such enabling legislation.

Sometimes state legislation mandates the creation of special districts but it is more usual that these districts are brought into existence by petition or by a local government resolution which may have to be ratified by referendum.

Governance and Funding

Special districts usually have special governing boards whose members are either elective or appointive or a combination of these procedures. Elective members are most frequently elected by the voters within the special district's boundaries. Appointive members are usually appointed by the local governments within or containing the special district's area of jurisdiction. County governments are the most frequent appointers of special district board members.

The powers and duties of special districts are set out in the enabling legislation and may be restated in the petitions or resolutions or ordinances bringing them into being. The powers may include eminent domain, taxing, the power to float bond issues, exemption from local taxes, the establishment of monopolies, and relative independence from outside supervision. The duties enumerated describe both required and prohibited functions and their degree of dependence on other governments in regard to approvals of their plans, activities, and budgets. In addition to being funded by taxation and bond issues, special districts may be funded by user charges, rents, or intergovernmental aids as specified in the legislation creating them.

The Problem of Proliferation

For the purposes of metropolitan planning, those districts functioning within metropolitan areas are of most interest. In the decade between 1962 and 1972 special districts within Standard Metropolitan Statistical Areas increased from 5,410 to 7,842 and these figures do not include state-wide authorities empowered to act within metropolitan areas.[8]

The proliferation of special districts has been of some concern because most of them are single-purpose and, being relatively independent, are difficult to coordinate. In 1964 the Advisory Commission on Intergovernmental Relations recommended the establishment of boundary commissions to control special district growth. Subsequently five states (California, Nevada, New Mexico, Oregon, and Washington) enacted legislation providing for commissions authorized to review and control the creation, consolidation, annexation, and dissolution of special districts on a statewide or countywide basis.

The Problem of Coordination

Because coordination of the development activities of all governmental entities in a planning area is an important function of the area's land use planning agency, the kind and degree of dependence of special districts on local government in regard to their developmental activities is important for the implementation of land use plans. This dependence may be organizational, fiscal, administrative or some combination of these.

The strength of the linkages between special district board members and the local governments within a district's jurisdiction may influence the degree of coordination of plans and policies of the district with those of the other local governments concerned. These linkages are determined by the organizational makeup of the special district's controlling board. Board members may be directly elected, appointed elected officials of the constituent local governments, appointed ex officio staff members of the constituent local governments, citizen appointees by state or local governments, or some combination of these. Directly elected board members are likely to have the weakest linkages with the constituent local governments. Citizen appointees may or may not have strong linkages to their appointing bodies. Elected officials and ex officio staff members of constituent local governments would seem to have the strongest linkages with local governments and therefore the strongest motivation to secure effective coordination between special district plans or policies and those of the local governments concerned. However, even strong organizational linkages may prove ineffective in achieving the desirable coordination.

Fiscal controls usually involve review of a special district's budget by the constituent local governments, control of grants to the district, and/or approval of special district bond issues by referendum. If this review does not involve participation in the capital budgeting process or item by item approval of the spending pattern it will not be very effective in ensuring orderly development in accordance with the land use plan.

Administrative control involves required review of a special district's policies and programs by the local general purpose government. It may also involve prior review and recommendations by the planning agency in regard to planning issues. This is one of the strongest forms of dependence, but even this may not be entirely effective if the special district does not wish to cooperate.

If local planning purposes are to be served through making special districts and authorities more dependent it is important that the form of dependence be structured so that the land acquisition and developmental activities of these entities be subject to review for conformance with the area's long-range comprehensive plan and the shorter-range implementation plans. Although planning recommendations are rarely binding they do bring attention to the probable results of actions counter to the adopted plan.[9]

FUNCTIONAL CHARACTERISTICS

Most special districts are single-function rather than multi-function in purpose. The most important purpose of these districts is usually to provide services rather than to undertake physical development. The development they undertake, then, is usually that which is necessary for providing their intended services. However, it is the attendant development which is of primary concern for land use planning because of its effect on the timing, location, and quality of overall development.

The relevance of special districts for land use plan implementation varies somewhat by the type of function and the interrelationships between functions. Accordingly what follows is an examination of some of the functions for which the special district device has been used or proposed to be used in urban areas.

Public Utilities

Utilities include water supply, sewerage and sewage disposal, solid waste collection and disposal, gas, electric, telephone, and cable TV services. These services may be provided by private corporations, special districts or departments of local government. The delivery systems for these services are located subsurface in public rights-of-way or in utility easements, and frequently several systems share the same corridors. Coordination of these delivery systems is essential if they are to be efficiently and economically provided. Together with the street and drainage systems and other public facilities they form the infrastructure on which sound urban development depends.

Historically water supply and sewage disposal systems grew up separately and are administered separately in most cities. However, it is becoming increasingly obvious that they are but two aspects of water resource management. In metropolitan areas where many independent local governments are close together, the quality of sewage treatment in some of them may affect adversely the quality of water supply in others. Commonly located in the street rights-of-way, both services are essential to development except in low density areas where septic tanks may be permitted for sewage disposal. Where combined systems are permitted, the sanitary sewers may carry storm drainage water as well. However, the use of combined systems is a poor practice because of its effect on sewage processing. It follows that drainage, water supply, and sewage disposal could be more easily coordinated if the responsibility for them lay with a single multifunction authority or department of local government in cases where watersheds and drainage areas are reasonably conterminous. Alternatively, the responsibility for building water supply and sewage disposal systems might remain the responsibility of individual local government agencies if the responsibility for coordinating their planning and policies were in the hands of an areawide authority. This situation is approximated in metropolitan areas where overall planning is performed by a council of governments responsible for the coordination of the utility plans of local governments into one unified comprehensive plan. While most such councils are voluntary and advisory to their component governments, they do exercise through the A95 review process de facto veto power over the requests of local governments for federal funds for building utility lines and plants.[10]

Transportation

Transportation special districts may be established to handle a wide variety of functions: mass transit and rail facilities; transport terminals and associated warehousing; public markets; highways, bridges, and tunnels; street improvements, including street paving, maintenance, and street lighting; parking lots and garages; airports and air terminals; waterways, dams, locks, port facilities and related functions. Of course, these facilities and functions may also be built and carried on by departments of local general purpose governments if they are so empowered.

All of the transportation functions are closely interrelated. Especially close relationships exist between the different modes of transportation, the corridors in which they operate, and their terminal facilities where intermodal transfer takes place. Nonetheless, it often occurs that these functions and facilities are managed by separate private or public entities. This fragmentation of the planning and administration of transportation functions makes their coordination very difficult and may result in conflicts of policy and marked diseconomies. For example, planning highways separately from mass transit may eliminate the savings to be gained from corridor development for multimodal use; parking policies in central areas designed to maximize revenues for a special district may encourage undesirable all-day parking at the expense of short-term parking badly needed for increased customer use of the central business district and at the expense also of increased mass transit ridership and possibly better people movement.

Multifunction transportation departments or authorities have the potential for better coordinating intermodal plans and policies than single-function districts. Two significant examples of such entities are the Port of New York Authority and the Metropolitan Dade County Department of Transportation. Both of them have broad responsibilities in regard to various modes of transportation and their respective terminal facilities and in the case of New York, port-related office space (e.g., the Port Authority built World Trade Center). A less common combination of functions is found in the Louisville and Jefferson County River Port Authority which combines development of port and riverside facilities with that of developing riverside industrial parks. But even combining all transportation functions in a single special district or department ignores the strong connection between transportation rights-of-way and utility rights-of-way and raises the question of the need for even greater integration of these functions and facilities.

Public Recreation and Open Space

Recreational facilities include the provision of ". . . major areas and facilities such as parks, water and winter sports facilities, neighborhood playgrounds, recreation buildings, athletic fields, indoor recreation centers, playfields, golf courses, and reservations".[11] Another aspect of the parks and recreation functions may be the acquisition and preservation of open space as a tool for the control of sprawl, protection of conservation areas, and of flood plains.

Because of the vast range of scale of recreation areas and facilities, and the boundaries of benefiting geographic areas, the question of which level of government is the appropriate one to handle parks and recreation is difficult. George Butler, the research director of the National Recreation Association, in considering the need for reallocating recreational facilities among the various levels of government concluded that the responsibility for these facilities should be vested in a unit which can establish an equitable relationship between the allocation of costs and receipt of benefits; that an adequate financial capacity of the unit should be achieved; and that the governmental units formed should be willing to undertake the function. He feels that areas and facilities that benefit only local residents can be administered by municipalities; and that only areas and facilities that serve a large number of nonresidents should be administered by counties, joint city-county agencies or special districts where the benefit areas cross city or county boundaries.[12]

Examples of area-wide special districts dealing with recreation cited by Advisory Commission on Intergovernmental Relations included the Huron-Clinton Metropolitan Authority in Michigan, the East Bay Regional Park District in California, the Metropolitan District Commission in Massachusetts, and the Hennepin County Park Reserve District in Minnesota. Another significant example is the Cleveland Metropolitan Park District. The use of the special district device for parks and recreation is usually confined to regional park systems and most park and recreation functions are handled directly by municipalities or counties. However, some major facilities such as sports arenas and stadiums may be built and operated by single-purpose authorities.

At the local level a special problem exists between park systems and school systems in coordinating the use of school recreational facilities both by school students and the general public. The use of school recreational facilities by the public can eliminate the need for costly duplicate facilities. The main issues are cost-sharing and management. Use of school facilities and grounds out of school hours costs extra money for operation and maintenance which school administrations can rarely afford. Recreation budgets are also usually tight and recreation departments do not like to pay school administrations what they want to charge for the shared use.

Park systems operating on the metropolitan level may undertake to protect future park sites, scenic areas, and other open space by the acquisition of land, the development rights in land, or scenic easements. However to have park systems undertake the acquisition of land for nonrecreational development would seem inappropriate because of their limited principal objectives and priorities.[13] The experience and competence of park departments in site selection is usually limited to looking at land from a point of view of its potential for park and recreational uses. For these systems to have the responsibility for acquiring land for other urban purposes would require them to have a broader than usual understanding of land use capabilities for urban development.

If the creation of a special district is the most feasible means of implementing park and recreational development in a given circumstance, it is critical in the interest of land use planning that there be a requirement for planning review of park and recreational sites for conformance with land use plans and full participation of the district in the financial planning process.

Education and Related Functions

Schools, colleges, libraries, civic theaters, public auditoriums, and convention centers all may be established and/or operated by special districts instead of by general-purpose governments. Although all might be combined in multipurpose districts there appears to be no example of this and it is common for each function to be handled by a separate single-purpose district. In many cases there are formal or informal relationships between them. Cultural centers may be organized to contain more than one of these facilities (e.g. Lincoln Center in New York City) but with administration by a single authority. Another combination involves the incorporation of school libraries into metropolitan library systems as is the case in the Cuyahoga County (Cleveland) Library System.

The location of educational and cultural facilities and places of public assembly is an integral part of the comprehensive land use and redevelopment planning process. The accessibility of these facilities, the amount of traffic they generate, and their influence on the timing of development are critical considerations for effective land use planning.

The location of school sites and buildings is of particular concern in residential development. Branch libraries, other than those in schools, need for convenience to be coordinated with private development such as major shopping centers. Other educational and cultural facilities serving the whole metropolitan area need to be located centrally where they are easily reached by private vehicles and mass transit. Therefore, their locations need to be coordinated with transportation plans.

Health Facilities and Services

Hospitals, clinics, medical laboratories, nursing homes, convalescent homes, public health centers and medical office buildings are among the included facilities. Whether in public or private ownership, health facilities are part of the community facilities aspect of the comprehensive land use plan. Accordingly their distribution and siting are a planning concern. Some facilities should be clustered in medical centers for reasons of convenience, mutual interdependence, and economies of scale. These include facilities which are too specialized or require such expensive equipment that only one such facility can be afforded by the community; they also include teaching hospitals which, for convenience, need to be near as wide a spectrum of health facilities as possible in order to give their students a maximum exposure to all the differing kinds of health problems and methods of treatment. In clusters of medical facilities the hospitals and clinics by sharing each other's specialized service and equipment can avoid unnecessary duplication. Medical services and facilities which can afford to be duplicated should be located at carefully spaced points throughout the community so they will be convenient to the people they serve. Emergency centers, which are sometimes very expensive, need to be located where they can be easily and quickly reached day and night by all those in the area they serve.

According to the Advisory Commission on Intergovernmental Affairs, in regard to public health facilities, there appears to be a trend toward transfer of functional responsibilities from municipalities to counties, or consolidation in city-county health departments. The Commission also reports that there has been a steady growth in health facilities districts as there has in special districts as a whole.[14]

Air Pollution Control

The control of air pollution was first begun at the local level through the use of performance standards in zoning ordinances, mainly in industrial zones. The standards applied were local in character although the problem often extended beyond the controlling jurisdiction.

Air pollution sources are varied and include odors, gases, smoke, and particulate matter from vehicles, from heating and power generation plants, from the burning of trash and leaves, and from waste incinerators, as well as from commercial and industrial enterprises. Control of these sources was first attempted through nuisance suits, then through zoning to control the location of pollution producers and in the case of industrial areas by the imposition of performance standards—all at the local level. These approaches have proven to be inadequate, primarily because polluted air is no respecter of boundaries, prevailing winds cannot always be relied on to carry polluted air away from inhabited areas, and in many urban areas temperature inversions allow pollution to build to levels that are hazardous to health. Other problems include those of poor administration and enforcement in the face of resistance on the part of polluters expressed by stalling tactics, the exertion of political pressure, and outright bribery.[15]

In 1955 the Federal government began to support state and local governments in their efforts to control air pollution through grants to these entities, including local special districts. By 1963 most states had adopted legislation for State air pollution activities. Their interjurisdictional nature encouraged the use of interjurisdictional control agencies. Washington is an example of a state with multicounty authorities.

In 1967 with the passage of the Air Quality Act the previous Federal legislation was expanded to include the designation of air quality control regions, the development of air quality criteria for these regions by state and local control agencies, and implementation programs establishing a time-table for compliance.[16] The Clean Air Amendments of 1970 gave the states the option of considering the state as one air-quality region or dividing the state into smaller multicounty air-quality districts. For convenience the boundaries of such smaller districts often follow county lines and in some cases they may encompass counties in more than one state.

Because of the nature of the problem, multijurisdictional special districts have become the logical instrumentalities for air pollution control. Usually the localities are permitted to impose stricter standards than required by state and federal guidelines but rarely do, and the economics and increased efficiency of control by "air-basin"-wide entities has led local governments to collaborate through inter-local agreements, or turn the air pollution control function over to multijuris-dictional special districts. In shifting the responsibility to higher levels, Crenson points out that this upward shift has not been the result of pressure from below but because of federal pressure in the absence of effective action by the lower levels of government despite federal financial incentives.[17]

Although air pollution often arises from polluting land uses, the air pollution problem has as yet only indirectly affected land use plans and their implementation. Air pollution control goals are logically a part of the policies expressed in comprehensive plans. Moreover, in the mid-1970s the Federal Environmental Protection Agency actively considered intervening in local land use planning with implementation of Section 110 of the Clean Air Act especially directed at the location of pollution sources such as concentrations of automobiles in central cities and regional shopping centers.[18] If carried through, this intervention, by way of funding air pollution programs, would have had disastrous effects on the rehabilitation of central business districts and the establishment of multipurpose suburban nodal areas. However, the 1977 Clean Air Act will directly affect land use activities through the designation of attainment and nonattainment areas in regard to National Ambient Air Quality Standards. Not meeting these standards carries the threat of losing Federal funding. In some localities new development will be possible only if air pollution from existing development is severely reduced.

Solid Waste Collection and Disposal

This service is usually a function of local government departments rather than special districts. There are a number of different methods of disposal such as: sanitary landfills, central incineration, on-site incineration, garbage grinding, sale of food wastes for animal feeding, composting, salvage and reclamation, and open dumps. The location of most of these activities is controlled by such provisions in the zoning ordinance as those for conditional uses rather than being shown on the land use plan.

Increasing use of combination facilities which provide for salvage and reclamation and incineration of the nonsalvageable material to produce district heating and/or electric power may mean that in the future these facilities will show up on the community facilities plan as a standard feature. Also, sanitary land-fill operations may be directed at the filling of low-lying land for recreation or other community facilities. However, at present special districts or authorities for solid waste disposal do not figure very significantly in the implementation of comprehensive land use plans.

Public Safety

Police protection, fire protection, and the handling of emergencies are the major functional components of public safety. These are usually handled by local government departments rather than special districts, but where districts cross governmental boundaries the services may be provided by intergovernmental agreements or special districts.

The location of police and fire stations is usually an integral part of the community facilities portion of the comprehensive land use plan. If the land and the stations built on it are developed by special districts, the extent to which they are located in conformance with the land use plan aids in the implementation of the plan. Especially in urbanizing areas where local governmental departments responsible for public safety have not been established because of financial, legal or jurisdictional inadequacies, the special district device is useful as a land use planning tool for providing public safety facilities.

Housing

With the passage of the United States Housing Act in 1937 creating the United States Housing Authority, the federal government entered into the housing business by lending money to local housing authorities, both municipal and county, to build and annually subsidize the rental of public housing for families otherwise unable to obtain affordable housing on the private market. This legislation mandated the use of the authority device and resulted in a widespread proliferation of local housing authorities.

Housing authority projects have often met with political resistance resulting in their defeat or curtailment, and it took over 20 years to meet the original national goal of 810,000 units.[19] More recently clearance resulting from urban freeway projects has been displacing more

TABLE 6-1. State Housing and Development Authorities Directly Engaging in Development and/or Planning Assistance

Connecticut Housing Finance Authority

YEAR ESTABLISHED   1971

PROGRAMS AUTHORIZED·
(1) To purchase mortgages;
(2) To make construction and permanent mortgage loans;
(3) To insure mortgage payments; and
(4) To make advances to nonprofit corporations for the planning and developing of housing to be financed or insured by the Authority.

Illinois Housing Development Authority

YEAR ESTABLISHED·   1967

PROGRAMS AUTHORIZED:
(1) To make mortgage loans;
(2) To make noninterest bearing development advances to nonprofit corporations pursuing low and moderate income housing programs;
(3) To plan, acquire and develop land for low- and moderate-income housing and new communities.
(4) To make housing assistance grants for the benefit of residents of developments in order to achieve lower rentals for some or all of the housing units in such developments;
(5) To make grants to local housing development corporations for administrative and operating expenses; and
(6) To purchase mortgages from, or make loans to, private lending institutions.

Michigan State Housing Development Authority

YEAR ESTABLISHED·   1966

PROGRAMS AUTHORIZED·
(1) To make mortgage loans for multifamily and single-family housing;
(2) To make housing development loans and grants to qualified recipients;
(3) To implement land acquisition and development programs;
(4) To provide technical services and assistance to sponsors of low and moderate income housing; and
(5) To undertake studies and analyses of housing conditions and needs in the State and to develop and implement programs to deal with such needs.

TABLE 6-1   (Continued)

Minnesota Housing Finance Agency

YEAR ESTABLISHED: 1971

PROGRAMS AUTHORIZED:

(1) To purchase securities issued by mortgage lenders, the proceeds of which are utilized to provide residential housing for persons or families of low- and moderate-income.

(2) To make or participate in construction loans to sponsors of low and moderate income housing developments;

(3) To make or participate in permanent mortgage financing of low- and moderate-income housing developments;

(4) To purchase, make or participate in loans for rehabilitation of existing housing to persons and families of low and moderate income;

(5) To grant "seed money" or development loans to non-profit sponsors of low and moderate housing; and

(6) To provide planning grants to local communities to defray pre-development cost of low- and moderate-income housing.

New York State Urban Development Corporation

YEAR ESTABLISHED.   1968

PROGRAMS AUTHORIZED·

(1) To supply housing for low-, moderate-, and middle-income families;

(2) To redevelop blighted areas;

(3) To assist industrial and commercial development in areas of unemployment and blight;

(4) To provide needed educational, cultural, community and other civic facilities; and

(5) To develop new communities through a combination of the above activities.

Tennessee Housing Development Agency

YEAR ESTABLISHED: 1973

PROGRAMS AUTHORIZED:

(1) To finance land development and residential housing construction;

(2) To make permanent mortgages;

(3) To purchase existing insured mortgages from lenders; and

(4) To provide technical, consultative and project assistance.

West Virginia Housing Development Fund

YEAR ESTABLISHED: 1968

TABLE 6-1 (Continued)

PROGRAMS AUTHORIZED:

(1) To make mortgage loans to sponsors of residential housing for persons or families of low and moderate income;

(2) To make loans to private mortgage lenders for the making of new residential mortgages to persons or families of low and moderate income;

(3) To purchase from private mortgage lenders mortgage loans on residential housing for persons or families of low and moderate income; and

(4) To acquire, hold, develop and finance land suitable for the construction of residential housing for persons or families of low and moderate income.

From: Paine, Webber, Jackson, and Curtis. Summary of Financing by State Housing Finance/Development Agencies, New York: P,W,J,&C, 1974, pp. 5–25 passim), reproduced by permission.

low-income families than public housing has been able to accommodate.[20] Furthermore, public housing is not available to some lower- and middle-income people who cannot afford federally insured middle-income housing. Accordingly many states (see Table 6-1) and some cities have used the authority device to finance and/or construct housing for those with incomes too high for public housing and yet too low for housing available on the open market.

Most notable of the state housing authorities is the New York Urban Development Corporation. Created in 1968 with the primary purpose of providing housing for low- and moderate-income families it was also empowered to assist industrial and commercial development and to provide needed educational, cultural, and other civil facilities. It was given the power of eminent domain, the power to waive local ordinances, independent financial resources, partial tax-exemption and a "full range of development powers" including the right to set up subsidiary corporations such as: UDC Greater Rochester, Inc.; Roosevelt Island Development Corporation; and the Harlem Urban Development Corporation.[21]

The UDC has been plagued with economic and political problems. In 1973 its power to override local zoning ordinances in towns and villages was stripped from it as a result of its attempts to build low income housing in nine suburban Westchester County towns.[22] More recently the UDC found itself unable to pay off $104.5 million in one year bond anticipation notes and was forced to turn to the New York legislature for help. UDS was reorganized, and has somewhat curtailed its development program, but now (1978) seems to be viable. Nonetheless there is no reason to assume that its problems resulted from the use of the public authority device.

In an analysis of state housing finance agencies Michael Stegman observed that: ". . . housing finance agencies have proved to be reasonably effective instrumentalities in filling gaps or voids left after the full arsenal of federal and urban development programs have been exploited . . ."[23] He also observes that they need more state support and concludes that: ". . . HFA's are unlikely to receive greatly expanded mandates from their legislatures and are certainly not about to be granted broad-based community development responsibilities which they can initiate on their own accord."[24]

Public housing, except for the aged with whom we all can sympathize, has never received much public support. The main beneficiaries should be the poor who have little political power to exercise on their own behalf. Also the locational policies of public housing authorities bring the threat of racial and social integration when public housing sites are sought outside of the poorest neighborhoods. As a consequence, the proportion of public housing to private housing being built is so small that it has no significant impact on the implementation of the residential portions of most long-range land use plans. The New York UDC in its new towns programs (Audubon, Radisson, Roosevelt Island) is the only authority carrying out most of the residential development entailed in large-scale land use plans. On the other hand the potential for the use of the authority device in residential development inevitably increases in times when rising costs of land, construction, and financing prevent private developers from satisfying the housing needs of the community.

Urban Renewal

James Lash defines urban renewal as the ". . . total of all private and public actions necessary for the continuous sound maintenance and development of the urban area."[25] Urban renewal is a continuous process which undertakes to maintain and renew the urban physical fabric. As such it is a powerful tool for carrying out land use plans in areas already largely urbanized.

Fostered in part by the housing acts of 1949 and 1962, it is now carried on as a joint federal-local government activity. The redevelopment, rehabilitation and conservation programs of urban renewal involve the functions of urban planning, zoning, housing code enforcement, housing rehabilitation, relocation of displaced persons and economic activities, and the acquisition, clearance, and disposal of land and buildings.

The housing acts previous to 1974 provided that federal monies be made available to ". . . any State, county, municipality, or other governmental entity or public body . . ."[26] or combinations thereof. The principal participation of the states has been by way of enabling legislation. Some states enabled the creation of local urban renewal authorities, some combined renewal with housing in joint authorities, some permitted the function to be located in departments of local general purpose governments, and others permitted more than one of these alternatives. There were approximately 2000 housing and/or urban renewal authorities by 1964, an indication of their widespread creation. A more recent survey by the International City Managers' Association showed that almost half of the reporting urban renewal agencies did their own project planning separately from the local planning agency.[27] This is a result of a number of factors stemming in part from their often relatively independent status, a feeling among renewal agencies that better project control is achieved by keeping all planning functions in-house, distrust of the planning agency as a result of poor liaison, and the inability of the planning agency to perform project planning because of the lack of experienced personnel or the prior demand of other planning functions on a limited staff.

Whatever the reasons for renewal agencies to go their own way, urban renewal is such a direct and strong tool for the implementation of land use plans that its separation from the planning function is likely to affect land use planning adversely unless there are effective coordination arrangements between the two functions.

George Duggar, in research into organization for urban renewal, comes to the conclusion that: ". . . no form of government can claim it

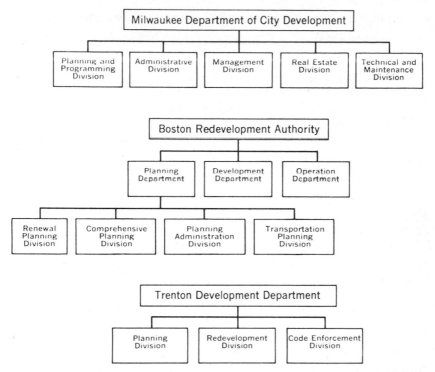

Figure 6-1. Organization charts for city development departments: Milwaukee, Boston, Trenton.

From Jerome L. Kaufman, *Principles and Practice of Urban Planning*, (Washington: The International City Managers' Association, 1968). Reproduced by permission.

has provided the only good foundation for pioneering in the field of urban renewal." On the other hand, he observes that urban renewal ". . . encourages the reorganization of some development activities in a new line department or as an area of responsibility for a coordinator."[28]

Jerome L. Kaufman[29] points out that at least 20 cities reorganized along the "department of development" lines in the mid-1960s. (See Figure 6-1.) This form of agency structure encourages greater cooperation and coordination between all developmental activities from planning to implementation.

The effect of block-grant funding under the Housing Act of 1974 which channels its community development funds through the local general-purpose governments rather than directly to renewal agencies, is yet fully to be seen, but where renewal agencies are retained better co-ordination is likely.

Land Banking and Development

Proposals for public land acquisition and development authorities of a general-purpose nature as an alternative to land use plan implementation by public regulation have been advocated in the United States at least as long ago as the 1930s. In 1937 the National Resources Committee advocated ". . . a more liberal policy of land acquisition by municipalities . . . in order to prevent urban authorities to acquire, hold, and dispose of land with greater freedom . . ." for better control of urban development.[30]

More recently, in 1967, John Reps proposed a public or public-private metropolitan authority in the form of a "Metropolitan Land Corporation" to purchase and resell or rent land in urbanizing areas for the purposes of controlling the form of development, citing European and Canadian as well as earlier American examples.[31] Two years later the National Committee on Urban Growth Policy recommended that a national agency be established to aid state agencies which would engage in urban development in urbanizing areas. In the same report Henry Bain proposed urban development districts to undertake land acquisition and multipurpose development.[32] The Puerto Rico Land Administration[33] and the previously mentioned New York Urban Development Corporation are examples of state land acquisition and development agencies with broad development powers. Fairfax County, Virginia recently began a land banking program with two million dollars of revenue sharing funds but, shunning the authority device, vested the program directly in the county's Department of Housing and Community Development.[34] There are also more limited land banks engaging only in industrial development in Baltimore, Philadelphia, and Milwaukee.

Commenting on the difficulties of establishing a land bank, Holbein says:[35]

However limited a land-banking program, the chances are that local government does not have the full legislative authority to do the job. Acquisition without a specifically advertised purpose is prohibited by most states.

Even for permitted uses, the local government may lack the ability to act directly. Acquisition of sites for parks, schools, housing, water and sewer lines, and economic development is often the rightful function of a special-purpose authority. These authorities may or may not be committed to the local land-use plan or show allegiance to the governing body itself. Therefore, local governments may be forced to approach land banking somewhat indirectly. To make land banking an effective growth management tool, all branches of local government must have a hand in the selection and acquisition of sites. Bringing these separate authorities back under the direct control of a local legislative body would be politically and practically impossible in most cases. One possible method is for the governing body to be more special about long-range goals and sites before granting approvals of budgets, capital improvement programs, or bond issues.

However, another approach is to make a loan to the special-purpose authority for a specific site. For example, many state laws not only inhibit local governments from direct general-purpose acquisition, but often fail to provide a single comprehensive piece of legislation for local community development. Due to the traditional conservatism of most legislatures, the revision of existing legislation to give local government the power of direct acquisition or to create a land-banking agency can be a long and arduous process. An alternative is an administrative program built on existing legislation, such as the creation of a revolving fund from which the governing body could make loans to its various community development authorities. In Fairfax County, this approach is based on the county's authority to give financial assistance to any political subdivision created by itself or the state. In this way, a grant can be given for the site at the time the site is to be acquired. The governing body is not committed to a long-range acquisition program which may be out of focus with local goals as circumstances change.

Planning

The location of the planning function in urban areas was discussed at some length in the first chapter. Because most state planning legislation is modelled after the Standard Acts of the 1920s, planning in most municipalities and counties is vested in autonomous advisory planning commissions which have some of the characteristics of special districts and public authorities. Multijurisdictional metropolitan or regional planning responsibilities, because of federal grant program requirements, have recently been vested in councils of government, which for the most part have as their only implementation tool the A-95 review process through which they influence the funding of local projects. The lack of implementation powers has generally weakened these agencies in their efforts to guide and control development. There are, however, some significant examples of innovative legislation in regard to state, regional and local planning agencies which will be described in the next chapter along with proposals for more effective land use guidance mechanisms. Some of these employ the special district or public authority device.

The question, however, is not the importance of special districts and authorities in carrying out strategic portions of comprehensive land-use plans; it is, rather, are they the best available tool for that function from a planning point of view? The answer is neither a clear "yes" or "no".

A regular unit of government could do virtually everything an authority could, were it so empowered, except when functions need to be unified across local governmental or state boundaries. However, the problem of local governmental boundaries and restrictions on the financial and legal powers of local general-purpose governments often make the creation of a public authority the only feasible alternative. In the light of these problems and those of governmental reform, Moore makes an especially persuasive argument for the immediate establishment of Metropolitan Planning and Development Authorities.[36]

Although the Advisory Commission on Intergovernmental Relations in its study of special districts generally recommends ". . . their abolition, consolidation, or subordination to general purpose units of government,"[37] it also makes a strong recommendation that planning and plan implementation programs for substate districts involving federal funds be vested in consolidated multijurisdictional umbrella agencies (UMJO) or authorities having the power ". . . to resolve any inconsistencies between . . . [federal grant] . . . applications and officially adopted regional policies or plans . . ." and planning implementation powers where possible.[38] These umbrella agencies would consolidate the planning and review required for the following ten federal programs:[39]

1. OMB—A 95 Clearinghouse Areas
2. EDA—Economic Development Districts
3. HUD—701 Metropolitan and Regional Planning Areas

4. USDA—Resource Conservation and Development Areas
5. HEW—Comprehensive Health Planning Areas
6. DOL—Comprehensive Manpower Planning Areas
7. DOJ—Law Enforcement Planning Areas
8. OEO—Community Action Planning Areas
9. EPA—Air Quality Control Districts
10. DOT—Metropolitan Comprehensive Transportation Planning Areas

They would undertake to:[40]

- adopt and publicize regional policies and plans along with a program for their implementation;
- provide planning and programming inputs into the State's planning and budgeting process;
- serve as the region's A-95 review agency;
- assume the responsibility for implementing all Federally encouraged areawide planning programming, coordination, districting, or even servicing programs, as well as all similar State undertakings;
- act as the basic policy board for multi-jurisdictional special districts;
- promote mutual problem solving among counties, cities, and towns and provide such services as these units may request singly or jointly;
- resolve differences between regional policies or plans and certain projects and actions of State agencies and local governments having a spillover effect;
- in certain instances, assume direct operating responsibilities under terms set in the State authorizing legislation, including the provision that at least a majority of the member local units representing three-fifths of the region's population must concur.

The UMJO then would be a comprehensive and functional planning, coordinating, programming, servicing, and implementing body—in short, a regional council with some meaningful, but limited authority.

CONCLUSIONS

In general, special districts, especially single-purpose districts, contribute to the fragmentation of governments and their use should be avoided where the same functions can be vested in general purpose governments. The proliferation and independence of special districts makes their coordination difficult for the implementation of plans and policies. On the other hand, if special districts have many functions consolidated within them, and serve as umbrella agencies with the purpose of planning for and coordinating the planning implementation programs of many separate governmental agencies, whose political consolidation would be much more difficult to achieve, they may be the best alternative for planning implementation purposes.

NOTES AND ACKNOWLEDGMENTS FOR CHAPTER 6

1. U.S. Bureau of the Census. *Governmental Organization, Vol. I, Census of Governments: 1962*, (Washington: U.S. Government Printing Office, 1963), p. 15.
2. Committee for Economic Development. *Modernizing Local Government*, (New York: The Committee, 1966), p. 32.
3. *Ibid.*; also see Alan Altschuler in *Hearings Before the Subcommittee on Urban Affairs, Joint Economic Committee of the Congress of the United States, Part 1*, (Washington: U.S. Government Printing Office, 1970), pp. 8–9.
4. See Metropolitan Study Commission, *Report on Sewage Disposal in the Milwaukee Metropolitan Area*, (Milwaukee: The Commission, 1958), p. 64, and Governmental Functions Committee of the Capitol Regional Planning Agency, *Governmental Organizations for the Capitol Region*, (Hartford: The Committee, 1967), pp. 15-3 to 15-4.
5. Advisory Commission on Intergovernmental Relations, *Regional Decision Making: New Strategies for Substate Districts, Vol. I, Substate Regionalism and the Federal System*, (Washington: U.S. Government Printing Office, 1973), p. 21. (Hereinafter referred to as ACIR, *Regional Decision Making*).
6. Manvel, Allen D., "Metropolitan Growth and Governmental Fragmentation," in *Governance and Population: The Governmental Implications of Population Change*, (Washington: The Commission on Population Growth and the American Future, 1972), Vol. 4, p. 185.
7. ACIR, *Regional Decision Making*, pp. 22–24.
8. ———, *Regional Decision Making*, p.25.
9. Kent, T. J., *The Urban General Plan*. (San Francisco: Chandler, 1964), pp. 69–71.
10. This refers to *Circular A95* of the Bureau of the Budget (July 1969) which together with Section 204 of the Demonstration Cities and Metropolitan Development Act of 1966 created metropolitan area-wide clearinghouses to undertake comprehensive planning and comment on all applications for federal funds within their jurisdiction for feasibility, soundness and conformance to the comprehensive plan.
11. From *Municipal Recreation Administration*, (Chicago: Copyright 1960 by the International City Managers' Association), pp. 233, reproduced by permission.
12. Butler, George D., "Recreation Administration in Metropolitan Areas, Part 2: Authorization and Function," *Recreation*, (October 1962), pp. 411–13.
13. Holbein, Mary Elizabeth, "Land Banking: Saving for a Rainy Day," *Planning*, **41**, No. 1, (January 1975), p. 21.
14. Advisory Commission on Intergovernmental Relations, *Performance of Urban*

Functions: Local and Area Wide, (Washington: U.S. Government Printing Office, 1963), p. 156, (Hereinafter referred to as ACIR, *Urban Functions.*), and ACIR, *Special Districts*, pp. 17-18.

15. Crenson, Matthew A., *The Un-Politics of Air Pollution*, (Baltimore and London: The Johns Hopkins Press, 1971), p. 5.
16. Rossano, Jr., A. T., *Air Pollution Control Guidebook for Management*, (Stamford: E.R.A., 1969), pp. 184–86.
17. Crenson, *op. cit.*, p. 10.
18. Stevens, David Ross, "How a U.S. Law May Sharply Change Planning Here," *The Courier Journal and Times*, (Louisville, June 9, 1974), and Barry Israel, "EPA Promulgates Land Use Regulations to Control Air Pollution," *AIP Newsletter*, **8**, No. 7, (July 1973), pp. 11-12.
19. Pynoos, Jon, Schafer, Robert, and Hartman, Chester W., eds., *Housing Urban America*, (Chicago: Aldine, 1973), p. 17.
20. Meyerson, Martin, Tyrwhitt, Jacqueline, and Wheaton, William L. C., *Housing, People, and Cities*, (New York: McGraw-Hill, 1962), p. 16.
21. *Goals, Policies, and Prospects*, (New York: New York State Urban Development Corporation, 1972), pp. 2-5 (pamphlet).
22. "Agency News," *Planning*, **39**, No. 6, (July 1973), p. 5.
23. Stegman, Michael A., "Housing Finance Agencies: Are They Crucial Instruments of State Governments?" *Journal of American Institute of Planners*, **40**, No. 5, (September 1974), pp. 310-11, reprinted by permission of the author and journal.
24. ———, *op. cit.*, p. 320, reprinted by permission of the author and journal.
25. Lash, James E., "Renewal: Area Problem," *National Civic Review*, Vol. LI, No. 4, (April 1962), p. 201, reproduced by permission.
26. ACIR, *Urban Functions*, p. 242.
27. *Municipal Yearbook*, 1972, Vol. 39, (Washington: International City Managers' Association, 1972), p. 72.
28. Duggar, George, "Local Organization for Urban Renewal," reprinted from *Public Management*, Vol. XL, No. 7, (July 1958), p. 159 and p. 162, by special permission, © 1958, the International City Management Association.
29. Kaufman, Jerome L., "Urban Renewal," Goodman, William I and Freund, Eric C., eds., *Principles and Practice of Urban Planning* (Washington: The International City Managers' Association, 1968), p. 509.
30. Natural Resources Committee, *Our Cities*, (Washington: U.S. Government Printing Office, 1937), pp. 76-77.
31. Reps, John, "The Future of American Planning: Requiem or Renascence?" *Planning 1967*, (Chicago: The American Society of Planning Officials, 1967), pp. 49-52.
32. National Commission on Urban Growth Policy, "Findings and Recommendations," *The New City*, ed. by Donald Canty, (New York: Praeger, 1969), pp. 172-75.
33. True Copy Act (No. 13), *Commonwealth of Puerto Rico*, (San Juan: Puerto Rico Land Administration, 1969), pp. 1-18, *passim*.
34. Holbein, Mary Elisabeth, "Land Banking: Saving for a Rainy Day," *Planning*, **41**,

No. 1, (January 1975), p. 19, the magazine of the American Society of Planning Officials, copyright 1975.

35. ———, *op. cit.*, p. 20, reprinted with permission.
36. Moore, Woodrow L., *Governmental Reorganization and Metropolitics: Determinants Central to a Normative Theory of Metropolitan Planning*, (Lafayette: Purdue University/Joint Highway Research Project, 1975), pp. 281–348.
37. As cited in ACIR, *Governmental Functions and Processes: Local and Areawide, Vol. IV, Substate Regionalism and the Federal System*, (Washington: U.S. Government Printing Office, 1974), pp. 40–47.
38. ACIR, *Regional Decision Making*, pp. 347–71.
39. ———, *Regional Decision Making*, p. 350.
40. ———, *Regional Decision Making*, p. 372.

7

Toward more effective implementation of land use plans

In previous chapters the traditional land use controls and other planning implementation devices, together with some limited experimental reforms in land use plan implementation techniques, were described and evaluated. This chapter will deal with how these diverse planning tools might be, or are being, more effectively coordinated and systematically used. Representative examples of proposed and existing land use guidance systems and reforms will be examined, as will the growing role of state governments in the guidance of land use and new directions in state planning legislation.

Most of the tools now used in the implementation of land use plans were created for other purposes and are not generally thought of as part of an implementation system. In fact many of them have been exercised at cross purposes, and attempts to coordinate them have proven to be very difficult. These devices have in many cases developed adherents who perceive of any reform or modification of them as a threat to their personal interests. Consequently it is the problems and failures in land use planning implementation that have given rise recently to both proposals and experiments in the development of "land use guidance" and "growth management" systems.

Consideration of these systems has been spurred on by the weakening of the American growth ethic and increasing realization of the costs of urban sprawl.[1] The use of growth controls and land use guidance systems has been experimented with most in areas undergoing rapid population growth accompanied by problems of diminishing resources, problems of providing sufficient additional urban services and community facilities, and various perceived threats to local life styles and/or the environment.[2]

This chapter deals successively with the components of land use guidance systems, an examination of selected proposals for such systems by professional planners and other urbanists, recommendations concerning growth guidance by governmental and professional organizations, examples of innovative federal and related state legislation affecting land uses, examples of innovative local land use guidance systems, and conclusions concerning land use guidance.

COMPONENTS OF A LAND USE GUIDANCE SYSTEM

On the basis of the strengths and shortcomings of the already described planning implementation tools, and by inference, it is possible to argue for the following components as necessary to a land use guidance system:

1. There must be an ongoing comprehensive land use planning program for the area covered by the system having long-range, middle-range, and short-range components in the form of both visual elements showing the proposed geographic distribution of land uses and policy instruments including land use and financial policies. The long-range plan is of necessity a very generalized statement of land use objectives and policies which are subject to greater definition and specificity in the middle-range and short-range plans. The latter, sometimes referred to as stage development plans, are necessary for designing implementation programs and for making land use control decisions.

2. There must be available an array of implementation tools sufficient for carrying out land use plans and policies. Different arrays of tools have been experimented with in guidance systems now in effect. The study by Einsweiler, et al., which will be described later in this chapter shows such differing combinations of planning tools and observes that few of the systems have been studied or monitored sufficiently for a determination of their relative effectiveness to be possible.[3]

Based on the shortcomings of the planning implementation tools pointed out in previous chapters, it is asserted here that the tools used in a guidance system should at least be capable of achieving the following ends:

a. The control of the location and timing of new development and redevelopment and the provision of the necessary infrastructure for both in accordance with adopted land use and financial plans and policies.
b. The control of land use interrelationships in order to minimize conflicts between uses (negative externalities) and maximize inter-use benefits.
c. The control of community appearance in the interests of preserving historic or esthetically significant structures and sites, preserving the character of esthetically pleasing old neighborhoods, and encouraging in new development and redevelopment a richness of variety within the bounds of esthetically and functionally harmonious relationships.
d. The provision of a means of economic compensation where land use controls inequitably restrict development or redevelopment; that is, where use of the police power could reasonably be construed as constituting a "taking" without due compensation.
e. The control of the physical design adequacy of new development, and maintenance of the quality of the built environment.

3. There must be coordination of the implementation tools into an implementation program so that they will be used in a mutually supportive and nonconflicting manner. This may require sacrifices of political and administrative independence as was pointed out at the beginning of this chapter, and may be made more difficult by the

failure of administrators, in some cases, to perceive their implementation actions as part of a system. Although integration of the implementation tools into one program is not in itself a criterion for existence of a land use guidance system, it is likely to influence the degree of operational efficiency.[4]

4. Where the planning area, as it usually does, contains a multiplicity of local governmental entities there must be an effective administrative means for coordinating the plans, policies, and implementation actions of these governmental entities to eliminate conflicts and in support of area-wide plans, policies and implementation programs. It was pointed out in the chapter on special districts, in the discussion of planning agencies, that the evidence of the need for an administrative authority capable of such coordination is both preponderant and convincing.

5. The guidance system, in its implementation program, must take into account the influence of federal, state, and substate regional plans, policies and programs (if the planning area is not conterminal with the region) in order to take maximum advantage of, and minimize conflict with these plans, policies and programs. The often conflicting effects of federal and state legislation and programs have already been noted at various places previously in this work, and the Einsweiler *et al* study observes concerning the systems it examined that: "Most of the systems tend to ignore levels of government other than the level of the agency proposing the system."[5]

6. If the guidance system is to receive the political support necessary for it to be effective it must provide for the full participation of the planning area's political representatives, civic and professional groups, citizens' organizations, and individual citizens in the planning, policy-making, and preparation of implementation programs. For some time federal legislation has been stressing citizen participation and the planning legislation, in particular, has not only required citizen participation in connection with its programs but by vesting metropolitan planning in councils of governments made up largely of elected officials has recognized the need to get elected representatives more extensively involved in the planning process. Such participatory planning is essential to the formulation of the goals and objectives upon which plans, policies, and implementation programs must be based if they are to be in the public interest.

7. The implementation programs must take full advantage of the

plan and policy implementation tools which are available and acceptable to the community; they must be carefully and subtly orchestrated for coordination of the timing of implementation activities, and achievement of the desired results.

GUIDANCE SYSTEMS PROPOSED BY PROFESSIONAL PLANNERS AND OTHER URBANISTS

In the last two decades there have been a number of differing land use guidance systems proposed as being more effective than the generally piecemeal and uncoordinated use of planning implementation tools current in most communities. Systems have been proposed both by individuals and organizations interested in land use planning implementation problems. Those chosen for presentation and examination here are representative of such proposals in both content and emphasis as they have appeared since the mid-fifties. They are presented in chronological order so the evolution of ideas can be more easily perceived.

The first to be examined is a briefly sketched proposal for the timing of development, made in 1955 by Henry Fagin, currently a Professor of Administration and Research Administrator in the Public Policy Research organization of the University of California at Irvine.[6] The second was made in 1963 by Stuart Chapin who is a Professor of Planning at the University of North Carolina at Chapel Hill.[7] The third was proposed in 1964 and elaborated on in 1967 by John Reps, a Professor of Planning at Cornell University in Ithaca, New York.[8] The fourth was proposed to the National Committee on Urban Growth Policy in 1969 (and incorporated in part in its recommendations) by Henry Bain, then Senior Associate at the Washington Center for Metropolitan Studies.[9] The fifth was proposed in 1970 by Frank S. So, Deputy Director for Advisory Services of the American Society of Planning Officials.[10] The last included is the proposal of Donald Canty when he was editor of *City* magazine in 1972.[11]

Henry Fagin: 1955

Referring to the (then) new emphasis on planning action programs, Fagin asserts that the timing of development is in need of attention equal to that paid by planners to the spacial distribution of land uses.

He adds that the programming over time of capital improvements made by local government is not enough and that programming of private development must be done as well.

He goes on to describe two aspects of coordination in time: the *tempo* or rate of development and the *sequence* or order of development. Both aspects of the timing of development need to be controlled because of five ". . . well-considered motivations . . . " of planning for the community. A description of these underlying reasons follows:[12]

1. The Need to Economize on the Costs of Municipal Facilities and Services. He explains briefly that efficient provision of urban services and construction of community facilities, street systems, and utility systems depend on keeping service areas compact and development coherently contiguous.

2. The Need to Retain Municipal Control Over the Eventual Character of Development.   For example, premature development at low densities may preclude redevelopment later at planned-for higher densities, creating inefficiencies in the provision of public facilities and services through their being designed for the larger planned-for population.

3. The Need to Maintain a Desirable Degree of Balance Among Various Uses of Land.   Fagin then points out that the economic viability depends on tax income from a balanced mix of developed properties because different types of uses give different tax yields. All land uses do not equally pay the costs of providing them with urban facilities and services.

4. The Need to Achieve Greater Detail and Specificity in Development Regulation.   Here Fagin describes the increasing use of special permits and "designed district" controls as evidence of a growing awareness of the need for more subtle and detailed land use controls than available through conventional zoning districting. He further observes that:[13] "With the current trend to specific changes for specific projects, however, timing has become an integral element in zoning administration." He bases his argument that greater specificity is desirable, on trends rather than reasons. These reasons have been discussed, however, in relation to conditional uses and planned unit development, in the chapter on zoning, and there are ample reasons to support his contention which need not be repeated here.

5. The Need to Maintain a High Quality of Community Services and Facilities.   Here Fagin discusses the ability of the community to absorb new development and the necessary infrastructure, especially in times of rapid growth. In these periods if the growth is scattered or too rapid the community may not be able to afford all of the needed facilities; some may be overloaded, others underused and service quality very uneven. As previously noted this problem was an underlying consideration in the development of the Petaluma and Ramapo growth guidance controls.

Having outlined what he felt were compelling reasons for controlling the timing of urban development, Fagin then goes on to suggest the land use controls necessary for achieving the desired growth guidance.

The first modification of controls he suggests is the creation of "reserve districts" in which undeveloped land for which it was not yet reasonable to assign specific, eventually permissible uses, would be placed. He would presumably allow predominantly open space uses such as parks, recreational uses, and agriculture or forestry, in these zones although he does not mention them. Overlaying these districts would be building sequence districts called "*zones of building priority*" which would indicate the order of priority in which development would be permitted. The priority accorded each zone would express the sequence of development most advantageous to the community from the point of view of economy and achievement of the character intended for the development.

From time to time the number of permits available would be derived from findings concerning the current balance between types of development, the status of private and public projects the local government especially wishes to encourage, and the capacity of local government to assimilate new development in view of its financial planning for public facilities and services.

In exercising this development timing system the local government, according to Fagin, should be obliged to relate its financial planning to expected development trends thus expediting development or, if this is not feasible because of lack of possible funding, give the developer the option of improving his priority rating by building the necessary community facilities and/or providing the necessary community services himself earlier than the local government plans to provide them or by granting tax relief in cases of extreme hardship.

Evaluation.   Because the article in which Fagin makes these proposals is extremely brief it is difficult to judge from what is stated and implied how complete a system is intended. An ongoing comprehensive planning program is implied rather than specified. The proposal for "reserve districts" takes into account the difficulties involved in translating a long-range land use plan into a zoning map. Whether short-range and middle-range plans figure in the monitoring of development specified is in doubt. Rather a process of detailed review of individual proposals within a framework of land use policies ("findings") is implied but not spelled out.

The crux of the problem of judging the completeness of the system is in the review process which is not explicated. From the list of reasons for justifying the timing of development it can be assumed that the review would involve financial planning, the historic and esthetic character of development, land use interrelationships, effective control of the details of development, and the presence or absence of an adequate infrastructure; economic compensation is also taken into account. It would appear by implication that an adequate array of tools would be involved if it is also assumed that all of the usual planning implementation tools would be in use. The description of the implementation program is rudimentary but again a definite system is implied by the program described.

Fagin's system is designed for a single local all-purpose government, and so the question of intergovernmental coordination does not arise; failure to deal with this issue limits the applicability of the system. It would have to be modified to provide for coordinating mechanisms in areas where multiple governments are involved. The proposal also fails to deal with interlevel intergovernmental cooperation, the problems of political support and citizen participation, and the need for taking advantage of all available planning implementation and policy tools acceptable to the government involved. Nonetheless it is a significant early guidance system proposal and does contain most of the elements essential to a complete land use guidance system.

Stuart Chapin: 1963

In 1963 in an article in the *AIP Journal* Chapin took a look at our planning implementation tools and developed a proposal for better coordinating their use. He observed that the land use planning techniques were ". . . a curious patchwork of devices . . . bearing the mark of fragmented governmental situations . . ."[14] but that the growing willingness to try new techniques should make the systemization of land use implementation easier.

Chapin listed the elements of a land use guidance system as:[15]

1. A general plan for the metropolitan region.
2. The urban development policies instrument.
3. A metropolitan area public works program.
4. An urban development code.
5. An informed metropolitan community.

The Metropolitan General Plan.   Although taking into account the various criticisms of the general plan, Chapin contends that it is nonetheless a powerful concept especially when set forth in three levels of detail having different time frames. The first of these levels is the "horizon" or final goals plan which is the most generalized, has no time schedule, and no price tag attached. The second is the more usual version envisioning development over a 20–25 year period with a general priority schedule, financial program, and implementation program. The third is a short-range, often 5-year plan representing the first period of the longer-range plans, and forming the basis of the capital improvement program and other short-range implementation programs.

In regard to the short-range plan Chapin warns that studies of liveability and urban design must be a continuing part of such plans if they are to be imaginative and gain public acceptance. In fact, at all levels the effectiveness of the plan will depend on its imaginativeness and power to inspire widespread support, its technical practicability and power to inspire confidence, and the extent to which planning is an integral part of the local decision-making process.

The Urban Development Policies Instrument.   The close keying of public policies to the general plan can be an effective technique for implementing land use plans. This is especially true for infrastructure extension policies involving transportation, utilities, and community facilities (including schools and recreation). Similarly state and federal policies affecting housing, air and water pollution, reforestation, and other resource and subsidy programs exert influences on development patterns.

Concerning the coordination of these policies Chapin says:[16]

> Clearly the effectiveness of policies as a means for shaping urban growth is dependent on one *modus operandi*—a framework for steering public policy—and whether such a framework becomes a recognized basis of coordinated action by all levels of government in policy decisions relating to urban development.

He goes on to credit Henry Fagin for having advanced the notion of such a policies instrument in 1959. Further, he contends that such a policies instrument would need to be sufficiently specific and politically acceptable to the local governments involved for it to be adopted.

Chapin cites the Metropolitan Regional Council in the New York area as an example of where such an instrument seemed to be developing. He suggests further that federal aid could be made conditional on the adoption of such an instrument. The content of the instrument would vary from area to area but would usually contain a statement of goals for urban expansion, policies for achievement of those goals, and a schedule for timing of development.

A Metropolitan Public Works Program.   This would go hand in hand with the policies instrument. All public improvement expenditures listed in the chapter on public improvements programming would be included and would, in turn, grow out of the general plans.

An Urban Development Code.   Because of the lack of uniformity and coordination of the various land use controls, Chapin proposes that they be integrated into a single regulatory code to be adopted by all jurisdictions within each metropolitan area, arguing that with the ". . . profusion of regulatory measures and the continual tinkering with these ordinances, even the most imaginative metropolitan plan loses its organizing force . . ."[17] The emphasis in such a code should be on coordination, simplification, and positive incentives.

An Informed Metropolitan Community. This element in the guidance system relies on a broad and continuing public education program focussed on the persuasive power of a sound and logical approach to urban development. It would make use of all available communications media directed at all segments of the community. It would involve the dissemination of public information, active citizen participation, and demonstration projects, as well as using the schools to develop an awareness of urban planning among students.

Chapin observes that civic education is a relatively underdeveloped technique but feels that it is essential for making planning more effective.

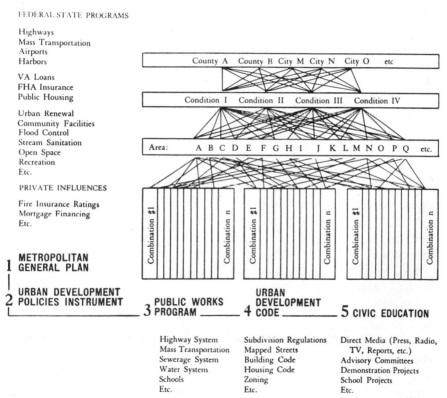

Figure 7-1. Diagrammatic representation of the elements of an urban development guidance system.

From the *Journal of the American Institute of Planners*, 29, no. 2 (May 1963), p. 83. Reproduced by permission.

The Guidance System.   The system consists of coordinated use of the described elements so that the concepts developed in the general plan give rise to the policies instrument and are implemented through the public works program, the urban development code and the public information, education, and participation programs. (See Figure 7-1, page 203).

Evaluation.   Chapin's proposed land use guidance system is more detailed than Fagin's and therefore easier to evaluate in the light of the components specified at the beginning of the chapter as essential to a complete land use guidance system. His system meets the requirement for including an ongoing comprehensive land use planning and policy-making process, including long, intermediate, and short range plans. It includes a broad array of tools of which the policies instrument, including an implementation program and the urban development code, are the principal new implementation tools. As in Fagin's proposal his development code would include development timing regulations. He neglects to say whether the development code would include control of community appearance and provide for historic preservation, but nothing in his system precludes this. Also the question of compensation is not dealt with specifically, although tax policies and subsidies are mentioned.

Chapin makes a point that in his proposal ". . . emphasis has been placed on a broadened approach and a fuller use of existing techniques."[18] The thrust of his proposal is on the development of *urban development guidance* systems, thus meeting another requirement for completeness. He also takes into account coordination with federal, state and regional plans and programs in the discussion of the policies instrument.

Although Chapin's proposal lays great stress on citizen education and participation, including the participation of civic groups, he is strangely silent about the participation of local elected politicians and the organizational and administrative framework necessary for the obtaining of mutual agreement on the plans, policies, and planning implementation program. He recognizes that his system would require ". . . some form of intergovernmental collaboration within the metropolitan area and the surrounding region."[19] However, he does not spell this out.

He does stress the need for taking full advantage of the tools at hand and the orchestration of "bundles" of policies into implementation programs tailored to community acceptability and the particulars of the implementation system. Overall, except for the shortcomings noted above, Chapin's proposed guidance system has most of the components of a complete land use guidance system, as judged by the criteria previously set forth, and it was a landmark proposal in the literature of the time.

John Reps: 1964, 1967

The idea of a land use guidance system was next furthered by John Reps in two addresses to annual conventions of the American Society of Planning Officials which were widely discussed and debated in the planning profession. The first of these addresses, "Requiem for Zoning,"[20] was a major attack on the land use implementation tool that planners have relied on most. It was also a plea for a drastic overhaul of existing implementation tools and direct public intervention in the land development market. He urged zoning reforms as part of a proposed land use guidance system bearing the acronym "ACID" from the four groups of proposed components: advice, controls, inducements or incentives, and direct public development.

Concerning planning advice, he notes that the first public planning agencies were purely advisory and that advice, in conjunction with persuasion and inspiration, still plays an important role in guiding urban development. Also all of the various controls—zoning, subdivision regulations, official maps, and building, housing and sanitary codes—influence development patterns, but their usefulness is limited by their negative character. Further, inducements and incentives such as subsidized financing, tax exemptions, direct subsidies, guaranteed loans, and direct subsidies have also played a part in guiding development. However, direct public development of the infrastructure necessary for private development to take place has been most effective in urban renewal areas and has a much greater potential for urban fringe development than contemporary American cities have been able to take advantage of.

After briefly outlining the elements of his guidance system, Reps concentrated the balance of the lecture on the flaws in zoning as now constituted. He proposed, instead, an integration of all land use controls into one set of "Development Regulations" involving the granting of much more discretionary power to the administrative agency within the framework of a plan for community development, and a related set of development objectives and standards both of which would be mandatory and adopted by the legislative body. The plan and objectives and standards would be subject to review and approval by a state agency which would also hear appeals from those opposing details of the plan. This would be more like European planning and development control procedures which Reps praises as having produced a high quality of urban development. He further proposes that the local "discretionary administration review body" be metropolitan area-wide in jurisdiction rather than a function of the constituent, smaller jurisdictions. An alternative to interlocal delegations of power would be direct intervention by the state in the exercise of planning controls.

Several years later in another address before the 1967 ASPO Convention, entitled "The Future of American Planning—Requiem or Renascence?" Reps dealt more extensively with the public development aspect of his land use guidance system. He summarized his proposal as follows:[21]

> I propose that land at the urban fringe which is to be developed for urban uses should be acquired by a public agency. Acquisition, in fact, should run well ahead of anticipated need and include the purchase or condemnation of idle or agricultural land well beyond the present urban limits. The public agency, therefore, should be given territorial jurisdiction which includes not only the present central city and the surrounding suburbs but a wide belt of undeveloped land. Land scheduled for early development should be designed in detail, conforming to a general, comprehensive, and long-range metropolitan growth plan. The public agency, directly or indirectly, should install all street and utility improvements and should identify and retain all sites needed for such public facilities as parks, schools, and other neighborhood and community needs. The remaining land should then be disposed of to private builders by sale or lease, the aggregate price to reflect full acquisition and improvements costs but no profit. The terms of the sale or lease should include adequate safeguards to insure development only in conformity to the detailed plans prepared for the area. In short, I am suggesting that a municipal, metropolitan, or state agency enter the field of land development in suburban or rural locations in a manner similar to that used in central city redevelopment projects.

Reps goes on to elaborate that his proposed metropolitan development agency, which might be wholly public, or semi-public like Comsat,[22] would operate primarily in the fringe areas. Development in central areas would be undertaken through urban renewal where necessary and control of the land use in the in-between, mostly developed areas would be managed by the reformed zoning controls he proposed in his earlier lecture.

The major control devices available to the proposed agency would be detailed deed or leasehold restrictions, similar to those used currently in urban renewal areas, and the withholding of land from the market until the intrastructure had been provided in a pattern consistent with the locations of uses and timing of development indicated in the metropolitan land use plans.

This proposal goes further than most land-banking proposals in that all of the infrastructure of streets, utilities, parks, and schools would be provided by the development corporation or other public agencies and therefore the building developers would have little latitude in regard to overall plans, traditional subdivision-control procedures having been eliminated. In order to avoid monotony much of the site planning would be farmed out to private practitioners through design competitions rather than being done in-house by the development corporation.

The benefits envisioned from this process include overcoming the land use pattern distortions caused by speculation, acquisition of land for public use in the right locations, providing an even flow of publicly improved building sites to the construction market, promoting more efficient, contiguous development rather than sprawl, providing land for relocating families displaced by urban renewal and improving the building process for private builders.

In support of his proposal Reps cites the effectiveness of large-scale advance purchase of land in achieving a high quality of design in Stockholm, Amsterdam, Rotterdam, Oslo, Helsinki, The Hague and Utrecht in Europe. In America the device was used in the late 1700s and early 1800s in New York, Washington, Detroit, San Francisco, and Savannah but only in Washington and Savannah was municipal ownership of land used to control the design of development.

Reps's proposal combines land banking with development powers similar to those of the New York Urban Development Corporation, both commented on in chapter six. He contends this kind of control is

". . . wholly compatible with our fundamental political beliefs and . . . economic system . . ." and ". . . absolutely essential to the satisfactory control of urban growth . . ."[23] His argument is persuasive, his examples compelling, and it seems certain that more cities and counties will experiment in this direction as Fairfax County, Virginia[24] is doing, and as is provided for in the American Law Institute's Model Land Development Code.[25]

Evaluation. Review of Reps' proposed land use guidance system reveals that it does have its basis in an ongoing comprehensive land use planning process having as elements: a long-range land use plan; shorter-range more detailed plans for areas scheduled for early development; and comprehensive development objectives and standards. In fact, the land use plans are the central elements by which the planner guides his increased discretionary decision-making authority. Clearly Reps' system meets the criteria concerning the planning process.

He proposes the rejection of, or less reliance on, zoning, districting (especially in urbanizing areas), in favor of giving the planner more discretionary power over land use and other development considerations. His proposal meets all the criteria for having an adequate array of implementation tools and for integrating them into a coordinated land use guidance program. He would consolidate all land use controls into one set of development regulations controlling land uses and use mixes, quality of development (including esthetic and historic preservation considerations), subdivision of land and the time of development, and provision for just compensation where the planning controls are very severely restrictive. He goes beyond the previous proposals in the amount of discretionary authority he would give to planning administrators, and introduces the concept of a metropolitan land acquisition and development corporation.

In discussing the problem of coordinating the development activities of many governmental entities he proposes that it be done by a public authority or an agency of the state. He does not deal directly with how metropolitan planning would be coordinated with the plans and policies of higher levels of government—although he discusses the utility of state coordination—or with civic group and citizen participation except through required public hearings and the normal political processes. He would place the responsibility for the implementation program, its efficiency, and local acceptability firmly in the hands of the planner.

With the exceptions noted above Reps' is a complete guidance system with more potential strength than those previously described. Furthermore, he argues very persuasively for giving the planner added flexibility through giving him more discretionary power within the constraints of adopted plans and policies and for increased involvement of local government in all aspects of urban development.

Henry Bain: 1969

Two years after the second Reps lecture, Henry Bain, in *The New City*[26] proposed an urban growth guidance strategy somewhat similar to Reps' proposal. Under the auspices of the National Committee on Urban Growth Policy, he espoused the use of "Urban Development Districts" to be created under state enabling legislation. These districts would be special districts created to plan and undertake development in those largely undeveloped metropolitan urban fringe areas ripe for development. As an alternative to sprawl they would insure a high quality of planned, contiguous development. They would assume all the development powers of local governments within their boundaries until development was complete, after which the districts would be dissolved and their development powers would be returned to the general purpose governments within their districts. They would not operate or maintain services; these functions would remain in the hands of the local governments.

These districts would be administered by the state, county, or local governments as provided for in the establishing enabling legislation. Bain also suggests the alternative of joint public-private development corporation as did Reps.

The districts would employ ". . . new and improved zoning techniques to stimulate and guide development . . ."[27] of areas for which low and medium densities were planned. Where plans call for high density development the districts would acquire the land for resale or lease to private developers with the appropriate restrictions designed to insure the execution of the land use plans. The districts would prepare and carry out a coordinated public improvement program in cooperation with the local agencies which, in turn, would operate the completed facilities.

The level of government establishing the agency would provide it with adequate capital to finance land acquisition and development. This capital would be reimbursed by the operating agencies in the case of public facilities and by the sale or lease of land to private developers.

The development process would involve the following steps:[28]

1. Designation of the development district. The area to be developed would not necessarily follow jurisdictional lines but might be larger, smaller, or interjurisdictional.
2. Declare a temporary moratorium on development in the districts to forestall anticipatory development and allow time for planning.
3. Ascertain predesignation land values to avoid paying speculative prices for land acquisition.
4. Prepare a district general plan.
5. Prepare detailed plans for the district stage by stage.
6. Prepare a private development program.
7. Prepare a public improvement program.
8. Prepare a development schedule.
9. Undertake the construction of public improvements.
10. Secure the construction of private development.
11. Administer the development program.
12. Provide public services through the responsible agencies.
13. Dissolve the urban development district.

Evaluation.   Bain's proposal provides for an ongoing comprehensive land use planning program with long-range and stage development plans, but the program appears to be limited to the area within the development district(s) rather than encompassing the entire metropolitan area. In fact, the problem of metropolitan area planning coordination is not raised. Bain does not go into detail about the array of land use controls to be used by the development districts except to specify new and improved zoning techniques, programming of public and private development, and the use of the district to carry out these programs directly or indirectly. Use by the district of all the usual land use controls is implied rather than stated. No mention of integrating the controls into a system is made but the use of district powers for land banking and direct development would seem to be enough for detailed development design control. Again, control of community appearance and historic preservation are not mentioned. Compensation in cases of severely restricted control of development is also not mentioned. The same is true for taking into account the plans, policies, and programs of other levels of government and the question of providing for involvement in the planning process of local elected officials, civic groups, and citizens with the exception of final approval by the affected local governments of district development plans.

The main thrust of Bain's proposal lies in the use of the special district device for planning and development in urban fringe areas. As a land use guidance system it is less complete than those proposed by Reps and Chapin or those discussed in the chapter on special districts. Too many questions were either not addressed, or were treated vaguely by Bain, such as the responsibility for initiating the districts, for controlling them, and the question of ongoing urban growth in relation to setting up and dismantling the districts.

Frank So: 1970

In a Planning Advisory Service report of the American Society of Planning Officials, entitled *Metropolitan Planning Policy Implementation*, Frank So examined the various strategies for metropolitan planning agencies to use in the implementation of metropolitan policies and plans, and devised the conception of an implementation program for more systematically using the available implementation tools. He observed that metropolitan planning agencies are ". . . still relatively weak institutions and possess very few strong implementation powers . . ." and therefore have to rely on ". . . more indirect and persuasive techniques . . ."[29] for carrying out their plans, policies, and programs. Accordingly, So argues that if the available techniques are to be used more successfully, they must be used more systematically. This is essential, he believes, because in examining existing metropolitan planning agencies he found ". . . a serious imbalance between policy development and policy implementation."[30]

He states that because for metropolitan planning agencies "implementation" as a concept must be broad, the objective of these agencies must be *planning and policies* implementation involving the whole planning process rather than plan implementation and that the former is far more difficult and subtle a process than plan implementation, being concerned with the exercise of influence and power in the interest of guiding development in accordance with the policies of the metropolitan planning agency. He argues further that plans or plan-making are not separable from implementation because of the interaction between them. Accordingly, at the metropolitan level policy guides have increasingly been prepared, rather than detailed plans, because of the uncertainty concerning implementation opportunities. He concludes this introductory part of the report by describing the complexity of the metropolitan development process as follows:[31]

> The growing metropolitan area is continuously being transformed from a rural into an urban area as a result of a conglomeration of public and private development decisions: decisions of state government affecting the area's capacity to grow; budgetary decisions of county and special district governments; decisions by government agencies, private corporations, and others to build or invest in something, to initiate a program of service, and so on. At times these decisions are complementary, and at other times they are in conflict . . . Not all such decisions are of equal importance. The most important decisions from a metropolitan development standpoint are those affecting major utilities, transportation, open space, and major economic activity centers.

From there he goes on to examine the major persuasive strategies which he classifies as: (1) "the classic," (2) gaining and strengthening allies, (3) information, (4) cooperation, (5) coordination, (6) ad hoc problem solving, and (7) education and indoctrination. He criticizes each of these techniques and concludes none is adequate in and of itself and many contain possible hazards.

After that he examines three legislative reforms: mandatory referral, institutional change, and development power.

Where there is mandatory referral to a metropolitan planning agency of specified planning and development questions it is usually not mandatory to follow the advice of the metropolitan planning agency. Only the Metropolitan Council in the Twin Cities area (Minneapolis-St. Paul) was cited as having enforcement powers in regard to some mandatory referrals.

In discussing institutional change So lists without comment the following possible types of change:[32]

(1) Combining a metropolitan planning agency with a metropolitan transportation planning agency (or, combining with a health facilities planning council).

(2) Changing the MPA from a planning commission with appointed members to a council of governments represented by government officials who themselves have been elected as chief executive officers of their own respective governments.

(3) For those MPAs which do not have it, obtaining mandatory referral powers; strengthening mandatory referral so that denial by the MPA means something.

(4) Having the governing body of the MPA elected rather than appointed.

(5) Establishing a greater degree of financial independence through, for example, obtaining non-earmarked funds from state government, or having the power to impose a tax levy to support the MPA's programs.

(6) Removing certain land-use control powers from local governments and placing them within the MPA.

(7) Obtain power to either indirectly or directly plan and operate certain regional facilities and systems and the power to raise taxes to operate and maintain them.

(8) Combining several regionwide special purpose authorities, and the MPA, into a metropolitan development government.

In the discussion of development power So cites the Twin Cities Metro Council as having planning and development control jurisdiction over land use within three miles of the new regional airport, and appointive power over the members of two seven-member boards, one of which would develop a metropolitan sewer system, and the other an areawide open space and recreational program. He also cites the Maryland-National Park and Planning Commission as having development powers over parks and recreation and the power to administer zoning and subdivision regulations within most of its jurisdictional area.

In the third section of *Metropolitan Planning Policy Implementation*, So proposes that metropolitan planning agencies should develop an instrument called an *implementation program*. He outlines it as follows:[33]

   I. A critical review of the MPA's field of action
      A. Identifying key decision-makers
      B. Examining constraints
  II. A review of the MPA's past performance
      A. The policy base
      B. Implementation strategies that have been used.
 III. Developing a new implementation strategy
 IV. Assessing the implications of carrying out the program
      A. Staff and budget considerations
      B. Establishing a monitoring system

Rather than a single detailed strategy it is an outline of a program to be tailor-made for each metropolitan area taking into account the local resources and constraints.

The critical review of the metropolitan planning agency's field of action involves: a study of the land development process; an inventory of all local governments and agencies to determine their relationship to, and influence on, metropolitan development; consideration of how the planning agency might best be related to these governments and agencies in influencing development; identification of constraints on the planning agency including lack of adequate enabling legislation, distrust of the planning agency as a possible stepping stone to metropolitan government, and assessment of the degree of political fragmentation with a view to determining how it might be ameliorated.

The review of the past performance of the metropolitan planning agency starts with an analysis of the adequacy of the agency's policy base to determine if policies are clearly spelled out, sufficiently comprehensive, consistent, being carried out (or if not, why not?), and an assessment of their usefulness. This is followed up by an appraisal of the implementation strategies used by the metropolitan planning agency with an emphasis on critical evaluation, reasons for successes and failures being determined.

After the review of past planning implementation comes the task of devising a new implementation strategy. Based on the review it is necessary to determine which past strategies were successful and should be continued as opposed to those which were unsuccessful and should be discontinued. With as much precision as possible those strategies should be identified which will be directed at the previously identified decision-makers. The constraints which cannot be changed must be identified as well as those the metropolitan planning agency has a reasonable chance of altering or removing. The question of desirable institutional changes must be examined with a view to making such reform proposals as are both reasonable and possible. And finally the agency's work program should be reviewed for determining the necessary changes in the light of the proposed new implementation strategy.

The new implementation strategy must be adequately staffed and funded in order to be put into operation, and some form of monitoring of implementation must be developed if the program is to become an effective part of the continuing planning process.

Evaluation.   So's proposal assumes an ongoing comprehensive planning program including stage development plans whose implementation elements are the focus of his concern. Because he is dealing with planning at the metropolitan level there is less emphasis on small scale planning than on plans and policies having areawide impact; he is less concerned with detailed physical planning than with policies planning directed at guiding all development decisions.

So's proposal is for the establishment of a *process* whereby an array of available planning implementation controls and strategies (usually used in piecemeal fashion) can be organized into more effective *implementation programs*. He does not propose one specific set of controls and strategies as being the most desirable but lists a variety of arrays which could be coordinated. The programs would be carefully tailor-made to fit individual situations and be monitored with a view to revising them as conditions warrant. He also does not go into detail about what the programs should accomplish beyond their being designed to carry out the adopted metropolitan planning policies. Coordination of the implementation tools into an implementation program as indicated above is the core of his proposal.

In dealing with the problem of coordinating the development activities of a multiplicity of local governments, he suggests alternative organizational reforms and grants of power to the metropolitan planning agency which would improve its implementation ability. He also fully takes into account cooperation and coordination with higher levels of government. He provides for full participation of the planning area's political representatives, civic and professional groups, and other citizens. Except for its lack of detail about small-scale plans and planning controls because of its focus on metropolitan planning, So's land use guidance system proposal is quite complete and is a significant contribution to the literature on the subject.

Donald Canty: 1972

Donald Canty in 1972 proposed the creation of elective Metropolitan Development Agencies (MDA's) to guide and/or undertake physical development and the provision of areawide services in and for metropolitan areas. These instrumentalities would do metropolitan planning, undertake urban renewal, undertake and/or guide peripheral urban development including the construction of satellite communities.

In constructing his proposal Canty first sets out four criteria that a land use guidance instrumentality for metropolitan areas should meet:[34]

1. It must be a multipurpose instrument, capable of dealing with the relatedness of metropolitan problems.

As one by one the areawide nature of some metropolitan problems has become evident, the response has been to create a special district or authority to deal with them—one-by-one. These entities add still more overlapping strands to the metropolitan web. Dealing individually with such matters as airports, highways, parks, and mosquitoes, they often fall over one another. Right and left hands work busily at cross-purposes.

2. It must be democratic instrument. That is, it should be politically accountable on an areawide basis. The special districts or authorities typically are not accountable at all. Their behavior to date is testimony of the danger of vesting great power in remote appointive officials.

Another widespread form of quasi-metropolitanism are the Councils of Governments, comprised of local elected officials who attempt to coordinate planning and action on area wide concerns.

. . . .

When it comes to difficult decisions, local officials serving on the COGs are likely to vote local rather than areawide concerns. How could it be otherwise, since their constituencies are purely local?

The elective leaders of the new instrument must have and serve an areawide constituency.

3. At the same time, the new instrument must be decentralized in terms of both decision-making and administration. It must widely share the new power that it creates.

Otherwise those in the central cities already pained by their remoteness from local government will be still further from influence over the public aspects of their lives.

4. The final specification for the design of the instrument is that it should not replace existing municipalities.

Many aspects of metropolitan problems are best left in local hands. These include curriculum design and staff selection in the schools and most aspects of law enforcement.

. . . .

Also, many municipalities, large and small, are held together by cultural, traditional, or geographical ties. There is little enough sense of community in any modern society. It should be encouraged, not disrupted.

Canty then goes on to examine city-county consolidation, the CED's proposal for two-tiered, federated metropolitan governments, and Burton's proposed metropolitan states. He rejects all of these alternatives and then advances his own. His initial presentation of it is brief enough to quote almost in its entirety:[35]

It would be an elective metropolitan development agency (MDA). Since it would be an instrument of national strategy, it would be entirely financed by the federal government. The federal money would be tied in some strong and sizable strings relating to such matters as representativeness, environmental protection, and priority attention to the widening of options and opportunities for the poor and minorities.

The MDA would be the primary delivery mechanism for all federal programs in the following categories anywhere in its area: housing and community development, transportation, environmental protection, and economic development. It would supplant such present mechanisms as local housing authorities and redevelopment agencies as federal funding channels. It would function as a secondary delivery system for federal employment and service programs aimed at helping localities meet needs generated by its development decisions.

The MDA would be comprised of population-equal community districts smaller than the central cities and larger than the smaller suburbs. Each district would elect its own governing board and officers. And these district boards, in turn, would choose delegates to form the areawide MDA governing board. Officers of the MDA would be chosen in an areawide general election, and would serve on a full-time basis. The MDA would have the powers of eminent domain and supercession of local building and land-use regulations. Specified powers would be reserved to the community districts. Both the areawide and district offices would have interdisciplinary professional staffs.

The federal government would seek to induce the states to create the MDAs through energetic use of fiscal carrots and sticks. But where the states did not do so, the MDAs would be created directly by the federal government.

The first step in an MDA's creation would be establishment of a metropolitan commission composed of local elected officials, federal representatives, and citizen members (plus state officials if the MDA were being created by the state). The citizen members would be chosen through area-wide general elections.

In recognition of the differences between areas, many decisions about the MDA's structure would be left to the commission, but within overall federal guidelines containing such strings as those cited above. Included in these decisions would be such crucial matters as the size of the community districts, the distribution of powers between the district and areawide levels, and the powers of the areawide officers vis-à-vis the board of district delegates.

The federal guidelines, in each case, would have to be sturdy enough to protect the presently powerless. In the matter of district vs. areawide MDA powers, for example, no district should be allowed to veto the development of lower-income housing allotted to it through an areawide MDA plan. And the areawide officers should have sufficient checks on them to prevent their becoming "metropolitan czars."

Once created, the MDA would be required to consult with local general-purpose governments on the impact of its activities within their boundaries, and to coordinate its plans and activities with theirs. The original commission would remain in existence (renewed by periodic areawide elections) to act as a fact-finding and arbitration board on disputes between the MDA and local jurisdictions.

The MDAs would contain a "self-destruct" mechanism in that they would become agencies of general purpose metropolitan governments as such were formed in their areas. The strings on their federal funding would remain however, including the requirement that decisions about its use be effectively decentralized.

He then goes on to elaborate. He describes the role of the MDA as involving programs to generate new jobs for the unemployed in the central cities, assisting in the development of low-cost housing near existing employment centers where there is a shortage of it, and creating new, relatively self-contained communities of various scales on open land within its jurisdiction. Having the power of eminent domain, the MDA could undertake land banking as a means of guiding development. It could do detailed planning for the land under its control, undertake the provision of the infrastructure necessary for development to take place and resell the land to private developers or public agencies willing to carry out the plans. The MDA would also administer federal "subsidy packages" providing funds to constituent local governments to help defray the extra costs of their providing services to their low-income families.

Evaluation.   Canty's proposal assumes an ongoing comprehensive land use planning process with an emphasis on short-and intermediate-range plans and policies keyed to detailed urban development and redevelopment programs. The emphasis is on solving the problems of the poor through increasing the supply of physically well-related low-cost housing and establishments offering appropriate employment opportunities. The planning process would be directed toward carrying out national goals within a local institutional framework responsible to the local electorate. Stage development planning is implied rather than explicitly stated.

His array of planning tools is narrow but powerful. Although the traditional planning controls would remain in the hands of local governments within the MDA's jurisdiction, the MDA could override them in regard to development it undertakes. The central tool is the control of development through the acquisition of land, planning for its use in detail, providing the infrastructure necessary for development or redevelopment and resale of the land to public or private developers subject to conformance to MDA plans. Also important is the MDA's carrot and stick control of the disbursing of federal funds to its constituent local governments. Because local planning controls remain in the hands of these governments there is no reference to the question of compensation for seriously restrictive controls.

The instrumentality Canty proposes would be charged with the coordinating of the planning implementation tools used in its development and redevelopment programs. It also would be charged with coordinating its plans and programs with those of the local governments within its jurisdiction.

The proposal adequately takes into account the programs of higher levels of government. Its directly elected council would satisfy the requirement for local political involvement although that wouldn't rule out conflicts between the MDA and its constituent local governments. Citizen and civic group participation is implied rather than spelled out. Presumably this would be more effective at the MDA subdistrict level.

Finally, Canty's proposal meets the requirement for making full use of the available planning tools in a manner acceptable to the community in that the necessary planning ordinances would have to have local popular support in order to be passed. The MDA's council being elective would further guarantee that in its developmental and other activities it would be politically accountable.

Canty's proposal seems to grow out of the ideas proposed by Reps and Bain, both of which use the public authority device. It goes beyond both in taking over the urban renewal function from its constituent local governments, and in being federally funded and acting as an administrator for disbursing federal funds to local governments within its jurisdiction and an instrumentality for carrying out federal urban development policies.

Comparative Summary

The guidance systems selected for examination on the preceding pages will be briefly reviewed here for a comparison of their major features, their major emphases, and for their contribution to the evolution of growth guidance system concepts.

Fagin argued for the need to control the timing of development: its tempo and sequence. He assumed the existence of a unit of local government capable of exercising land use controls over urbanizing areas. He proposed modifying zoning to include reserve districts in which the options for future land uses would be left open until they were ripe for development as determined by overlay zones establishing priorities for development according to which building permits would be issued or denied. The highest priority districts would be planned in detail and requests for building permits issued if the proposed development met the requirements of the plan. Land owners having low development priorities would receive tax relief as part of the guidance system. Four years later Fagin proposed integrating the development policies aspect of land use planning into a single "policies plan," an idea which Chapin incorporated into his guidance system.[36]

Chapin took a broader approach based on a metropolitan general plan, an urban development policies instrument (after Fagin), a metropolitan public works program, an urban development code consolidating zoning and subdivision controls, and a public information program for gaining public understanding and support for carrying out the plan. Unlike Fagin's proposal, Chapin's does not rely on new implementation techniques or on tax relief, but does strive to organize planning and plan implementation into a systematic land use guidance system.

Reps, though despairing of zoning, also proposes that existing techniques of planning and controlling land use continue where appropriate in the community, but that they be supplemented by the more powerful tools of economic incentives and direct public involvement in land acquisition and development through a metropolitan development agency (exempt from conformance to local land use controls), which would go beyond land banking to provide directly the whole infrastructure necessary for development; it would then dispose of land for development through sale or lease, subject to discretionary approval of the individual development proposals.

Bain, like Reps, proposes a land acquisition and development agency or agencies to plan and undertake development in urbanizing areas. Bain's development districts would preempt local land use controls and would exercise them within district boundaries until dissolved, rather than simply having the override powers of Reps' agencies. The difference between the two proposals is in the details rather than in basic concepts. The significance of Bain's proposal lies rather in its influence on the recommendations of the National Committee on Urban Growth Policy for whom it was prepared and on

Canty who edited *The New City* in which it appeared.[37] (The relevant parts of the Committee's recommendations will be presented and discussed in the next part of this chapter).

So's proposal, like Chapin's is aimed at metropolitan *planning* and *policies* implemented through a systematically organized *implementation program.* He does not propose new land use controls but he examines the possible strengthening of metropolitan planning agencies by giving them the right of mandatory referral over local plans and development proposals, strengthening them through institutional change (possibly including agency conversion to a development authority as proposed by Reps, Bain, and Canty). However, the principal emphasis of So's proposal is on making more systematic use of existing land use guidance techniques while attempting to strengthen metropolitan planning agencies through improved state legislation.

Canty's proposal is built around the establishment of metropolitan development authorities like those proposed by Reps and Bain (and discussed as an alternative by So), but with the requirement that their governing boards be elective, their funding come from the federal government, and that they be empowered to undertake urban redevelopment and the development of new satellite communities as well as the development of the urban fringe.

All of the guidance systems examined show a concern for more systematic organization and use of planning implementation techniques. Starting with Reps' proposasl the idea of a metropolitan planning and development agency capable of guiding new development through land acquisition, improvement, and resale or lease under stipulated planning requirements has been increasingly proposed as the major element necessary for effective land use guidance systems especially in metropolitan areas.

The next section will examine the recommendations of selected government and professional organizations concerning land use guidance.

RECOMMENDATIONS OF GOVERNMENT AND PROFESSIONAL ORGANIZATIONS CONCERNING LAND USE GUIDANCE

The recommendations selected for examination here are those of the National Commission on Urban Problems in 1968,[38] the National

Committee on Urban Growth Policy in 1969,[39] the National Policy Task Force of the American Institute of Architects in 1972,[40] the Committee on Growth and the Environment of the International City Management Association in 1973,[41] the Advisory Commission on Intergovernmental Relations in 1973,[42] and the American Law Institute in 1975[43] which will be reviewed in relation to the relevent national planning policies of the American Institute of Planners.[44] These proposals were chosen because they were made by organizations deeply concerned with land use and development and have been widely circulated and commented upon.

Members of the American Institute of Planners participated in the AIA Task Force study and the drafting of the ALI Model Land Development Code, and AIP responded to the ALI Code with an analysis and recommendations for modification. AIP has also disseminated information about land use guidance systems through its periodicals.

The quasi-professional American Society of Planning Officials, (now consolidated with AIP in the American Planning Association), while not proposing a specific guidance system, has become interested in developing policy positions and has widely disseminated information concerning land use guidance systems and innovative legislation affecting the implementation of land use plans through its various publications.

National Commission on Urban Problems: 1968

This Commission, chaired by Senator Paul Douglas, was appointed by President Lyndon Johnson in 1967 to carry out the purposes defined in section 301 of the Housing and Urban Development Act of 1965. In this report to the Congress and President, the National Commission made recommendations, among which were several affecting urban growth guidance. These are quoted and commented on here. The recommendations are pursuant to the following Commission findings concerning which levels of government should have assigned to them particular governmental functions:[45]

(1) *Local initiative*—Local governments—i.e., governments below the State level—should bear primary responsibility for detailed guidance of urban development.

(2) *Larger local governments*—So that local governments can take effec-

tive initiative in guiding urban development, the size of local governments in many metropolitan areas must be substantially increased.

(3) *Stronger local governments*—Local governments must be strengthened through the grant of additional powers and through substantial financial and technical assistance.

(4) *Stronger voice for neighborhoods*—In recognition of the special interests of property owners and residents in their immediate surroundings, increased efforts must be made to enhance the ability of neighborhood residents to effect changes and protect desirable features of their environment.

(5) *Effective implementation of State and National policies*—The range of local actions must be effectively limited by the States and the Federal Government both to assure fair treatment of property owners and minorities in each locality and to assure that local decisions will not place unfair, uneconomic, or unrealistic burdens on people who live outside a given local jurisdiction.

Interim reallocation of regulatory powers. Substantial time will be required to achieve major changes in governmental structure of the kind recommended in part IV of this report. During this time, continuing development will determine the quality of urban environment in large areas for decades to come. The Commission therefore believes it appropriate to recommend interim measures which, though insufficient to secure the full local initiative which is the Commission's objective, may nevertheless be partial steps in that direction and may reduce certain abuses associated with the present regulatory system.

The first relevant recommendation is:

Recommendation No. 1—Enabling competent local governments to guide urban development effectively.

The Commission recommends that State and Federal agencies take steps to assure that local governments bear primary responsibility for the guidance of urban development, and that they are capable of effectively performing this function.

Recommendation 1(a)—County or regional authority in small municipalities.

The Commission recommends that State governments enact legislation granting to counties (or regional governments of general jurisdiction, where such governments exist) exclusive authority to exercise land-use control powers within small municipalities in metropolitan areas. Although conditions vary from State to State, it appears that municipalities within metropolitan areas should not have regulatory powers if (1) either their population is less than 25,000 or their area is less than 4 square miles, or (2) in the case of a municipality hereafter incorporated or not now exercising regulatory powers, their population is less than 50,000.

Recommendation 1(b)—State requirement of a local development guidance program.

The Commission recommends that State governments enact legislation denying land-use regulatory powers, after a reasonable period of time, to local governments that lack a "development guidance program" as defined by State statute or administrative regulations made pursuant to such statute. Powers denied would be exercised by the State, regional, or county agencies as provided in the statute. The existence and enforcement by the States of such local development guidance program requirements should, after a reasonable period of time, be made a condition of State participation in the Federal 701 planning assistance program.

Recommendation 1(c)—Study of Government structure in relation to land-use controls.

The Commission recommends that the Department of Housing and Urban Development require as a condition of Federal 701 grants to States for local planning assistance, the submission of a comprehensive State study of (1) the allocations of planning and land-use control powers and other decisionmaking activities significantly affecting land use within metropolitan areas, (2) the need for regional decisionmaking or regional review of local decisions within such areas, (3) the need for State action to redistribute control powers, and (4) such other matters as may be required to assure more orderly urban development. Such study should be submitted within a reasonably short period after promulgation of the Secretary's requirements and should be published and distributed within the State. Revisions of such studies should be undertaken not less than every 5 years and should report progress made toward implementing recommendations contained in previous studies.

Recommendation 1(d)—Restructuring local planning and development responsibilities.

The Commission recommends that State governments enact legislation authorizing but not requiring local governments to abolish local planning boards as traditionally constituted.

Recommendation 1(e)—State recognition of local land-use controls.

The Commission recommends that State governments enact legislation granting to large units of local government the same regulatory power over the actions of State and other public agencies that they have over those of private developers.

This group of recommendations is concerned with making land use guidance programs mandatory and putting land use controls in the hands of local governmental units capable of making them effective yet close enough to those affected for them to be responsive to local needs.

Recommendation 1(a), by denying land use controls to small local governmental units would simplify the problem of coordinating planning implementation in metropolitan areas. It would, as the Commission points out, make sure guidance programs are exercised by local units large enough to recognize their land use problems, large enough to be able to solve them, and large enough to be able to coordinate their guidance programs with other governmental units at all levels.

Recommendation 1(b), making land use guidance programs mandatory for local governments exercising land use controls, is in line with criticisms by the American Institute of Planners of the ALI Model Land Development Code. Oregon is an example of a state which has put this recommendation into effect. Both the ALI Code and Oregon legislation will be dealt with later in this chapter.

Recommendation 1(c) addresses itself to the dynamic aspects of planning and the exercise of land use controls in metropolitan areas. It would require monitoring of local government structure in relation to land use controls as a means of maintaining or improving the effectiveness of land use guidance systems.

Recommendation 1(d) would enable local governments to abolish independent planning commissions in favor of placing the planning function in local government departments directly responsible to the executive of the local government and through him to its elected representatives. The intent of this proposal is to make the planning agency more directly accountable to its constituency and facilitate the coordination of the planning-related activities of local government departments.

Recommendation 1(e) is intended to ensure that the development activities of higher levels of government do not run counter to the local guidance program.

The second recommendation concerns the establishment of state agencies for development planning and review:[46]

The Commission recommends that each State create a State agency for planning and development guidance directly responsible to the Governor. The agency should exercise three types of functions: (1) research and technical assistance to localities in land-use planning and control; (2) the preparation of State and regional land-use plans and policies and (3) adjudication and supervision of decisions by State and local agencies affecting land use.

Implementation of this regulation would establish a framework for state and regional planning and policies within which local guidance programs would have to be organized. Together with the previous recommendation it would insure mutual coordination of developmental plans and policies by all levels of government. The technical assistance provision would strengthen the planning efforts of the smaller units of government as well as being a resource for all planning activities. The adjudication provision, also proposed by Reps, would help develop state-wide uniformity of administrative policies and interpretation of land use regulations.

Recommendation 3 has to do with housing policy. Only subrecommendation 3(d) is relevant to guidance systems:[47]

Recommendation 3(d)—Public acquisition of housing sites.

The Commission recommends that State governments enact legislation authorizing State, regional, and local agencies to acquire land for present or future use or disposition to provide sites for low- and moderate- income housing.

Implementation of this recommendation would enable land banking for housing. This would be a more limited use of land banking than proposed earlier by Reps and subsequently by Bain and Canty.

The fourth recommendation is concerned with the unified planning and design of new neighborhoods:[48]

The Commission recommends that States enact legislation enabling localities to encourage unified planning and design of new neighborhoods and to prevent wasteful and unattractive scattered development. Specifically the Commission proposes the following actions:

Recommendation 4(a)—Restriction of development through holding zones.

The Commission recommends that State governments enable local governments to establish holding zones in order to postpone urban development in areas that are inappropriate for development within the next 3 to 5 years. Local governments should be authorized to limit development within such zones to houses on very large lots (e.g., 10 to 20 acres), agriculture, and open space uses. The State legislation should require that localities review holding zone designations at least every 5 years.

Recommendation 4(a) is similar to Fagin's proposal for reserve districts.

Recommendation 4(b) and (c) deal with planned unit development:

Recommendation 4(b)—Regulatory process for planned unit development.

The Commission recommends that State governments enact enabling legislation for, and local governments adopt, provisions establishing a regulatory process for planned unit developments. Such legislation should authorize provisions to vary according to size of projects (e.g., to permit high-rise buildings or light industry only in projects of more than a specified size).

Recommendation 4(c)—State authorization for planned development districts.

The Commission recommends that State governments enact legislation enabling local governments to classify undeveloped land in planned development districts within which development would be allowed to occur only at a specified minimum scale. Such statutes should make clear that such minimums could be sufficiently large as to allow only development which created its own environment.

This important regulatory tool was discussed in the chapter on zoning. What is new here is the proposed regulation establishing a minimum scale for all development in undeveloped areas. This has also been proposed by Downs[49] and is often a precondition for the "industrial park" zoning classification.[50] The purpose is to prevent piecemeal unplanned peripheral development.

Recommendation 5 deals with the fair allocation of infrastructure costs and is usually covered in subdivision regulations. (See chapter three). Recommendation 6 deals with strengthening land use controls in developed areas and is generally a recommendation for improved zoning regulations.

Recommendation 7 is concerned with the use of land purchase and compensative techniques for development control:[51]

The Commission recommends that States and localities with the assistance of the Federal Government, use public land purchase and compensation techniques for the control of development in situations where such approaches would accomplish better results than traditional police power regulations.

Recommendation 7(a)—Compensative regulation.

The Commission recommends that the States enact legislation enabling property-owners to compel the purchase of property rights by regulating governments when regulations (or certain types of regulations specified by the statute) would constitute an unconstitutional "taking" of property without just compensation. Land so purchased would then be placed in a public reserve of urban land for present or future disposal and use in accordance with approved plans.

This recommendation goes beyond Fagin's tax relief proposal and Reps' just compensation proposal by tying compensation in with a land banking program:[52]

Recommendation 7(b)—State authorization for land banking.

The Commission recommends that State governments enact legislation enabling State and/or local development authorities to acquire land in advance of development for the following purposes: (a) assuring the continuing availability of sites needed for development; (b) controlling the timing, location, type, and scale of development; (c) preventing urban sprawl; and (d) reserving to the public gains in land values resulting from the action of government in promoting and servicing development. At a minimum, such legislation should authorize the acquisition of land surrounding highway interchanges. At such times as development of such land is deemed to be appropriate and in the interests of the region, such land could be sold or leased at no less than its fair market value for private development in accordance with approved plans. Wherever feasible, long-term leases should be the preferred method of disposing of any public land, and lease terms should be set so as to permit reassembly of properties for future replanning and development. Legislation should specify a maximum period that such land may be held by the public before lease or sale.

This recommendation expands that of 3(d) to include land banking for all forms of development as proposed by Reps, Bain, and Canty.

The final recommendation is as follows:[53]

Recommendation 7(c)—Provision of Federal assistance for land acquisition.

The Commission recommends that the Congress enact legislation establishing a Federal revolving fund to facilitate the purchase of land by local governments in owner-initiated compensation proceedings and as part of direct-purchase programs, with the Federal contribution to be returned to the fund upon disposition of the property. Furthermore, the Congress should enact legislation authorizing the Department of Transportation to assist States in acquiring land surrounding federally assisted highway interchanges.

Federal funding of the land banking aspect of local land use guidance systems is an option under Reps' proposal and the sole source of funding under Canty's proposal.

Commentary. The recommendations of the National Commission on Urban Problems follow in time the guidance system proposals of Fagin, Chapin, and Reps and seem to have been influenced by them in the respects commented on. They also foreshadow some of the elements of later guidance system proposals. Rather than being a description of a specific guidance system, they are directed toward encouraging action on the part of the federal, state, and local governments to bring into being effective local land use guidance systems.

They place heavy reliance on land banking and improved land use controls as the major guidance tools. Though the use of these techniques is to be vested primarily in the larger scale local governments, they intend that local planning and development be required to be coordinated with the plans and policies of higher levels of government. They also provide for compensation to land owners whose property uses are so restricted as to approach being confiscatory.

They do not specify the elements of the local planning process or the extent of citizen involvement but otherwise they address themselves to all of the concerns expressed in the seven criteria for guidance system completeness previously set forth.

National Committee on Urban Growth Policy: 1969

This committee, chaired by Congressman Albert Rains, undertook a study directed by Laurence Henderson under the joint sponsorship of the National Association of Counties, The National League of Cities, The United States Conference of Mayors, and Urban America, Incorporated. About half of the Committee members were drawn from the Congress and most of the rest were elected officials from state and local government. They examined firsthand the European countries noted for their successful urban growth policies and heard statements from an impressive array of urban planning and development experts, many of whose papers are included in *The New City* along with their recommendations. These recommendations are strongly directed at the development of new communities and the creation of development agencies to undertake both peripheral and new community development as follows:[54]

The Committee recommends that there be in the Executive branch a mechanism to serve as a focal point of policy-making on matters dealing with urban growth policy. It should annually report to the nation and the Congress on the status of urban growth in America, and make recommendations for dealing with urban growth problems. It should be sufficiently staffed and have adequate power to reconcile, among Executive branch agencies, interagency and inter-program differences.

The Committee further recommends that the Executive branch and the Congress, with the assistance of the new mechanism, mold a national policy which coordinates a range of programs designed to assure more rational patterns of urban growth and development in the United States. These programs should include new measures to further assist existing cities to redesign and rebuild, to organize new growth on the peripheries of metropolitan areas, and to strengthen and expand smaller communities in rural areas designated as "accelerated growth centers."

As still another essential component of that program, the Committee recommends that financial assistance be extended from the federal government to enable the creation of 100 new Communities averaging 100 thousand population each and 10 new communities of at least 1 million in population. The British experience shows that only new communities approaching this size can be an effective instrument of urban growth policy. This dimension of community building, while it may seem ambitious, will accommodate only 20 percent of the anticipated population growth in the United States by the end of this century. The cost of this program, as seen by the Committee, will be small compared to the cost incurred by the inefficiencies in the current approach to development and the lack of coordination among existing programs. The Committee finds that building of new communities at this scale will produce efficiencies and returns to the national economy which dwarf the direct outlays involved.

The Committee recommends that a national program of this magnitude, established to promote and assist new community development, be predicated on the following principles.

1. New communities developed under this program must significantly contribute to an increase in housing, education, training, and employment in the area in which it is built, with particular attention to the needs of central cities.
2. New communities under this program should result in socially and economically adjusted communities. Special account should be taken of the needs of low and moderate income families. Special opportunities should be provided to afford gainful, varied, and satisfying employment to such families. They should not, however, be induced to migrate to new towns without the assurance of having there employment, adequate housing, recreation, and like facilities.

   New towns should be attractive to all classes, creeds, and races; to all types of businesses and industries; to a mix of citizen talent that will insure new town success.
3. New communities developed under this program should be carried out in accordance with the announced planning objectives of the state and local governments of the region in which the development is located. They must be consistent with existing and future national objectives and policy for orderly urban growth and development.
4. New community developments under this program must provide full opportunity for the private sector to be engaged in both long-term financing and construction within the larger planning objectives established by the governments involved.
5. New community developments assisted under this program should not encourage the proliferation of special service districts, and should, to the maximum extent possible, build upon the powers of general purpose state, county, and local governments.
6. New communities developed under this program should encourage the use of the latest technological advances in construction.
7. New communities developed under this program should follow the highest standards of planning and urban design.

The Committee recommends that the Congress enact a program of long-term loans or loan guarantees to assist agencies empowered under state law to assemble land, install public facilities, and plan for large-scale new community development. These loans or loan guarantees should provide for deferment of payment of principal and interest for no more than 15 years, or at such time within 15 years as revenue of the agency allows repayment.

The Committee recommends to states that they authorize the creation of agencies at the state, county, or local level power to use federal financing tools mentioned above. The agency—the key development instrument of an urban growth policy—should have authority to operate in at least the following kinds of areas:

1. In existing metropolitan areas, including central cities where sprawling suburban development is the norm, or where inefficient design has seriously retarded growth, and where such agencies can operate as an arm of state or local governments for the purpose of ordering metropolitan development in accordance with the development objectives of the region. Thus, in these areas, the function of the agency would be to utilize the existing dynamic of growth to bring about a stronger ordering of the forces of growth thereby making the development more efficient and opening new opportunities to all the people of the region.
2. Outside of metropolitan areas, these agencies would operate as new community builders with the ability to assemble large quantities of land and install the public facilities systems required. These agencies would be empowered to create genuine new communities away from the increasingly congested metropolitan centers of the country thereby bringing about greater balance in the nation's development.
3. In smaller communities designated as "accelerated growth centers" these agencies should be empowered to stimulate growth through the acquisition of large quantities of land, the orderly installation of new public facilities, and the inducement of business and industry to locate in these areas.

Thus, the Committee is recommending federal financing for development corporations, authorized under state law, which could stimulate needed large-scale development in and out of existing metropolitan areas and would have ample authority to bring about genuine balance in urban growth.

Without specifying a specific organizational mechanism to implement this program, the Committee recommends that an appropriate federal agency be established to administer the program and to coordinate with other federal agencies in the administration of their respective programs which relate to and have a bearing upon new community development.

In recognizing the urgency of the problem, the Committee recommends that the federal agency proceed immediately to develop model state enabling legislation under which new community development agencies could be established and operate at the city, county, or state level. These agencies should be public corporations with powers of condemnation and eminent domain and with an authority to bring about genuine balance in urban growth.

Without specifying a specific organizational mechanism to implement this program, the Committee recommends that an appropriate federal agency be established to administer the program and to coordinate with other federal agencies in the administration of their respective programs which relate to and have a bearing upon new community development.

In recognizing the urgency of the problem, the Committee recommends that the federal agency proceed immediately to develop model state enabling legislation under which new community development agencies could be established and operate at the city, county, or state level. These agencies should be public corporations with powers of condemnation and eminent domain, and with an authority to issue bonds and develop other financial instruments as may be required to carry out their purposes.

The Committee recommends that the appropriate federal agency provide a substantial and positive program of technical assistance to state, county, and local governments and to agencies empowered under state law to engage in new community development. The federal agency should also establish a program of research into the latest advances in building technology.

The first set of recommendations is concerned with the establishment of a national growth policy of which the development of an extensive new communities program would be a key part. Subsequently Congress passed the 1970 Housing Act, Title VII of which required the Executive Branch to report biennially, rather than annually as recommended, on national growth and development. However, in regard to the establishment of a national growth policy, the reporting Committee on Community Development in its 1972 and 1974 reports agreed with the three principles asserted in the National Goals Research Staff's 1970 report as follows:[55]

That the process for formulating growth policies is long term, expansive, and evolutionary.

That our social, economic, and governmental systems are not conducive to the establishment of a single national policy on growth.

That it is essential to achieve greater policy coordination.

The New Communities Act of 1968 provides for the recommended assistance to the developers of new communities and implements several other of the recommendations in that regard. It does not, however, establish a new communities development program within the framework of coordinated national, state, and local growth plans and policies.

The second set of recommendations is concerned with the establishment of development agencies at the state and local levels with the power to ". . . assemble land, install public facilities, and plan for large-scale . . . development."[56] This mechanism, similar to that proposed by Reps earlier and that of Bain, would be used for urban renewal, peripheral development, and/or building satellite new communities in metropolitan areas. The further recommendation that these agencies be federally funded under a federally administered program finds its way into the later proposal by Canty, the editor of the Committee's report.

Commentary. Although this set of recommendations does not provide the details of a complete land use guidance system, it does propose a strong guidance tool in the establishment of local development agencies with the power to plan and undertake urban development and redevelopment. The recommendations concerning existing cities lack the extent of consideration given to those concerning new communities.

National Policy Task Force of the American Institute of Architects: 1972

The AIA Task Force Recommendations for a "National Growth Strategy" deals with both planning/policy issues and proposed mechanisms for land use guidance, summarized as follows:[57]

A. Scale and Form: The building and rebuilding of American communities should be planned and carried out at neighborhood scale (ca. 500–3,000 residential units along with a full range of essential facilities and services) and in a form appropriately called a "Growth Unit."

B. Priorities: The value most to be respected is free choice. First concern should be given the condition of those trapped in the poverty and deterioration of older neighborhoods, especially of the central cities.

C. Changes in the Ground Rules of Community Development:

Free choice should be expanded:

(1) by ensuring open occupancy throughout the entire development in central and peripheral areas of the metropolis.
(2) by directing needed housing subsidies to people rather than to structures.
(3) by providing locational options, especially by linking development in central and peripheral areas of the metropolis.
(4) by providing for diverse living styles, through Growth Units of varying densities, housing types, and service patterns; also, less restrictive building and zoning codes.
(5) by expanding the possibilities and scope of citizen participation in the design and governance of neighborhoods.

Financing patterns should be revised:

(1) less reliance should be placed on the local property tax.
(2) state and federal governments should assume a greater share of:
    a. infrastructure costs, and
    b. costs of social services, especially health, education and welfare.
(3) the appreciating value of land benefited by public investment should be recaptured and recycled into community facilities and services.
(4) categorical aids should be broadened—especially the Highway Trust Fund which should be expanded into a more general fund in support of community development.

Government structure should be reshaped and adapted:

(1) Private–public ventures should be encouraged.
(2) Development corporations should be created by federal, state and local governments.
(3) Metropolitan planning and development agencies should be encouraged.
(4) State governments should participate more directly in planning and regulating the use of land, especially in areas defined as

"critical" (e.g., flood plains, coastal regions, areas of acute housing shortages, and areas in the path of rapid development).

Capacity to build at neighborhood scale—both public and private—should be strengthened:

(1) Financial, legal, and other constraints should be reviewed and eased.
   a. A steady flow of mortgage money at low and stable rates should be ensured.
   b. "Front money" for Growth Unit development should be made available.
   c. Public investments in infrastructure should be properly phased and coordinated.
(2) State governments and metropolitan agencies should take a more assertive role in acquiring and preparing land for development—and in building a network of utility corridors to accommodate and give shape to Growth Units.
(3) Tax and other incentives and disincentives should be revised to encourage high quality urban development.
(4) Environmental controls and design standards should be strengthened.
(5) New patterns for the delivery of critical services should be encouraged.
(6) Industrialized building processes should be encouraged.
D. Special Program for Areas Impacted by Rapid Growth and Deterioration:

Priority should be given to the 65 metropolitan areas over 500,000 population.

Within these areas, the public should acquire and prepare one million acres for Growth Unit development.

This development should be explicitly designed to benefit not detract from, the improvement of the quality of life of those now residing in the older and deteriorating sections.

At average densities of 25 per acre, this special program should accommodate one-third of the expected growth of the U.S. population between 1970–2000.

Only those elements of the recommendations pertaining to land use guidance will be elaborated on and discussed.

The "Growth Unit" Concept. The Task Force goes on to say that the "growth units" might vary in size from 500–3,000 dwelling units and could be applied to renewal areas as well as to peripheral development and new communities. They would be the basic building blocks for all development and would be large enough to contain a good range of community facilities and to ". . . realize the economies of unified planning, land purchase and preparation, and the coordinated design of public spaces, facilities, and transportation."[58] In proposing the establishment of a minimum scale of development this recommendation is similar to those of the National Commission on Urban Problems (1968) and Downs (1970).

Changes in the Ground Rules of Community Development. Under *expansion of free choice*, recommendation (5) concerning citizen participation is an important guidance system element. It was a key element in Chapin's proposal and meets one of the criteria for guidance system completeness. The proposals for the creation of development corporations and for metropolitan planning and development agencies, (2) and (3) under *government structures* are consistent with the earlier proposals by Reps, Bain, and So and partially meet the criteria for completeness concerning an ongoing comprehensive planning process, an adequate array of implementation tools, and for coordination of local plans, policies, and implementation programs. Furthermore, in the detailed elaborations of the recommendations the Task Force covers fully the considerations necessary for meeting the guidance system completeness criteria.

Strengthening Capacity to Build. Recommendation (2) under this heading further expands on the role of state and local agencies in initiating development through land acquisition and provision of the infrastructure of utilities and community facilities necessary for development. Recommendations (3) and (4) under the same heading call for providing economic incentives and disincentives and strengthened land use controls in the interests of ensuring high quality urban development. Carrying out this recommendation would add to the effectiveness of the array of land use guidance tools.

Mechanisms. The elaboration on the mechanisms for carrying out metropolitan growth guidance plans and policies is worth further examination and comparison with the previous proposals. The relevant sections of the Task Force's suggestions concerning mechanisms are as follows:[59]

Execution of the Growth Unit concept requires governmental mechanisms or institutions. Their creation requires federal incentive legislation and state-enabling or institution-creating legislation. These mechanisms can be in several forms. Those discussed below are examples.

At the metropolitan scale, one needs a metropolitan planning and development agency to deal with the rebuilding of the wornout portions of the metropolitan area, with control over the direction and form of peripheral growth, and with building of the interstices, in-filling those areas leapfrogged by development.

The metropolitan planning and development agency should be responsive, in an electoral way, to the residents of the metropolitan area. Methods of election and representation would be determined by the interests of the individual state.

Although such a metropolitan planning and development agency should exercise the metropolitan planning function, it must also have authority, with teeth, to see that its development plan is actually carried out. Development follows urban umbilical cords—transportation, communications, and utilities. To direct growth, one must control the infrastructure. Thus, this agency must have authority over the location and timing of major infrastructure development—major roads, mass transit, major water and sewer lines, airports, open space, state and federal office buildings, publicly owned or financed hospitals, and any other public investment that influences economic development and determines the pattern and character of future urbanization.

The metropolitan planning and development agency must also have the authority of eminent domain to do the following
(1) acquire vacant, or quasi-vacant, land in the urbanized portion of the metropolitan area to encourage the building of Growth Units in these areas. This is the in-filling process.
(2) acquire land in the deteriorated portions of the metropolitan area at a scale to enable the building of Growth Units redevelopment.
(3) acquire land in the path of development to at least diminish speculation in land and to establish the character of future development.
(4) acquire raw land on the somewhat removed periphery of the urbanized area in order to build Growth Units or multiples of Growth Units.

Once such land is acquired, the planning and development agency should prepare broad-based plans for its development, install the necessary utilities and public facilities, and then lease or sell the land to those developers who agree to build in accordance with the prescribed plan and who also agree to provide housing for a specified spectrum of economic groups. The rate of land disposition should be geared to the rate of urban growth for the metropolitan area; and the metropolitan planning and development agency would, by this method of land acquisition and disposition, determine the pattern and character of future growth.

A metropolitan planning and development agency should be able through this process to acquire sufficient land so that the prices of its offerings keep in line the speculative land values of private holdings in other portions of the metropolitan area.

The metropolitan planning and development agency should also be given the authority over the location of housing for low- and moderate-income families. Real freedom of choice requires not only that there be housing for all races and income groups throughout the metropolitan area, but that it be in sufficient quantity to assure the actual availability of housing units.

Within the inner city, the metropolitan planning and development agency should concentrate on relatively long-range (15–20 years) Growth Unit development plans, recognizing that the transformation of inner-city areas takes time and that housing must be available prior to displacement if large-scale land acquisition and development are to take place. Emphasis should be on early installation of good public facilities, particularly schools, to improve the area's public investment character. When rebuilding takes place, it must be for all income groups and all races.

. . . .

In order to maintain control over development, the metropolitan planning and development agency should have control over all major (relatively large and large-scale) zoning decisions in the metropolitan area. There should be a uniform building code for the metropolitan area.

Such a metropolitan planning and development agency would not serve as a municipal government, carrying out normal municipal services such as police, fire, street repair, library services, etc. Existing political jurisdictions would continue their municipal, governmental functions, but they would be relieved of the functions previously itemized. In fact, one would hope for the establishment of some form of neighborhood, quasi-governmental institutions, within the central city, to deal with neighborhood municipal functions on a neighborhood (Growth Unit) scale.

And finally, but still most important, is the necessity of equalizing the property tax throughout the metropolitan area so as to remove locational bias for economic development.

The Task Force goes on to say that the public determination of where development takes place is essential and that while citizen participation is important it should not be translated into a veto power by the local citizens in renewal areas or suburban areas; that is, a minority of the citizens in an urban area should not be put in a position where they can prevent development which is in the general public interest. It also calls for better coordination of federal, state, and local development policies.

Commentary. The AIA Task Force recommendations constitute the basis for a very complete land use guidance system whose emphasis is on the concept of a basic unit of development having a minimum area, thus assuring more coordinated development, and on an elective metropolitan planning and development agency as the major implementation means. Although having different emphases, these recommendations are similar to those of the National Commission on Urban Problems but more detailed. On the other hand they are less detailed than Reps', especially in the area of economic incentives and compensation.

The Committee on Growth and the Environment of the International City Management Association: 1973

This Association has been very active in the field of urban planning as well as urban management. It has published the most comprehensive description of the many aspects of the planning process: *Principles and Practice of Urban Planning*, previously cited. The recommendations to be examined here were first published in the Association's monthly magazine, *Public Management*, in September 1973 and have just recently been reprinted in the Urban Land Institute's three-volume work, *Management and Control of Growth*.

Those recommendations bearing directly on planning and growth guidance at the various levels of government are as follows:[60]

To the profession:
  1. Managers and administrators should work with their governing bodies

in assessing their communities' growth program which includes a set of goals, directives, and objectives and a set of companion environmental standards. Assessment of needs should include peoples' attitudes toward the desirability of various levels of population growth as well as population projections, and the present and future capacities of city and county services and infrastructure (e.g., sewer and water systems, solid waste disposal facilities, transportation systems, recreational facilities, etc.).

Assessment also should include the cost of anticipated future growth in terms of higher levels of services and improvements of physical facilities. Further, assessment should consider peoples' physical and psychological tolerances for congestion and technical development designed to cope with pollution. From the assessment, managers should guide their councils in the adoption of a community growth program. The program should include desirable levels and rates of growth, ways to guide growth to those levels, and programs for meeting the cost of further growth.

2. Managers should see that desirable levels of growth are defined in terms of both the timing of growth and the area to be covered by future development. Community comprehensive plans often are expressed in terms of the population levels and land to be used at a given point in time, for instance the year 2000. Few plans explain how a community gets to year 2000. Few plans are timed or staged in any sense. Few say what the population and land use will,or should, be in 1975 . . . or 1980, 1985 and so on.

Managers should ensure that in the process of setting growth goals the goals are expressed first in terms of the timing of growth—the levels desired in 1975, 1980, 1985 and so on. Managers also should see that growth goals are expressed in more than aggregate numbers, but also in terms of the specific land on which the additional population and industry will be located. Specific areas for future growth also should be timed.

. . . .

3. In preparing community growth programs, managers should thoroughly investigate and utilize the available techniques of land use control or create new ones as tools for limiting growth.

4. Managers and administrators should recognize the critical interrelationship between capital projects and growth in communities. People follow sewers, roads, and other community facilities. The existence

and location of these facilities should be an integral part of any growth program. The absence of water and sewer facilities, for instance, will greatly retard growth, especially high density growth where septic tanks are ineffective.

Growth programs should not end with land use plans; they should be accompanied by capital programs and plans, which extend for at least five years and, if possible, longer. And, they should specify the phased development of capital facilities within a locality.

. . . .

5. Managers should create within the municipal attorney's office a division devoted to land use, the environment, and other growth related issues.

. . . .

6. Managers should propose policies that cause local land developers to pay the secondary costs of their development and construction.

. . . .

Programs which facilitate correct identification and apportionment of secondary growth costs include: (a) growth impact statements much like (but not necessarily as extensive in smaller communities) environmental impact statements, prepared by developers and city officials before construction is approved to determine secondary costs and effects; (b) public education programs to create greater awareness of the real cost as well as benefit of growth and development; (c) planned unit developments, an especially effective concept that requires inclusion of infrastructure as well as open space costs along with land use planning in new developments; (d) use privilege charges for utility tap-ins, to assure that new developments pay their fair share of the costs of existing and future community infrastructure; and (e) construction taxation on new buildings, as a percent of the cost of buildings, designed to reimburse cities and counties for secondary costs.

7. It is the responsibility of administrators to see that programs directed toward controlling or influencing growth do not erect barriers to equal access to community resources and amenities because of economic status, race, ethnic origin, or religion.

One of the greatest objections to local control of growth policy nationally has been that land use controls and other growth control programs tend to discriminate against persons because of race or economic status. Zoning ordinances have been struck down by the courts for this reason.

. . . .

To regional organizations:

8. In order to deal with growth, it is especially important that regional bodies be constituted as umbrella, multijurisdictional organizations, made up of at least a majority of locally elected officials, as recommended by the ICMA Committee on the Problems of Regionalism. The emphasis on multifunctional, multijurisdictional, locally controlled regional bodies permits local officials to have a major role in regional decision-making, not only in land use, but in many other areas related to growth regionally.

It is important that regional planning organizations encompass entire urbanized areas and their surrounding corridors for possible growth. Any smaller region will tend to diminish the effectiveness of regional planning and the input of local officials. In nonmetropolitan areas, it is anticipated that local officials will be working more closely with state officials in making growth-related decisions because of the greater state interest in the recreation facilities, roads, natural resources, and other statewide land uses in rural areas.

9. Regional bodies should seek to coordinate area development and local policies and programs related to growth and land use that have regional significance. Coordination should include determination of the implications of development in a given locality for the whole region, and the ability to recommend or reject such development depending upon its impact on the region. Coordination also should extend to the uniformity of utility service charges.

. . . .

10. Regional organizations should provide local governments with information and technical assistance that will enable them to make informed and rational growth decisions.

. . . .

To states:

11. States should act to protect the overall interests of citizens in the state with regard to land use, conservation of resources, and protection of the environment by the issuance of standards and guidelines for land use development and other aspects and growth.

. . . .

12. States should delegate growth policy coordination and development in urban regions to the umbrella, multijurisdictional organizations charged with land use and growth planning and policy development in the region. In urban areas, the major locational decisions of concern to states have either been made or are precluded because the land is already used. The remaining land use decisions relate to the use of the small amount of land available for development and the improvement of existing structures on the land. These decisions should be left to local determination with regional coordination.

13. States should provide local government with funds for planning and management, technical assistance, and information relevant to growth. The role of states should be one of overall guidance and support for essentially local decisions.

. . . .

14. States should enact legislation that permits local governments to assume a strong role in land use regulation. In many states, the failure of local government to control growth is due in part to a dearth of authority to act. Land use and taxation laws are too restrictive to permit local innovation. It is important that states provide local governments with maximum flexibility in terms of legislation to control growth effectively and in an innovative fashion.

To the federal government:

15. National concerns related to growth should be cared for through federal growth programs. Many needs are national when it comes to growth policies and the needs should be dealt with nationally.

. . . .

16. Existing and future federal programs should be consistent with efforts of local officials to manage growth. The inadvertent national growth policies, expressed through mortgage guarantees, transportation networks, environmental protection, and tax laws, must be reviewed seriously to remove their undesirable effect on local growth.

17. Funds should be provided to assist local planning and management of growth policy. The role of providing overall direction and support extends to the federal government as well as to the states. In this role, the federal government must seek to direct its funds to support local growth planning and implementation.

The first two recommendations deal with most of the essential elements of an ongoing comprehensive planning program. Especially noteworthy is the emphasis on stage development plans. The third recommendation is directed toward ensuring full use of planning implementation tools and the fifth is a related one directed toward ensuring adequate legal help in determining which implementation techniques are or would be likely to be viable in the courts. The fourth recommendation prescribes capital budgeting as one of the necessary planning tools. The sixth deals with requiring the developer to share in the costs of the infrastructure necessary for development to take place. This is usually set forth in subdivision regulations as was pointed out in the chapter on subdivision regulations. The sixth also deals with such other implementation tools as growth impact statements, public education programs, planned unit development, and financial features designed to help defray local government secondary costs in relation to new development. The seventh recommendation is a policy against guidance programs being misused to maintain racial or economic status exclusivity.

The next group of three recommendations, 8–10, have to do with the establishment and function of elective regional umbrella agencies to undertake regional planning and the coordination of growth guidance. These agencies would be limited to dealing with development of regional significance over which they would have a veto power, to coordinating planning within their areas together with coordinating it with the plans and policies of higher levels of government, and to providing planning assistance to their constituent local governments. This proposal falls short of the previously discussed proposals for regional agencies in that the umbrella agency would not have land acquisition and development powers.

The next four recommendations, 11–14, are directed to state governments calling on them to prepare standards and guidelines for development, to delegate the power necessary to coordinate growth policies and development in urban areas to the proposed umbrella agencies, to provide local governments with economic and technical assistance for planning and growth management, and to strengthen the local planning implementation controls together with allowing for more innovative techniques. This group of recommendations is consistent with all of the previously examined land use guidance system proposals and recommendations to the extent that they deal with action on behalf of the states.

The last three recommendations examined (ICMA recommendations to its own organization are omitted here because they do not deal directly with growth guidance) are directed to the federal government and call for national growth programs internally consistent at the federal level and also consistent with local growth guidance efforts. Federal financial assistance for and overall direction of local planning and growth guidance is also recommended. The content of the "national growth programs" called for is not specified nor is the extent of the federal government's "overall direction," so it is difficult to compare these recommendations for federal involvement in urban growth guidance with those of Canty, the National Commission on Urban Problems, the National Committee on Urban Growth Policy, and the AIA Task Force except to say that the ICMA Committee does not seem to ask for as strong a role for the federal government in growth guidance as do the others.

Commentary. Under this proposal the growth guidance activities would be divided between regional multifunctional, multijurisdictional agencies whose directing boards, like councils of governments, would be composed of local elected officials. What functions other than regional planning would be undertaken by these agencies is not made clear. This proposal for urban growth guidance meets the criteria for completeness in regard to planning. It implies an adequate array of implementation tools without specifying them in detail. It does require the tools to be integrated in a growth guidance program. It provides for coordination of local government guidance activities by the regional agency and for coordination with the plans and policies of higher levels of government. It does not deal with citizen participation but provides for local political input to the regional agencies. And, finally, it calls for taking advantage of all implementation means available through a carefully coordinated program. Except for the indicated omissions the recommendations, if followed, would bring about fairly complete growth guidance systems as measured by the criteria for completeness.

Advisory Commission on Intergovernmental Relations: 1973.

The key aspects of the ACIR recommendations were introduced in the previous chapter. The recommendations themselves are too lengthy to quote here in their entirety but the central ideas will be presented and examined.

The first recommendation deals with federal assistance programs of all types which ". . . encourage or mandate areawide planning, programming coordination, and/or districting . . ."[61] It would require that these programs rely on an officially designated multijurisdictional umbrella organization (UMJO) in each substate region as the basic policy-developing, comprehensive and functional planning and, where empowered, implementing institution for reviewing federal grant applications and guiding and/or undertaking urban development. Funding areas for the ten federal programs listed in the previous chapter would be brought into boundary conformance for areawide planning and development. Funding of the separate grant programs would be combined into a single support grant for each of the UMJO's. The regional agency would also review and resolve differences in the plans and policies of local governments, the region, and state agencies in regard to grant applications before submitting them to the federal agency or agencies concerned.

The second recommendation begins as follows:[62]

The Commission recommends that the governors and legislatures of all applicable States, after appropriate and adequate consultation with representatives of units of general local government and their respective State associations, develop and enact a consistent, comprehensive statewide policy to provide a common framework and a clear set of State and local purposes for existing and future substate regional planning, programming, coordination, and districting undertaking.

This is then elaborated on, with a description of the minimum set of objectives. These include developing methods of determination and procedures for establishing and revising UMJO district boundaries; requiring the involvement of UMJO's in relation to state administered programs; establishing a process for state conference of legal status on UMJO's; adopting a membership formula for UMJO governing boards requiring state representation on them (at least sixty percent of the board members being required to be elected officials from the constituent local governments); devising an equitable voting procedure taking into account the size of population represented by the various board members; requiring each UMJO to adopt and publish regional plans and policies including implementation programs, requiring systematic regional inputs to the state planning and budgeting process; designation by the state of its UMJO's as the A-95 clearinghouses for their respective areas; endowing UMJO's with the power to review state plans, policies, and projects directly affecting their respective areas; assigning to UMJO's a policy controlling role in respect to multijurisdictional special districts within their respective boundaries; provision of state financial assistance to the UMJO's, and establishment of gubernatorial veto power over UMJO actions found to be in conflict with official state plans and policies having statewide impact or in conflict with the plans and policies of other affected UMJO's. This recommendation takes into account that the states are in a key position in regard to the establishment of adequate mechanisms for planning and development at the substate regional level and regardless of federal policies should take the initiative in creating the necessary institutions.

Recommendation three is directed at local governments urging that they support the formation of UMJO's as a vehicle for local participation in areawide planning, programming, and coordination of development, that they make regular financial contribution to these institutions, that they make maximum use of them for regional policy making, that they fully recognize their officially adopted plans and policies in guiding their own local planning and policy making, and that local governments through their representation on UMJO boards should seek to have the UMJO's designated as the official policy making bodies for their respective areas. Active and effective participation of all local governments in the work of the regional planning UMJO is the general purpose of this recommendation. It is recognized here that state mandating alone cannot bring into being an effective regional planning and policy making process.

Recommendation four deals with local and federal action to create UMJO's if the states fail to take the initiative in creating them. It provides for local governments representing at least two thirds of the population in a proposed substate region joining in a petition for such a regional agency to be enabled under federal policy to designate their own UMJO and be granted the same rights and benefits which are conferred by state-adopted districting systems. The Commission observed that at the time of making its recommendations at least six states had not yet adopted substate districting legislation and that most of such legislation passed was less comprehensive than they proposed in their second recommendation. Their proposal would not preempt state initiatives and would be in accord with the provisions of such federal legislation as the Water Pollution Control and Coastal Zone Management statutes of 1972.

Recommendation five is concerned with joint federal-state-local strategies in regard to UMJO's in *interstate* metropolitan areas because after studying the situation, the Commission concluded that the unique problems of these areas had been given inadequate attention by the states and federal government. The recommendation proposes the following: that all three levels of government join in an agreed strategy leading to the establishment of a single interstate UMJO in each interstate metropolitan area; that the affected states ". . . recognize in their substate districting the existence and integrity of interstate metropolitan areas . . ."[63] when delineating the boundaries of these districts; that the President initiate changes in Office of Management and Budget Circular A-95 review requirements, so that in interstate metropolitan areas the officially designated UMJO's boundaries and its policy review would be recognized for all federally assisted planning, programming, coordination, and districting programs; that ". . . the affected states initiate and Congress . . . approve amendments to all interstate compacts . . ."[64] in interstate metropolitan areas conferring on the UMJO the power to review and approve all capital programming and projects of interstate compact bodies within its boundaries; that the Intergovernmental Cooperation Act of 1968 be amended to give the interstate UMJO's the power to approve or disapprove all federal grant applications from all units of local government including special districts within their respective boundaries; that all three levels of government join in drafting interstate compacts defining the legal status, membership formula, functions and powers of interstate UMJO's; and that the federal government and affected states make adequate provision for the financial support of interstate UMJO's.

Commentary. The recommendations of the Advisory Commission on Intergovernmental Affairs are directed toward the coordination of regional planning, policies, and implementation programs. They are directed toward achieving integrated areawide development. The instrumentality recommended for planning and development guidance at the substate regional level is the umbrella multijurisdictional organization (UMJO), a multifunctional special district (public authority) having power at the regional level to effect coordination of all regionally significant plans, policies, and implementation programs of local governmental entities within its jurisdiction, and state or federal programs as they affect the region within the context of officially adopted regional plans, policies, and implementation programs. Also a complete, continuing comprehensive planning process at the regional level is recommended with plans, policies, and programs (including implementation programs) having a range of time horizons.

The array of planning tools recommended includes the organizational tool of the UMJO itself, the review of all local grant applications for state and federal funds with the power to approve or disapprove them, the right to review state and local capital expenditure programs as they affect the region for conformance with regional implementation programs and the responsibility for resolving conflicts between them, and the right (where enabled by state) to regulate development of regional significance and to deliver various substate services. This array of planning tools, being directed only at regional planning is not complete enough for detailed land use guidance, the latter function being left in the hands of the local governments. In this respect the ACIR would accord less control to the regional agencies than the other organizations whose recommendations have been previously examined here. Unlike ACIR the other organizations explicitly recommend that the regional agency engage directly in land acquisition and development activities as a principal guidance technique as Reps, Bain, and Canty also recommend.

Implementation programs are central to the ACIR recommendations and it is made clear that taking full advantage of the tools available and acceptable to the community would be necessary.

The ACIR recommendations are very strong in the areas of coordination of the planning and development activities of all levels of government. Although participation in the planning process of citizens and civic groups is not dealt with explicitly, the participation of local elected officials through their membership on the directing boards of the UMJOs is an essential part of the proposals.

The ACIR recommendations provide for most of the guidance system elements described at the beginning of the chapter but they lack explicit provisions for detailed control of development and provision for direct public participation in the development process.

The American Law Institute Model Land Development Code: 1975

Not since the *Standard Zoning Enabling Act* and the *Standard City Planning Act* prepared by the United States Department of Commerce in the 1920s has there been a nationally promulgated and accepted model act to serve in the revision of the largely outdated state planning and land use controls enabling acts until the recent effort by the American Law Institute in cooperation with planners and others interested in the guidance of land development. Begun in the 1960s and adopted by the ALI in May 1975,[65] the draft adopted is organized as follows: it is divided into twelve articles dealing with general provisions, power to regulate development, local land development planning, discontinuance of existing land uses, acquisition and disposition of land, land banking, state land development regulation, state land development planning, judicial review, enforcement of land development regulations, public records of development regulations, financing and coordination of governmental development and transitional material.

Because of the difficulty of including consideration of social and economic planning, building codes, fire codes, housing codes, health codes, taxation, and the effects of federal environmental legislation on land development, this code is confined to considering ". . . that part of the whole which seems to have most directly the objective of coordinating physical development."[66]

Article 1, General Provisions, starts with a statement of purpose as follows:[67]

It is the legislative purpose to protect the land, air, water, natural resources and environment of this state, to encourage their use in a socially and economically desirable manner, and to provide a mechanism by which the state may establish and carry out a state land use policy, including,

(1) the designation of the local governments of this State as the primary authorities for planning and regulating development in this State according to a system of uniform statewide procedural standards:

(2) authorization of the acquisition and disposition of land development having a significant impact beyond the boundaries of a single local government or affecting an area of critical state concern;

(3) provision for state review of decisions involving land development having a significant impact beyond the boundaries of a single local government or affecting an area of critical state concern;

(4) encouragement for the adoption of local and state Land Development Plans to guide the use of land, water, and natural resources of this State;

(5) establishment of a system of administrative and judicial review of local and state land use decisions which encourages both effective citizen participation and prompt resolution of disputes;

(6) provision of fair and efficient means for enforcement of land development regulations including the discontinuance of existing uses;

(7) establishment of a system for permanently recording development regulations and decisions in a manner that will enable the most efficient and accurate dissemination of this information;

(8) the encouragement of cooperation among governmental agencies to help achieve land use policy goals, and

(9) provision that financial support for capital improvements be made in accordance with state and local land use policy.

This statement is intended to make clear that the Code is concerned with the process by which public purposes within the concept of "general welfare" are brought to bear on land and people.

Article 1 authorizes each local government, as defined by the Code to plan and regulate or undertake land development in accordance with the Code. It also provides a list of definitions for use in interpreting the rest of the Code precisely. Here the most significant definition is that of "development" as meaning ". . . the performance of any building or mining operation, the making of any material or land, the division of land into two or more parcels, and the creation or termination of rights of access or riparian rights".[68] This definition is more in line with the language of British planning law than with American legislative use of the term. It brings zoning and subdivision regulation together in dealing with a common subject and paves the way for "development permission" to be concerned with either or both, and to include esthetics among other things.

Article 2, entitled "Local Land Development Regulations," enables the enactment by local governing bodies of a "development ordinance" combining most of the features of zoning and subdivision ordinances. It provides for the granting of "development permits" for all uses permitted as a right in given areas and for "special development permits" where the Land Development Agency (LDA) in accordance with specified criteria may exercise discretionary powers in granting such permits to which the Agency may attach conditions designed to make the development compatible with adjacent development and in conformance with the Land Development Plan.

The conditions for granting "special development permits" include compliance with approved plans, land subdivision, time limitations for starting and completing development, hours of use, intensity of use, sequence of development, duration of use and removal of structures (nonconforming uses), assurance of proper maintenance, location and nature of use, the supplying of detailed records (maps, plats, specifications, drawings), deeding of land for streets, utilities, parks and open space, or monetary equivalents.

The Article allows "special development permits" to be used for historic and esthetic preservation, for planned unit development, for "specially planned areas" (for LDA planned fringe development and urban renewal), for handling exceptions involving minor variations for exceptional parcels, for minor incremental revisions of district boundary lines, for necessary community service facilities, and for other specified special circumstances.

The Article provides for the administration of development regulations, including organization of the Land Development Agency, a description of its powers, a description of its procedures and functions, provision for hearings and a citizen participation, and a description of its decision-making process.

Donald Hagman observes that the Code's first two articles owe an unacknowledged debt to British planning law and represent ". . . a highly desirable wedding of Anglo-American practices".[69]

Article 3, entitled "Local Land Development Planning," deals with the process of land use planning and natural resource conservation. Although it requires that social and economic effects of land use plans be taken into account, the emphasis is on land use. The Article specifies that the Local Land Development Plan include ". . . information concerning present problems and conditions, . . . future probabilities if present trends continue, and statements of objectives, policies, and standards to solve the stated problems and to set forth desired patterns of development. . . . The Plan must also include a specific 'short term' program of public action to move in the direction of long term goals."[70] Also the Plan must ". . . be prepared to withstand a test in court in regard to its reasonableness or its appropriateness and completeness in relation to any particular governmental action which may later be taken . . ."[71] Further, the interagency review and adoption is outlined and the preparation of periodic reports of progress on plan implementation and effects is mandated.

Article 4, entitled "Discontinuance of Existing Land Uses", provides a means of eliminating uses which are clearly harmful or incompatible in any particular district. The Article covers the designation of land uses to be discontinued, the grounds for requiring discontinuance, and enforcement procedures. The concept in conventional zoning of "nonconforming uses" has been dropped as questionable and, in any case, ineffective. In its place this Article starts with a new premise: ". . . that existing uses of land should be encouraged to conform to new land development regulations only if those regulations embody a policy that a specifically defined neighborhood character should be maintained over a substantial period of time . . ." and ". . . the power to eliminate existing uses for failure to comply with development regulations should be limited to situations where such a policy exists."[72] The order to discontinue land uses must be based on careful land use planning to be valid. Payment of compensation need be made only ". . . where the agency feels that the elimination of existing uses would impose too great a burden on the property owner."[73] Offensive uses in areas for which there is no detailed plan may be required to be discontinued if not permitted as new uses and no official plan or policy indicates that the uses would be compatible with adjacent uses.

Article 5, "Acquisition and Disposition of Land," gives consideration to ". . . the use of the power to acquire land *for the purpose of securing land development in the manner proposed by the development objectives of the community*."[74] It consolidates in one article the grants of eminent domain usually scattered among a large number of state statutes. The Article describes the powers and purposes for land acquisition, the acquisition of land for large-scale development, procedural requirements for land acquisition, and the disposition of land held for planning purposes.

New among the purposes for using eminent domain is its use to encourage large-scale development in the interest of overcoming the lack of coordination and costs of sprawl involved in incremental piecemeal development. (As previously mentioned this was suggested by Anthony Downs in his book, *Urban Problems and Prospects*).[75]

Land could be acquired for the discontinuance of existing uses, to facilitate development, for conservation of "Specially Planned Areas," to provide replacement land or facilities, and for preservation of landmarks and "Special Preservation Districts."[76] Eminent domain also may be exercised extraterritorially subject to specified limitations.

The section on "Land Acquisition for Large Scale Development" spells out the public purposes for which this may be done, the eligibility of repurchase applications, and related administrative procedures. The following section covers general procedural requirements including the effect of local regulations in condemnation, application of the law of eminent domain, assumptions regarding development permission, valuation of temporary interest and acquisition of land from public employees.

The last section on "Disposition of Land Held for Public Purposes" defines planning purposes, describes the provisions for land disposition, discusses the conditions regarding covenants, disposal price, methods of disposition, and other restrictions regarding disposition.

Article 6, Land Banking, provides for a "State Land Reserve Agency," sets forth its general powers and obligations, deals with the acquisition and disposition of land, and describes the participation of local governments in the "Land Reserve System."

Rather than vesting the land reserve function directly in a local government or metropolitan agency as suggested by Reps[77] and others, it follows Abrams' proposal to vest land acquisition in the state.[78]

The public purpose outlined for the agency includes the ". . . purpose of achieving the land policy and land planning objectives . . . of the state and authorizes various means of financing land acquisition as being a ". . . valid public purpose."[79] The organization of the agency as a part of state government and the authorization of one or more advisory committees are dealt with. The agency is required to adopt a land reserve policy which is not inconsistent with a "State Land Development Plan".

Under the part concerning powers and obligations ". . . the land reserve agency is treated for administrative purposes as an office within a general state agency. Its powers granted under this Article are analogous to those of a large public corporation."[80] In addition to the management of land holdings, the agency's tax status is delineated.

The part on land acquisition sets forth the purposes of acquisition, the methods of acquisition, the method of payment for land acquired and the grant of condemnation powers to the agency.

The part on land disposition also outlines general provisions relating land banking to state law and other parts of the Model Code and prescribes legal procedures including required public notice and limitations on legal contest of the actions of the agency.

The part on participation of local governments in the land reserve system details the powers of local government participation as including the power to raise funds for making land purchases through the state agency, and the power to contract with the state agency. It also describes the process for local governments in requesting and securing and disposal of agency land holdings in the interest of the local governments concerned.

Article 7, State Land Development Regulation, ". . . is designed to assist the states in finding a workable method for state and regional involvement in land development regulation."[81] It is not intended that the state become involved in that detailed local development control which more properly is of local concern but only to ". . . those decisions involving important state or regional interest . . ."[82] The Article is divided into parts dealing with general provisions, areas of critical state concern, development of regional impact, analysis of overall impact of development, and appeals to a state land adjudicatory board.

The general provisions deal with the subordination of local development regulation and procedures to the state regulation and procedures in the cases where state control is superimposed in accordance with this Article. They also set standards for exempting regions or development from state control.

The part dealing with areas of "critical state concern" establishes criteria for designating critical areas, requirements for public notice and public hearings in connection with designating critical areas, the establishment of interim control of development while regulations for designated areas are adopted, adoption of local land development regulations consistent with state plans and policies for critical areas, the adoption of state regulations binding on local government for critical areas where the local governments fail within six months after designation to adopt adequate regulations, the amendment of regulations and notification to the State Land Planning Agency by the local Land Development Agency of development applications in areas of critical state concern.

An area of critical state concern may be designated only, if according to the Code, it is:[83]

(a) an area significantly affected by, or having a significant effect upon, an existing or proposed major public facility or other area of major public investment;

(b) an area containing or having a significant impact upon historical, natural or environmental resources of regional or statewide importance;

(c) a proposed site of a new community designated in a State Land Development Plan, together with a reasonable amount of surrounding land; or

(d) any land within the jurisdiction of a local government that, at any time more than (3 years) after the effective date of this Code, has no development ordinance in effect.

Because many areas may need protection before the State Land Development Plan can be properly prepared, designation can be justified by the other reasons cited above. Only in the case of new communities is the adoption of the state plan a prerequisite.

The part dealing with "development of regional impact" requires the State Land Planning Agency to adopt rules defining ". . . categories of development which, because of the nature or magnitude of the development or . . . its effect on the surrounding environment, is likely in the judgment of the Agency to present issues of state or regional significance."[84] And in adopting these rules the Agency must take into consideration:[85]

(a) The extent to which the development would create or alleviate environ mental problems such as air or water pollution or noise;
(b) The amount of pedestrian or vehicular traffic likely to be generated;
(c) The number of persons likely to be residents, employees, or otherwise present;
(d) The size of the site to be occupied;
(e) The likelihood that additional or subsidiary development will be generated; and
(f) The unique qualities of particular areas of the state.

These rules may vary from area to area according to differing local conditions.

This part also provides for "Development of Regional Benefit," allowing developers to proceed under the same rules as for development of regional impact if their development qualifies as:[86]

(a) development by a governmental agency other than the local government that created the Land Development Agency or another agency created solely by that local government.
(b) development which will be used for charitable purposes, including religious or educational facilities, and which serves or is intended to serve a substantial number of persons who do not reside within the boundaries of the local government creating the Land Development Agency;
(c) development by a public utility which is or will be employed to a substantial degree to provide services in an area beyond the territorial jurisdiction of the local government creating the Land Development Agency; and
(d) development of housing for persons of low and moderate income.

Development may be undertaken under this article only if within local jurisdiction having adopted a development ordinance in accordance with the Code or if the developer by notifying the State Land Planning Agency has ". . . given it an opportunity to appoint a Land Development Agency . . ."[87]

This part goes on to describe "Special Development Procedures for Development of Regional Impact," and standards for granting development permits.

The fourth part deals with the "Analysis of Overall Impact of Development" including the balance of benefits and detriments, the consideration of other relevant factors and the character of related geographic areas, and the requirements for reporting the results of the analysis. The externalities generated by the development and its relationship to the State Development Plan are among the factors to be considered.

Part five deals with "Appeals to State Land Adjudicatory Board." It sets forth the requirements and procedures for the establishment of such a board, describes how appeals to it must be made, what decisions must or may be made, and the procedures for the Board making rules or issuing orders. By establishing an appeals board at the state level this Article would create a board dealing exclusively with land use with the hope of it developing a more consistent and informed body of land use decisions than result now from appeals to the regular courts.

Article 8, State Land Development Planning, deals with the establishment of a state land planning agency, the enumeration of its powers, official mapping for the reservation of land for governmental agencies, the content of state land development plans, local planning assistance, and the establishment of a long-range planning institute.

The part concerning the state land planning agency provides for its creation and organization within the executive office of the Governor, for the establishment of regional planning divisions where deemed desirable, and for the establishment of state and regional advisory committees at the Governor's option.

The part concerning general powers grants the state agency the power to adopt rules and issue orders; the power to engage in land use educational programs; the power to intervene in judicial and administrative procedures in issues related to the Code; the power to issue rules concerning local administrative procedures; the power to regulate fees and forms for required public recordation; the power to appoint and establish training for hearing examiners; the power to appoint local land development agencies under conditions specified in the Code; the power to engage in interstate planning, and the requirement that the agency publish a weekly land development notice listing applications for permits concerning development proposals or changes in regulations.

The part about official mapping provides for the adoption of an official map under specified conditions, for the granting of development permission in designated areas under specified conditions, and the expiration of designation of reserved land not covered by the short-term program of actions in the state land development plan.

The part concerning state land development plans describes the state plan and its regional components, requires statements of objectives, policies, and standards for such plans, requires consideration of local and state agency plans in their formulation, requires a short-term program and provides for the adoption of state land use plans.

The local planning assistance part of the Article authorizes the state land planning agency to furnish planning assistance to local governments and other government agencies. It also provides for state agency review and comment on local land development and for the promulgation of rules specifying the date, projections, and forecasts which must be used in the preparation of plans reviewed by the state agency.

The last part of this article provides for the creation within the state planning agency, or affiliated with a state university, of an independent long-range planning institute to undertake or contract for research in support in the state's long-range planning activities.

Article 9, Judicial Review of Orders, Rules, and Ordinances, describes the necessary circumstances and eligibility of persons for seeking relief in the courts concerning land development decisions. The article ". . . prescribes a method of judicial review of all actions that may be taken under this Code: legislative ordinances, administrative rule making, and administrative orders issued with or without an adjudicatory type of hearing."[88] It also describes the basis for relief and the type of relief available and provides for appeals from court decisions.

Article 10, Enforcement of Local Land Development Regulations, contains general enforcement provisions and procedures for giving notice and ordering enforcement. It outlines the procedures for local government and for enforcement by other qualified parties. It outlines the issuance of enforcement notices, the holding of hearings, provisions for entry to correct violations, and provisions for noncompliance fines.

Article 11, Public Records of Development Regulations, deals with orders, rules, and ordinances affecting specific parcels, with generally applicable plans, rules, and ordinances, and with the duties of the state land planning agency in regard to public records. This Article is devoted to the details of maintaining adequate public land development records.

Article 12, Financing and Coordination of Governmental Development, deals with the undertaking and coordination of governmental development. It authorizes governmental expenditures for land development, enables joint and cooperative action between government agencies, requires compliance with local development ordinances and conformance to state land development plans, establishes conditions on capital grants, and establishes the State Land Development Plan as the basis for governmental agencies and regulated public utilities to estimate future service needs.

In addition to the twelve articles, the Code has a section concerning the transitional problems of implementing the Code including the effective date, relationship to existing law, and repeal of enactments it replaces.

Commentary. This Code, the first attempt in nearly fifty years to draft comprehensive state enabling legislation affecting land use planning and management, is deserving of careful evaluation. The committee of the American Institute of Planners which reviewed it observed that: "While the Code does suffer some deficiencies . . . it does offer a starting point for those legislatures considering a state level land use program," and, "It could well serve as a useful compilation of some of the basic constituent parts of a standard land use act . . ."[89] However, because it is limited to establishing a framework for a new relationship for state and local participation in the land use decision-making process, it does not offer ". . . a comprehensive state land use program responsive to all the needs of the human environment."[90]

This commentary on the ALI Model Land Development Code consists of a summary of the AIP review of the Code followed by general conclusions concerning the Code's potential for the establishment of land use guidance systems.

Summary of AIP Review.[91] AIP national planning policy is much broader than the Code and addresses all of the main issues raised by it with the exception of Land Banking. Otherwise, AIP Planning policy is considered by the reviewers as providing guidance for the issues raised by the Code in the drafting of state land use legislation. The AIP discussion deals with: "1) what development is controlled; 2) who manages the development; and 3) what comprises the decision-making process under the Code."[92]

1. The "development" to be managed is comprised of tangible and intangible activities including most (tangible) land uses except agriculture (a shortcoming in view of AIP policies regarding the best development for rural lands) and (intangible) development activities such as land subdivision and the creation of access rights. The Code includes regulation of private and public development not including unimproved public lands. Except for reducing or eliminating the ability to control wildlife preserves under the Code, this provision is consistent with the AIP policy.

The ALI Code provides for coordination of public facilities related to the development of land acquired in Specially Planned Areas (e.g. urban renewal areas) and for Large Scale Development. This is consistent with AIP policies for these kinds of development.

Under the Code, land development regulations must be supported by necessary studies and programs, but the Code is deliberately limited to dealing with regulatory devices and land acquisition. In view of broader AIP policies this may pose the problem that ". . . in adopting the ALI model and repealing the existing broadly constructed statutes . . . the legal support for contemporary development guidance systems . . ." may be eliminated.[93]

Although providing for state and local land development plans, the lack of a more comprehensive planning requirement going beyond "functional" planning has the effect of limiting the scope of considerations on which land use planning will be based at the expense of concern for social, economic, cultural, and environmental factors. Such limitation is contrary to AIP policies in regard to the scope of comprehensive planning.

2. "Management of land development under the Code is based on the premise ". . . that total localism in land use control is no longer possible or desirable."[94] Although under the Code most land use decisions would be made by local governments, the state, ". . . under a State Planning Agency, sets standards to which local regulations must conform"[95] in "Areas of Critical State Concern" and "Development of

Regional Impact" and provides an administrative appeals board for settling controversies concerning these areas. These Code provisions are in conformance with relevant AIP policies.

The management functions of the state under the Code may be exercised directly or through unspecified types of *regional divisions of the state planning agency*. This excludes the Council of Governments type of regional planning agency and is contrary to AIP policies calling for flexibility in forms of regional organization.

The Code would substitute administrative decision-making based on legislative standards for the case by case legislative decision-making now prevalent and is in accordance with AIP policy. This of course, presupposes the existence of adequate legislation dealing with the competence and ethics of administrative personnel.

Planning is optional at the state and local levels under the Code, but the Code grants certain extra land use control powers where there is a land use plan. This is contrary to AIP policy specifying both mandatory planning and land use regulation. The failure of the Code to make land use planning mandatory is the most important issue raised by AIP which presented its case strongly to ALI but was unable to obtain the requested changes. There is also a failure in the Code to clearly fix responsibility for coordinating functional and comprehensive plans as called for by AIP policy.

3. "Decision-making" under the Code entails many significant changes from prevailing practices. Those aspects of decision-making under the Code which are in accordance with AIP policies include the provisions that require most local land use controls to be consolidated into a single ordinance document incorporating the standards for making land use decisions, that potentially reduce the level of political land use decisions-making in favor of professionally administered, legislatively determined, general standards (except, possibly, where the local governing body declares *itself* under the Code to be the "land development agency"); for flexible procedures and standards for large scale development; that state and local public development shall be subject to the same standards and procedures as private development; that recognize the state has a legitimate interest in land use decision-making in large scale developments having significant impact beyond the local jurisdiction(s) within which they are located.

Those aspects of decision-making under the Code not in accordance with AIP policies are the failure of the Code to mandate adoption of a plan as a prerequisite for any level of government exercising land use controls except for planned unit developments and specially planned areas, the failure of the Code to make planning an integral part of the land use decision-making process except as noted above, and the failure of the Code to be truly comprehensive.

The AIP Code reviewers go on to point out some of the "dramatic shifts" in the Code away from prevailing land use decision-making standards and procedures such as: the abandonment of much of traditional land use terminology, including the term variance, special exception, nonconforming use and permitted use; the new procedures with their emphasis on professionalism in decision-making; the avoidance of defining the role of local governing bodies in individual land use decisions except when made under specified conditions providing for authorization of development by "special amendment;" the local "land development agency" being not only a planning and administrative body but a quasi-legislative body with the power to make rules and a quasi-judicial body with the power of review; the vesting in the "land development agency" of the authority to exercise wide discretion in making decisions concerning development; the procedures providing for designated neighborhood organizations to participate in administrative hearings; the provision for joint hearings where multiple permits are required, and the recapture for the state of previously delegated land use decision-making power in areas of state and regional concern.

AIP Review Conclusions. The AIP review of the ALI Model Land Development Code comparing its provisions to adopted AIP planning policies indicates Code strengths and weaknesses from the reviewers' professional planning points of view. The concern here, however, is with the extent to which the Code provides for or would inhibit complete land use guidance systems at the local and regional levels meeting the criteria previously established.

Although planning is not mandated by the Code, it is both enabled and encouraged at the local, regional, and state levels. At the local level land use planning is intended to be comprehensive, taking into account the social, economic, and environmental factors necessary for establishing the desired ". . . sequence, patterns, and characteristics of future development," together with a short range plan and an implementation program.[96] Although the prescribed planning studies are primarily physical and demographic, the phrases "or other appropriate characteristics" and "any other matter found to be important to future development" would seem to enable a broad planning endeavor provided the studies undertaken had some input to land use planning. The state and regional development planning is similar in scope both in regard to the breadth of studies as they affect land use and the requirement for long- and short-range plans. Undertaking social and economic planning unrelated to land use would probably require separate enabling legislation because they are beyond the scope and intent of the Code.

The land development regulations together with land banking provide for a wide array of land use guidance controls and techniques meeting the criterion for implementation controls. The integration of controls in a single set of Development Regulations and the coordination of implementation into a single program satisfies two other guidance system criteria.

Under the Code the state, directly or through its regional agencies, would have the power to coordinate the plans, policies, and implementation programs of local governments, and take into account the plans, policies, and programs of all levels of government.

Except for provision for participation in local planning of the previously mentioned neighborhood organizations and for required public hearings the Code is weak in regard to participation by elected officials, civic and professional groups, citizens organizations, and individual citizens. The means for achieving local acceptability for implementation programs is in doubt under the Code.

Although the Code is in many ways a great improvement over the Standard Acts on which most state planning enabling legislation is based, it has some serious shortcomings. Its provisions for state and regional intervention in the planning process are salutory as are the provisions for land use controls and land banking but the provisions for regional and local planning lack appropriate accountability and adequate citizen participation. The provisions for giving more discretionary authority to professional planning administrators within the limits of legislated standards would increase the flexibility of the decision-making process and, hopefully, expedite it, but the elimination of planning commissions or other advisory bodies, especially those composed of elected officials, might make securing support for planning and policies implementation more difficult.

As the AIP review committee observed, the Code is a good beginning for a basic revision of the land development guidance process and as will be seen in the next section, some states have already adopted variations on those parts of the Code dealing with state and regional planning.

Comparative Summary

Although there is considerable variation in emphasis and detail among the organizational recommendations just examined, there are many common threads running through them.

Except for the American Law Institute whose Code is directed only at the state and lower levels of government, all of these organizations recommend continuing or accelerated federal financial assistance for planning at the state, regional and local levels. Most of them also call for the establishment of national growth policies and more effective coordination of federal programs as they affect regional and local development.

All cited organizations call for increased participation by the states in regional and local development through local planning assistance programs, the establishment of state plans, policies, and guidelines for development, state intervention in regional and/or local planning and plan implementation where specified circumstances warrant, and the passage of state planning enabling legislation strengthening and allowing for more flexible regional and local development controls and other implementation techniques.

Regional umbrella organizations for coordinating planning and development are called for by all of the cited organizations. The employment of public land acquisition for conservation and the guidance of development is also recommended by all of these organizations except ACIR and ICMA, usually to be exercised for a variety of purposes by state, regional, and local units of government.

The major feature of the recommendations by the National Committee on Urban Growth Policy is the large scale development of satellite and independent new communities after the British example. This would also be possible under the recommendations of the AIA

Task Force and the ALI Code though is not central to them. Establishment of a minimum scale for new development is a salient feature of the AIA and National Commission on Urban Problems recommendations and is implied in some of the others.

This body of recommendations demonstrates the significant attempt of major professional and governmental organizations to come to terms with the pressing need for strengthening and improving public control of land uses and the coordinated guidance of physical development.

INNOVATIVE STATE REFORMS IN LAND USE LEGISLATION

In recent years there has been innovative state legislation in the field of land use controls, some of which was prompted by related national legislation. The Council on Environmental Quality reported in late 1974 that ". . . forty-eight states have now enacted legislation or are seriously studying proposals to expand the previously limited role of state government in the regulation of land use."[97] Some states have enacted broad state control over land use decisions in coastal zones, wetlands, and other areas of ecological importance. Some have concentrated on "areas of critical state concern" and "development of regional impact" as proposed in the ALI Model Land Development Code. Still others have established regional bodies to deal with land use problems in particular areas within their states.

The state legislation to be described here was selected for its pioneering innovation, its range of differing concerns (as described in the previous paragraph), and its contrasting legal and administrative approaches. A comparison of the examples reveals their significance in contributing to the improvement of land use guidance systems. State-wide legislative examples precede those affecting particular regions where this difference is distinguishable.

Hawaii: 1961

The rise of development pressures, scarcity of buildable land, desire to protect agriculture and avoid urban sprawl, and the need to conserve its scenic assets all combined to produce a political situation in which the Hawaii Land Use Law was passed in 1961.[98] The state had a tradition of strong, centralized government which contributed to the passing of this act vesting strong land use control powers in the state which elsewhere are usually vested in local government.[99]

The Law sets up a State Land Use Commission consisting of seven citizen members plus the Directors of the Department of Land and Natural Resources and the Department of Planning and Economic Development. As specified in the statute, the Commission has divided all of the state into four districts: urban, rural, agricultural, and conservation.

Urban districts include most of the already urbanized land plus a reserve sufficient to accommodate an additional ten years of urban growth. Rural districts include low-density residential development of the rural nonfarm type. Agricultural districts include crop and grazing lands and associated industrial and extractive uses. In addition, lava flow areas and other land unsuitable for agricultural uses are included in this zone when they are not deemed necessary for conservation. Conservation districts include state forest and water reserve zones and a substantial amount of private land, especially land in steep mountainous areas. They also include a 40-foot strip of shoreline around all of the state's coastlines.

The uses in urban districts are controlled in more detail by the counties through their own zoning regulations which are not necessarily confined to providing for urban uses. Because of this dual authority development permission in urban districts must be obtained from both the county and the state.

Uses in rural and agricultural districts are controlled by the Land Use Commission. Changes in zoning district boundaries in these areas may be made only by the Commission on petition or on its own initiative. In addition the Commission must review district boundaries comprehensively every five years.

In conservation districts the Department of Land and Natural Resources is the sole administrator of land use controls. These districts are subdivided into two subzones, the Restricted Watershed Zone and the General Use Zone, plus three special subzones for colleges, cemeteries, and nursing homes.

Although the Department of Planning and Economic Development has produced plans and revised them periodically they are not considered binding because ". . . the State Land Use Plan may be identified at any moment with the district boundaries established under provisions of the Land Use Law."[100] This is reminiscent of court declarations in zoning cases which declare the zoning map to *be* the general plan as was discussed previously. Curiously enough though, the Hawaii Supreme Court has insisted that county zoning be based on comprehensive plans.

Bosselman and Callies point out that there appear to be three basic policies guiding the Commission's administration of the Land Use Law:[101]

(1) Prime agricultural land should be preserved for agricultural use.
(2) Tourist-attracting development should be encouraged without disturbing the attractions of the natural landscape.
(3) Compact and efficient urban areas should be provided where people can live at reasonable cost.

Although they observe that the internal conflicts between these policies inevitably lead to public controversy over the Commission's decisions, they conclude that in spite of its imperfections almost no state citizen would advocate more than moderate changes in the system.

N.E.P.A.: 1969/California: 1970

The National Environmental Policy Act passed by the National Congress has led to direct and indirect intervention by various federal agencies in local development in cases of development requiring an environmental impact statement under the Act. The Department of Housing and Urban Development, the Department of Transportation, the Corps of Engineers, and other agencies also must consider environmental impact statements for certain types of development they fund, sponsor, or otherwise are involved in. The Environmental Protection Agency, for example, was requiring environmental impact statements for such attractors of automobiles as "indirect sources."[102] Such indirect sources include: highways and roads; parking facilities; retail, commercial, and industrial facilities; recreation, amusement, sports and entertainment facilities; airports; office and government buildings; apartment and condominium buildings; education facilities; and other unspecified indirect sources. The decision of EPA to require control of indirect sources set up a four-way tug-of-war between the agency, local government, developers, and environmentalists, resulting in EPA abandonment of this approach. However the 1977 Clean Air Act will affect land use through the designation of nonattainment areas as indicated in the previous chapter.

The review of environmental impact statements is carried out by the federal agency(s) concerned excepting where review authority has been delegated to state or local agencies. If the required environmental impact statements are approved (possibly subject to conditions) a permit is issued without which the development cannot legally be undertaken. This constitutes the federal government's most direct and pervasive intervention in local development and growth decision making and, as such, has been widely controversial.

In 1970 California passed an Environmental Quality Act. The Council on Environmental Quality said that: "It has become one of the most important tools for land use control in California, mainly because of the court ruling that the law applies to private as well as public projects."[103]

The law requires that environmental impact statements be prepared and considered in the process of making decisions concerning carrying out or approving projects ". . . which may have a significant effect on the environment."[104] Criteria and procedures for determining whether an environmental impact statement is necessary for a particular class of project is the responsibility of the Resources Agency with the assistance of the State Office of Planning and Research.

Rather than exerting state land use control it is the purpose of this act to ". . . require governmental agencies at all levels to consider qualitative factors as well as economic and technical factors and long-term benefits and costs, in addition to short-term benefits and costs and to consider alternatives to proposed actions affecting the environment."[105]

This act intervenes less drastically in local decision-making than the Florida act but may affect more development decisions because the Florida act limits state intervention at any one time to five percent of the state's total land area.

California has also passed coastal zone legislation (1972),[106] created the San Francisco Bay Conservation Commission (1965), and entered into a bi-state arrangement with Nevada creating the Tahoe Regional

Planning Agency (1970) for planning and protecting the environment of the area around Lake Tahoe.[107]

Massachusetts: 1963/68/71

In a series of legislative acts Massachusetts has sought to protect its coastal and inland wetlands from the adverse effects of development. The value of wetlands for the fishing industry, wildlife preservation, flood protection, and recreation had been established previously by the state's Department of Natural Resources.

Under the Coastal Wetland Act of 1965 the Department of Natural Resources is empowered after extensive local hearings to issue coastal protective orders which cover entire wetland areas. These orders may regulate, restrict, or prohibit ". . . dredging, filling, removing or otherwise altering, or polluting coastal wetlands."[108] After notice is given, owners have a time limit of 90 days in which to appeal to the courts and the courts, on appeal, are restricted to confirming or vacating the orders. The Department may use eminent domain to condemn and acquire sites where its orders have been vacated.

The Hatch Act of 1965 concerning inland wetlands requires developers wanting to alter inland wetlands, other than agricultural land and seasonally wet flood plain areas, to obtain permits from the Department of Natural Resources.

Bosselman and Callies point out that this act is much weaker than the coastal act because there is no system for informing owners of the protective orders and the permits must be granted and cannot prohibit or severely restrict the uses applied for. They conclude that the coastal program has been a qualified success but that the success of the inland program is highly questionable.[109]

In 1971 Massachusetts attacked the problem of exclusionary zoning through enactment of a Zoning Appeals Law providing a mechanism whereby qualified developers of low-income housing can apply for the granting of a "comprehensive permit" consolidating all required local approvals. If the locality denies the permit request the developer can then appeal this decision to a State Housing Appeals Committee empowered to overturn the local denial or modify conditions attached to a granted permit. On appeal the developer must show that local denial of the permit or conditions attached were not reasonable and consistent with local needs. Because of the cost involved developers have been reluctant to make appeals and the effectiveness of the law remains to be demonstrated.[110]

Florida: 1972/75

The Florida *Environmental Land and Water Management Act* of 1972 attempts to deal with "critical areas" and "developments of regional impact" through modifications of traditional techniques and significant innovations. It is modelled on Article 7 of the ALI Model Land Development Code. It was passed in response to a number of serious and growing problems resulting from a high rate of insufficiently controlled development resulting in adverse effects on the natural environment. At the time of passing the Act it was estimated that forty percent of the state's estuaries were polluted, fifty percent of the coastal shellfish were unsafe for harvest, and filling operations had destroyed 262 square miles of estuarine habitat in the previous decade. Despite high rainfall several major cities were suffering from freshwater shortages and about a dozen major counties experienced air pollution problems.[111]

The "critical areas" portion of the Act empowers the state to designate specific areas as of "critical state concern" and to guide development of those areas according to newly established principles and standards. These areas can include: historical, environmental or archeological resources of state-wide or regional concern; areas of major public investment or proposed public development; or areas having a major development potential. The Act gives an opportunity to local governments and regional planning agencies to propose critical areas within their purview. However, as previously noted, the Act limits state designation of critical areas to no more than five percent of the State's area at any one time. This portion of the Act was challenged in the state courts in 1978, declared unconstitutional, and appealed to the Florida Supreme Court which upheld the lower court decision later that year. Subsequently the legislature itself designated two critical areas and the 1979 session had two bills under consideration designed to meet court objections concerning delegation of legislative authority.

After designation the local government(s) within whose jurisdiction the critical area is located has six months to develop land use controls which would implement state principles and standards. If they fail to develop adequate controls and administer them, the state must implement the controls itself. Administration of the critical areas provisions was contingent on Florida voter approval of a bond issue for land acquisition in areas of environmental concern to the state and in November 1972 the required bond issue referendum was overwhelmingly passed.[112]

The second major element of the Act empowers the state to adopt guidelines and standards for determining whether certain land developments are "developments of regional impact (DRIs)." Before being applied these criteria have to be reviewed and approved by the state legislature. They went into effect on July 1st, 1973.[113]

As in the case of critical areas, regional planning agencies and local governments may suggest kinds of development for designation as DRI's. In issuing permits for a DRI the local government having jurisdiction must take into account: ". . . (1) the conformity of the proposed project to a state land development plan, and (2) the project's regional impact as analyzed in a report to be prepared by the designated regional planning agency for the area in which the project is located."[114]

Under the Act the Division of State Planning has the responsibility for devising a state land development plan, making recommendations to the governor and the cabinet in regard to areas of critical concern and the criteria for determining DRIs, approving local development controls in critical areas, and giving technical assistance to local government agencies which fail to devise suitable regulations. The Act also created an Environmental Land Management Study Committee to serve temporarily as a major advisory body to the Division of State Planning in the areas of land resource management and the development of additional legislation to achieve a pattern of sound, economic, and well-planned development, and protection of the environment.

Another body created by the Act is a Land and Water Adjudicatory Commission which has the responsibility for hearing and ruling on appeals relating to both the areas of critical concern and development of regional impact.

In 1975 Florida strengthened its planning legislation even further by passing the Local Government Comprehensive Planning Assistance Act of 1975 which requires all municipal and county governments to adopt comprehensive plans and gives them legal status; also it passed ". . . a bill reorganizing the state's environmental agencies, and a New Communities Act providing for special districts having implementation and enforcement powers for the purpose of developing new communities."[115]

Oregon: 1973

In 1973 Oregon passed new legislation strengthening and broadening its 1969 compulsory planning and zoning law. The new Act establishes a Land Conservation and Development Commission having three basic functions: to establish goals and guidelines; to decide whether land use activities of statewide significance should be allowed; and to review local land use plans and controls for conformance with LCDC goals and guidelines.[116]

Under the Act three types of goals and guidelines were to be established: those for land use activities of statewide significance; those for specified priority areas such as estuarine areas, flood plains and lands adjacent to freeway interchanges; and those for use in relation to the comprehensive planning process. These goals were to be adopted by the Commission by January 1, 1975 and all city and county plans and land use controls brought into conformity with them within the following year.

The Legislative Assembly named five land use activities as being of statewide significance: ". . . public transportation facilities, public sewerage systems, water supply systems, solid waste disposal sites and facilities, and public schools." Permits for planning and development of these activities are required from the Commission in conformance to the goals and guidelines adopted for them. The Commission reviews city and county land use plans and land use controls for conformance to Commission guidelines, has the power to bring them into conformance when they are not and the power to develop, adopt and administer land use plans and land use controls where they are lacking.[117]

The Act also mandates greater citizen participation and the Commission has held hearings all over the state in order to obtain recommendations on specific land use problems related to the formation of its goals and guidelines. The Commission also was required to create a State Citizens Involvement Advisory Committee to review the local citizen participation plans required under the Act. That the Oregon Act has teeth was demonstrated when in 1975 the Oregon Supreme Court ruled ". . . against a local government which allowed development not in accordance with its plan."[118]

In addition to the 1973 Planning Act Oregon has other innovative land use legislation. In 1971 the Legislative Assembly estalished the Oregon Coastal Conservation and Development Commission (OCC & DC), and four regional coordinating committees which are ". . . charged with submitting findings and a proposed plan for the preservation and development of the natural resources of the coastal zone . . ."[119] to provide standards for evaluating proposed uses in the coastal areas. And in the previous year the voters approved scenic waterways legislation which now protects all or portions of seven rivers and the adjacent land from deleterious development through regulations differing according to classification of river areas as ". . . natural river areas, scenic river areas, recreational river areas, natural scenic view areas, accessible natural river areas and river community areas."[120]

Vermont: 1970

Faced with a second home and ski-resort boom with attendant commercial and industrial expansion and concerned about the effect of this growth on the character of the state, Vermont in 1970 passed an Environmental Control Law. This law created a State Environmental Board to issue development and subdivision permits through seven district commissions and to adopt a statewide comprehensive land use plan to be prepared in three stages and designed as a guide for the Board and district commissions in making decisions.[121]

Under the law "developments" for which a permit is necessary include: commercial or industrial improvements on plots exceeding 10 acres and under one ownership or control, residential development involving 10 or more units within a radius of five miles, development by state and local governmental agencies and all development above the elevation of 2500 feet. Applications are processed by the Protection Division of the State Agency of Environmental Conservation which insures that all interested agencies hear about each application and review it for conformance to departmental requirements. After all comments and recommendations are in, the application is taken before the Agency 250 Review Committee (named after Act 250). This Committee is made up of representatives of various state departments having an interest in and expertise concerning development. It is the Committee's job to consolidate together with their recommendations the information in each application and forward it to the district commissions.

A district commission may grant a permit only if it finds that the proposed land use:[122]

(1) Will not result in undue water or air pollution. In making this determination it shall at least consider: the elevation of land above sea level; and in relation to the flood plains, the nature of soil and subsoil and their ability to adequately support waste disposal; the slope of the land and its effect on effluents; the availability of streams for disposal of effluents; and the applicable health and water resources department regulations.

(2) Does have sufficient water available for the reasonably foreseeable needs of the subdivision or development.

(3) Will not cause an unreasonable burden on an existing water supply, if one is to be utilized.

(4) Will not cause unreasonable soil erosion or reduction in the capacity of the land to hold water so that a dangerous or unhealthy condition may result.

(5) Will not cause unreasonable highway congestion or unsafe conditions with respect to use of the highways existing or proposed.

(6) Will not cause an unreasonable burden on the ability of a municipality to provide educational services.

(7) Will not place an unreasonable burden on the ability of the local government to provide municipality or governmental services.

(8) Will not have an undue adverse effect on the scenic or natural beauty of the area, aesthetics, historic sites or rare and irreplaceable natural areas.

(9) Is in conformance with a duly adopted development plan, land use plan or land capability plan (the statewide plans required by the Law).

(10) Is in conformance with any duly adopted local or regional plan under Chapter 91 of Title 24.

District commissions may also consider additional criteria but Bosselman and Callies comment that they do not appear to have done so. Appeals from the decisions of these commissions are made to the Environmental Board which may open the case for a rehearing on any issues requested by any party.

The three kinds of state plans adopted by the Board under the Law are an interim capability plan indicating current land uses and use capabilities, a capability and development plan, and a land use plan. These are intended to provide criteria for issuing development and subdivision permits, to guide state and regional agencies and local governments in planning and plan implementation, and to serve as a means of communicating public goals and policies to the public.

Bosselman and Callies point to ". . . ambiguities in the lines of authority and the different interests represented at all levels . . ." as ". . . examples of the problems which were faced in creating a state plan."[123] There have also been funding problems for the regional planning commissions which have had to rely strongly on federal and foundation sources. The substantial number of exemptions also weakens the effectiveness of the law. Nevertheless, the administration of the law seems to be going smoothly and it is an innovative attempt at the coordination of planning and development on a statewide basis.[124]

U.S. Water Resources Planning Act: 1965/New England River Basins Commission: 1967

The Water Resources Planning Act of 1965 established at the federal cabinet level a Water Resources Council made up of the Secretaries of the Army, Agriculture, H.E.W. and the Chairman of the Federal Power Commission ". . . for guiding the Nation's planning effort in the water resources field and keeping the President and the Congress informed on the water needs of the Nation . . ."[125] This Council has adopted procedures for the creation of interstate river basins commissions on the initiative of a state governor with the concurrence of not less than half of the affected states.

The fourth to be created under this act, the New England River Basins Commissions, is singled out here as an example because of the availability of information. The jurisdiction of the Commission includes all the New England States plus New York. Represented on the

Commission are ten federal departments, state agencies from seven states, six interstate commissions, and a chairman appointed by the President. The Commission's daily work is carried on by an eight-man staff, aided by the staffs of member agencies.[126]

There are eleven river basins within the Commission's jurisdiction. Its responsibilities for these areas are to:[127]

(1) Serve as the principal agency for coordination of water and related land use plans in the region, including federal, state, interstate, local and non-governmental plans;
(2) Prepare and keep up-to-date a comprehensive, coordinated joint plan for use in development of water and related land resources (the plan may be prepared in stages, is to identify alternatives, and is to be directed at specific action projects);
(3) Recommend long range schedules of priorities for collection of needed basic information, for planning, and for action projects;
(4) Foster and undertake studies.

The Water Resources Council supervises the Commission's work and reviews all their plans. Implementation of the plans is up to the constituent states.

The Commission has planned or is planning a number of comprehensive river basin plans. It has participated in or conducted studies of many smaller problems involving the siting of power plants and small dams and the preparation of flood plain regulations. Its primary goal, however, is the ". . . creation of a comprehensive plan for coordinated federal-state management of water and related land resources in the New England region."[128]

A weakness of the Commission is that its plans are only advisory and it has no implementation powers, but it is nonetheless influential because of the parent Council's control over the funding of state water resources programs. The Commission also depends on the publicizing of its proposals to create public pressure within the states for their implementation. But, in discussing it Bosselman and Callies conclude that: "Without authority to truly regulate land use . . . river basin commissions will remain yet another form of regional planning agency which . . . will have minimal effect on the actual use of land within their regional jurisdictions."[129]

Twin Cities Metropolitan Council: 1967/69/74/76/77

In 1967 the Minnesota Legislature created the Metropolitan Council of the Twin Cities Area as an agency to coordinate the planning and development of the Minneapolis-St. Paul metropolitan area. Concerning this the Advisory Commission on Intergovernmental Affairs points out that: "the really innovative and significant development was the creation by the legislature of a truly representative and politically responsive general-purpose, policy-making body at the areawide level". ACIR goes on to comment:[130]

> The central purpose of the Metropolitan Council is to provide the general framework of regional policy for . . . implementing agencies.
>
> . . . .
>
> Further, by providing representation directly from the citizenry and by structuring the Council explicitly on an equal-population-district basis, the legislature was making a conscious effort to design into the Council a system of representation and voting genuinely able to resolve conflict and produce a consensus with a political validity.

The 1967 session Act directs the Council to make recommendations on the prevention and control of air pollution; to develop a program of major parks and open spaces; to develop a program for the control and prevention of water pollution; to make recommendations for long-range planning programs in the area; to make recommendations concerning the tax structure and ways to equalize tax resources and assessment practices; to develop a surface water drainage program; to study and make recommendations concerning the advance acquisition of land for development purposes; and to make recommendations concerning the organizational and financial aspects of the various proposals.

With respect to a broad range of social and physical problems the Act directs the Council to make specific proposals for action by all relevant public and private agencies. These are set forth in the council's Development Guide which addresses such subjects as sewers, solid waste, parks and open space, transportation (including airports), health care, criminal justice, and housing.

The 1969 legislative session was rewarding for the Council. It passed a bill establishing a separate Metropolitan Sewer Board which gave the Council control over the Board through its authority to appoint board members, formulate the Board's plans, and provide for its financing. This legislature passed an act directing the Council to prepare a plan and program for solid waste disposal in the Twin Cities metropolitan area to be implemented by the counties. It also established a board to operate a state zoo to be located by the Council and provided financing for a metropolitan open space program through the Council's budget.[131]

In 1970 a Metropolitan Health Board was established by the Council which subsequently absorbed the preexisting voluntary Metropolitan Hospital Planning Agency. In this same year the Council completed the transportation and housing sections of the Development Guide and brought them to hearings in early 1971. First steps were also taken in 1970 to begin development of the public transit system.[132]

The 1971 legislative session was less generous to the Council. It failed to approve the metropolitan parks and housing programs and to bring the Metropolitan Airports Commission under the Council. It also failed to pass a bill making the Council directly elected. However, it obtained financing for the Metropolitan Transit Commission and subordination of transit plans to the Development Guide. Watershed districts were brought under the Council's planning controls, county plans were made subject to the same review as municipal plans and the commercial-industrial tax-sharing plan (see chapter four) was approved.[133]

Subsequent legislative acts in 1974 increased the powers and responsibilities of the Council. The Metropolitan Reorganization Act of 1974 further clarified the role of the Council in the planning and coordination of development, established a consistent planning review process, provided for planning assistance to local governments by the Council, provided for a uniform reorganization of other metropolitan agencies, and stipulated that the Council formulate policy plans for all metropolitan commissions. This Act also established a Metropolitan Waste Commission, modified the powers and duties of the Metropolitan Transit Commission, and gave the Council veto power over the construction of limited access highways within the metropolitan area.[134]

The Metropolitan Parks Act of 1974 provided for a regional

recreational open space system to be planned and financed through the Council but implemented by the units of local government.[135] The Council had been promoting the establishment of an independent metropolitan parks commission but failed to receive sufficient support from its constituent local governments. A related act, the Protection Open Space Act of 1974, provided for the establishment of standards for the protection of natural resources and the natural environment in the regulation of subdivisions in the metropolitan area.[136]

The metropolitan Housing and Redevelopment Act of 1974 granted the Metropolitan Council the powers of a municipal housing and redevelopment authority in those of its constituent local governments lacking such an authority, with the limitation that all Council-proposed projects would be subject to the approval of the units of government in which they were to be located.[137]

The next legislative session added further to the powers and responsibilities of the Council through two acts in 1976. The Metropolitan Significance Act directs the Council to ". . . adopt and implement regulations for reviewing major development projects proposed in the Metropolitan Area . . ." establishing ". . . criteria that identify which projects are subject to . . ."[138] review regulations and procedures. The other, The Metropolitan Land Planning Act, establishes a two-level planning process with cities, towns, and counties mandated to prepare land use plans with functional elements which parallel the Council's Metropolitan Functional Plans. This Act also specifies the contents of the plans including programs for sequential implementation. In addition to the Development Guide and related to it, the Council must prepare Metropolitan Systems Plans for transmittal to all affected units of local government to which local plans must conform. One important outstanding issue remaining in 1976 was that of making the Council membership elective, and the Metropolitan Significance Act contained a provision for a joint committee of both houses of the Minnesota Legislature to study this issue and report back to the Legislature in 1977.[139] In 1977 the Council was given responsibility for providing sports facilities . . . and in 1978 a bill to make the Council membership elective failed to clear committee.

The Twin Cities Metropolitan Council is an innovative and increasingly viable institutional solution to the problems of coordinating planning and guiding development in a multijurisdictional metropolitan area where the establishment of metropolitan government might be a much more difficult reform to achieve. The Advisory Commisslon on Intergovernmental Affairs in discussing the Council made a special point of its having been a child of the state (in some cases reflecting federal initiatives) rather than local government. Although the Council has had its setbacks, the overall record has been promising.[140]

Comparative Summary

Although the examples of state legislation examined were chosen for their diversity rather than their similarities, they reveal a considerable overlap in conceptual approaches to various planning problems and all of them involve increased state intervention in local land use guidance. The major important features of this legislation will be briefly reiterated here and a few additional examples noted.

State Land Use Planning. The requirement for a *state land use plan* as a guide for regional and local planning is a central feature of the Hawaii, Florida, and Vermont legislation. California requires the state planning office to prepare *guidelines* for the preparation of environmental impact statements required to be considered in making local planning determinations for specified types of development, and Oregon requires its state planning office to prepare both *goals* and *guidelines* for use in judging the adequacy of local plans and planning controls.

State-wide Zoning. This is unique to Hawaii where it is supplemented by more detailed local zoning in areas designated by the state as urban zones.

Planning and Controls for Critical Substate Areas. The more generalized legislation of this sort reflects the concepts of the ALI Model Land Development Code. In Oregon it is directed to "areas of statewide significance" and in Florida it is directed as well to "development of regional impact." In both cases the state can adopt plans and controls for such areas if the localities fail to do so. Vermont has legislation dealing with a state-regional-local process for the planning and control of development involving more than ten dwelling units or constructed on mountainsides at elevations above 2500 feet. Several states have legislation dealing with coastal zones and coastal or inland wetlands some of which was prompted by the federal Coastal Zone Management Act of 1972. The Massachusetts, California, and Oregon legislation has been described. Rhode Island, Connecticut, and Georgia also have similar legislation.

State-wide Mandatory Local Planning. Both Florida and Oregon have legislation making local planning mandatory. The Oregon act provides for the state to prepare and adopt plans for localities which fail to do so.

New Communities. Florida has passed a New Communities Act to assist in the development of New Communities, and, as has already been discussed, the New York Urban Development Corporation is building a number of new communities.

Regional Planning and Development Organizations. The Twin Cities Metropolitan Council is probably the most powerful of these, but others worth mentioning are the Hackensack Meadowlands Development Commission in New Jersey, and the San Francisco Bay Conservation and Development Commission. As an interstate example the Tahoe Regional Planning Agency of the California-Nevada border is also of interest.[141]

Conclusions. The recent legislation concerning land use controls reflects an increasing concern for the impact of new development on the natural and man-made environment, an increasing understanding of the interrelatedness of land uses, and a growing consciousness of the need for the higher levels of government to assume more responsibility in this regard because of the interjurisdictional nature of so many of the problems arising from land use decision-making at the local level. The states, particularly, are increasingly willing to experiment with new kinds of land use controls. This proliferation of approaches is likely to continue until the innovative legislation has been in effect long enough for it to be properly evaluated for its effectiveness. Although recently there have been a number of bills put forward in Congress for establishing a national framework for state and local planning and providing stronger support for statewide planning, none had succeeded in being enacted as this is being written.

INNOVATIVE LOCAL GUIDANCE SYSTEMS

Recently a few local governments have been developing innovative implementation programs for land use plans and policies. Those most widely written about have been the previously described Ramapo, Boca Raton, and Petaluma growth guidance programs. Few of them have been systematically described and analysed, mostly for the lack of sufficient information. There has, however, been a landmark study in this area. It was financed by the National Science Foundation and carried out at the University of Minnesota School of Public Affairs and reported in two volumes in 1974.[142] The University of Minnesota study which compares and analyses thirteen selected growth guidance systems will be briefly described here.

The number of cases selected for the comparative study was limited to those reflecting a range of approaches being used in different parts of the United States. The cases chosen vary in relation to such criteria as ". . . time of beginning, stage of evolution, actors initiating the system, sophistication of the decision and management process and capacity to execute."[143]

The cities and counties initially selected for study were: Boca Raton, Florida; Ramapo, New York; Fairfax and Loudon counties in Virginia; Montgomery and Prince George's counties in Maryland; Boulder, Colorado; Petaluma and Sacramento County in California; and Salem, Oregon. Before the study was completed Brooklyn Park, Minnesota and Pinellas County, Florida were included. A summary of the major features of each system follows:

Boca Raton, Florida

The objective of this system is the limitation of the city's ultimate developed population to that which can be housed in a maximum of 40,000 dwelling units. The elements of the system include a charter provision specifying the maximum number of dwelling units, planning moratoria and interim development controls embodying density limitations more restrictive than those under the previous controls, the granting of special approval for minor variances, recreational land acquisition, and the adoption of new minimum lot sizes. At the time of this writing (Spring 1978) the system was still being challenged in the courts.[144]

Boulder, Colorado

The objectives of this system are to reduce heavy growth rates placing a strain on the ability of the city to provide the necessary related community facilities, to reduce the impact of growth on the environment by restricting or preventing development of the scenic mountainous areas and the flood plains through creation of a greenbelt, and to reduce the costs of development by keeping it compact. The elements of the system include acquisition of all or partial rights in land, influencing the timing and location of development through the scheduling and location of community facilities, environmental controls, provisions for planned unit development and flexible zoning, height restrictions, mandatory dedication of land and/or capital facilities or the making of payments in lieu thereof, a low- and moderate-income housing requirement, the payment of user and benefit fees, provision for annexation and timed boundary adjustments, capital improvement programming, and a comprehensive land use plan.[145]

The city is the source of the area's urban services but because it is completely built-up all development must take place in the county. As a consequence developers have to negotiate with the city or have their development annexed by the city in order to obtain the necessary services. The acquisition of open space and scenic easements is supported by a one-percent sales tax and community facilities are financed on a pay-as-you-go basis. In June, 1976 a local court test of Boulder's refusal to extend sewer and water services to a developer whose development did not conform to the comprehensive plan's growth projections was decided against the city and this decision upheld on appeal.

Brooklyn Park, Minnesota

The objectives of this system are to guide development so that already constructed sewer and storm drainage facilities come to be fully utilized before the city is forced to construct additional ones in the unserved, agricultural, largely undeveloped northern two thirds of the incorporated area. The system elements include land acquisition, influencing growth through the location of facilities, agricultural zoning, minimum lot sizes, subdivision regulations having provisions relating approval to the adequacy of off-site facilities, mandatory dedication of land and/or capital facilities, preferential taxation, a comprehensive land use plan with a development timing schedule, and administrative processing.[146]

Since 1962 the system has been successful in restricting development to those areas provided with adequate community facilities. As of September, 1974 the system had not been challenged in the courts.

Dade County, Florida

Motivated by widespread piecemeal rezoning, a very rapid growth rate, and fear of environmental depredation, especially in the coastal areas of Dade County, the objective of the system devised there is to restrain or prevent development where the 1965 comprehensive plan and/or current zoning are outdated or inappropriate. The elements of the system include moratoria on the issuance of building permits and on the granting of zoning changes in specific portions of the County together with studies to update the plans and zoning ordinance for the affected areas.

The system was initiated in 1972 when the moratoria were put into effect and planning and zoning studies got underway. As these studies are completed and adopted the moratoria for the areas replanned and rezoned are repealed. As of May, 1978 there had been no test of the system's constitutionality although there had been several unsuccessful attacks on portions of it and an attempt to evade it through boundary revision.

Fairfax County, Virginia

This rapidly growing suburban county just west of the District of Columbia found itself faced with the problem that over three-quarters of its area, the largely undeveloped part of the County, was either unsewered, under a state Water Control Board sewer moratorium, or had soil conditions constraining development. Also the provision of community facilities and the infrastructure necessary for development was lagging behind the rate of growth, and there developed a public concern for controlling growth, improving the quality of life, preventing environmental degradation, and improving the quality and quantity of public services.[148]

The growth guidance system evolved for coping with these problems contained the following elements: control of access to existing facilities, planning and environmental moratoria with interim development controls, the updating of land use controls and both large- and small-scale plans, land banking, capital improvement programming, environmental impact review, and monitoring systems with improved methods of analysis.

The system was initiated in 1973 with the passing of an interim development ordinance which was subsequently struck down by the Virginia courts. The land banking has been successful mainly for housing and redevelopment, but lacks adequate funding.

Loudoun County, Virginia

This predominantly rural county west of Fairfax County, Virginia and south of Montgomery County, Maryland was concerned with its potential for large-scale suburban growth in view of the lack of an adequate tax base to support the construction of the necessary related public facilities. Determined to protect the area's economy and way of life, to prevent environmental degradation, and keep public expenditures within the limits of what the County could afford. In 1972 it evolved a growth guidance system based on a policy plan and zoning ordinance.[149]

The elements of the system include the policy plan delineating those areas of the County to remain rural and those to be urbanized, a new zoning ordinance with provisions for two large-lot zones (three acres and ten acres), the location of public facilities to influence the location of new development, controls relating development permission to the adequancy of off-site facilities, the mandatory dedication of land and/or capital facilities, the payment of money in lieu of land and/or capital facilities, preferential taxation, and capital improvement programming.

The system was put into operation with the adoption in 1972 of a zoning ordinance based on a previously adopted plan, with the adoption in 1973 of a premature-subdivision ordinance, with state legislation passed in 1973 enabling taxation to be based on current land use, and a capital improvement program adopted in 1974. Under the system developers are required to share in the cost of or provide the public facilities necessary for their projects if these facilities are not already existing, included in the capital improvement program or shown on the comprehensive plan. These requirements were upheld in a court test in 1972. Rural areas are protected from development pressures by both large-lot zoning and preferential taxation.

Montgomery County, Maryland

Just north of the District of Columbia, Montgomery County has for some time come under the same development pressures as the two Virginia counties just described. It has the same problems in providing the necessary public facilities and urban services for new development. This was recognized in the 1964 plan for the County which emphasized the desirability of controlling the timing and location of development. Also a concern was expressed for providing more low- and medium-income housing in the County.[150]

In addition to the plan, the elements of the growth guidance system adopted include influencing the timing and location of development through the location of public facilities, controlling access to existing public facilities, pollution controls, both conventional and incentive zoning, establishing minimum lot sizes, controls relating development to the adequacy of off-site public facilities, a low/moderate-income housing requirement, preferential taxation, capital improvement programming, locational restraints in relation to serviced areas, and environmental moratoria.

The system was put into effect through a series of actions beginning with securing state legislation in 1966 requiring a ten-year county sewer and water plan. This was followed by capital improvement programming and sewer moratoria in 1970, and the other elements were activated by 1973. The system has never been put to a court test but in view of the Prince George's County court test would undoubtedly be upheld.

Petaluma, California

This system, briefly described in chapter two, is concerned with controlling the rate of growth in order to prevent environmental degradation, limit the cost and improve the quality of public services, preserve the city's character, achieve orderly and attractive development and establish a permanent surrounding greenbelt of hills, marshes and recreational open space.[151]

First proposed in 1971, the growth guidance system includes the following elements: open space land acquisition, the location of public facilities to influence the pattern of growth, a system of special permits, controls relating development permission to the adequacy of off-site facilities, mandatory dedication of land and/or capital facilities, payments in lieu of land and/or capital facilities, a low/moderate-income housing requirement, a program of annexation including timed and conditional boundary adjustments and servicing, locational development restraints tied to the serviced area, and annual building permit quotas.

Based on an adopted General Plan and an Environmental Design Plan delimiting the area to be urbanized and locating the greenbelt, an annual quota of building permits is determined. Permit approvals take into account the impact of the proposed development on public facilities, site plan design, and other factors. A competitive point system is used in determining the awarding of permits. As previously mentioned this system was challenged in the courts all the way up to the U.S. Supreme Court which upheld its validity.[152]

Pinellas County, Florida

The County-owned and operated water system supplies water to 18 of 24 municipalities within the County. The largest city, St. Petersburg, has its own water system. These systems are drawing water from the Floridan Aquifer with production limited by drawdown of the water table to sea level after which there would be saltwater intrusion into the aquifer. A shortage of water because of several years of drought and increased consumption prompted the County to declare a 45-day ban on new water connections in mid-1973, followed by putting into effect a managed growth policy and water allocation system.[153]

The elements of this growth guidance system include control of access to existing facilities, conventional zoning, pollution controls, minimum lot sizes, mandatory dedication of land and/or capital facilities, user and benefit fees, annual permit limits, provision of information, monitoring, and technical assistance.

The County Water Department reviews all building permit applications. Water allocation from the County based on the County Water Allocation Plan or an arrangement to use a nonCounty water system is necessary before building permits will be granted. Similarly, the County Department of Pollution Control reviews building permit applications for approval of connection into the County sewer service or agreement to use a private sewer service. If sewer capacity is not available, no permit is granted. Agricultural zoning is used also to limit growth. An attack on the legitimacy of the County Planning Council and zoning by the City of Clearwater was defeated in the State Supreme Court in early 1978.

Prince George's County, Maryland

An urban county just east of the District of Columbia, Prince George's County has been under development pressure similar to those of the other suburban counties in the Washington metropolitan area. The impact of sprawl and rapid development on the environment and the cost of providing public facilities prompted the County to consider undertaking the carefully staged development proposed in the 1964 General Plan.[154]

The elements of the growth guidance system include the location of facilities to influence the timing and location of growth, conventional zoning with minimum lot sizes, planned unit development controls relating development permission to the adequacy of off-site facilities, preferential taxation, capital improvement programming, locational restraints, and environmental moratoria.

The capital improvement program and extension of services are based on annual targets for growth of population and employment, coupled with the channelization of growth into areas programmed for or already provided with adequate facilities and services.

The system was put into effect starting in 1966 with a state-required ten-year water and sewer plan. This was followed by capital improvement programming in 1967, a state health department ban on new construction, and passage of an "adequate public facilities" subdivision ordinance in 1970, initiation of the growth staging policy in 1972, and adoption of a sectional zoning map amendment procedure in 1973. As of May, 1978 there had been only one unsuccessful challenge of the adequate public facilities ordinance.

Ramapo, New York

This system, described briefly in chapter two, is concerned with improving the management of growth problems resulting from its location in the northwestern part of the burgeoning New York metropolitan area. The issues were the increasing costs and character of sprawl and a lack of low-income housing. The objectives were to control the character of development, minimize the costs of providing a satisfactory quality of public facilities and services, and to establish and maintain a desirable mix of land uses.[155]

Initiated in 1965, the system includes the following elements: acquisition of less-than-fee-simple rights in land, location of public facilities to influence the timing and location of development, conventional zoning, a system of special permits, provision for variances, conventional subdivision controls, controls relating development permission to the adequacy of off-site facilities, mandatory dedication of land and/or capital facilities or monetary payments-in-lieu-thereof, preferential taxation, official mapping, capital improvement programming, comprehensive land use planning, and locational restraints in relation to public services.

The system was put into effect through a series of legislative and administrative actions ranging from the adoption of a Master Plan in 1966 through the adoption of a point system in 1969. Under the point system development of two or more lots requires a special permit from the Town Board as a prerequisite for obtaining building permits. The awarding of special permits is dependent on acquiring ". . . fifteen development points based on readiness of the site for development with respect to . . ."[156] public facilities in place or scheduled in the 18-year capital improvement program. The permit gives the developer the right to apply for building permits as of the date when the necessary facilities are to be completed. However, this date may be advanced if the developer furnishes enough of the required facilities (at his own expense) to increase his points to the required number. Variances are obtainable for public and low-income housing and specified public uses which are in conformance with the plan. Tax relief is available for properties whose development is to be long delayed under the system.

As previously indicated, the legal validity of the system was upheld in a decision of the New York Court of Appeals which the U.S. Supreme Court refused on further appeal to rehear.

Sacramento County, California

Sacramento County, northeast of San Francisco Bay, is an extremely productive agricultural county, part of which is being urbanized even as the area intensively farmed increases. It contains important mineral lands and some lands subject to infrequent flooding. The location of growth as it affects the economical provision of public facilities and the protection of prime agricultural land are more important issues there than the rate of growth. The County states its goals as being to:[157]

> . . . develop a diversified economic base for the county; enhanced agriculture; protected use of land, water, other resources; a balanced ecological system, a distinctive character of each community, a wide range of urban living options; a wide range of recreational opportunities, safe and adequate housing, safe and efficient transportation, public services and facilities.

First proposed in 1970, the growth guidance system includes the following elements: land acquisition, location of facilities to influence the timing and location of development, environmental controls, conventional and flexible zoning including agricultural zoning and minimum lot sizes, planned unit development, preferential taxation, comprehensive planning, and locational restraints.

The strategy involves using the system to direct growth exclusively to planned areas adjacent to existing development thus preserving prime agricultural land and natural resource areas from development. The system was initiated by a regional plan in 1969 and a County plan in the following year embodying, respectively, the concepts of timing development and establishing urban limit lines outside of which urbanization would not be permitted. Subsequently, detailed community plans were prepared. The state took action providing for preferential taxation for agricultural land, prohibited the use of septic tanks in 100-year-flood areas, restricted the location of septic tanks with respect to property lines, made central sewage disposal plants mandatory for large developments (over 99 units), required that zoning be consistent with land use plans, and limited the frequency of amending land use plans.

Two court challenges in 1972 were dismissed, one for lack of cause and the other for insufficient evidence.

Salem, Oregon

Salem, Oregon is located between Portland and Eugene in the Willamette Valley. This valley produces about half of the state's agricultural output, is predicted to be where three-quarters of Oregon's new residents will settle, and is identified by the Environmental Protection Agency as one of two areas in the nation with the greatest potential for serious air pollution problems. The city is bisected by the boundary between Polk and Marion counties. The objectives of its growth guidance system are: ". . . to preserve valuable agricultural lands, reduce fragmentation in the provision of public services and prevent environmental damage."[158]

First proposed by the Governmental Coordinating Committee of the two-county Mid-Willamette Valley Council of Governments whose staff serves as the planning staff for Salem and Polk County, the system includes the following elements: location of facilities to influence the timing and location of development; control of access to existing facilities; pollution control; conventional and conditional zoning including the control of minimum lot sizes, exclusive agricultural zoning, and flood plain zoning; conventional regulation of subdivisions; controls relating development permission to the adequacy of off-site facilities; urban and rural service areas; user fees; special assessments; preferential taxation; annexation involving timed, conditional boundary adjustments and servicing; capital improvement programming; comprehensive planning; locational restraints; and provision of public information, monitoring, and technical assistance.

The development management concept (guidance system) was proposed by the local council of governments in 1970 following the previous action of the Local Government Boundary Commission halting annexation of areas not shown to be serviced in the Salem Sewer Plan and the formation of additional special districts. Among other system implementing actions were the adoption in 1972 by Marion County of a Rural Development Policy, the signing in 1973 by Salem and both counties of a letter of intent to undertake the development of plans and policies consistent with the Urban Growth Boundary Concept, and the adoption by Salem in 1974 of a three-year capital improvement program. By the spring of 1978 there had been no court tests of the system and the State of Oregon had required the

Urban Growth Boundary Concept to be adopted by all cities to accommodate growth through the year 2000.

Commentary

The University of Minnesota study group comes to the following tentative conclusions concerning these growth guidance systems:[159]

1. Most development management systems have a problem-solving orientation and give little consideration to the side effects of system operation. In contrast, Prince George's County with its two criteria for monitoring, one dealing with tax base per capita, and the other dealing with the ratio of jobs to homes, can "observe" whether or not operation of the system is producing certain desired effects.

2. There is relatively little research on the effects of land use controls in operation. Therefore, the choice is to delay action until exploratory research can be completed, or to proceed and monitor for desired and undesired effects and to alter the controls as the negative effects emerge. The former is not politically practical in most instances, but the latter is rarely being followed, either. No body of knowledge or insight is being recorded for future use by the operating agencies themselves, and no comparative evaluations across systems have been made.

3. In virtually all of the systems examined, the emphasis is on regulation or restraints. Very few systems incorporate or are considering emphasis on incentives. There is little doubt that the trend in court decisions over the last several decades has been to significantly increase the scope of police power restraints on individual use of land. Furthermore, the scope of eminent domain is expanding as the interpretation of what constitutes a public purpose continues to be broadened. Transfer of development rights and bonus and incentive systems are examples of responses to the need to achieve public purposes without the levels of restraint supported in some recent court cases.

4. Most of the systems tend to ignore levels of government other than the level of the agency proposing the system. For example, none mention or take into account the effect on development of federal income tax policy on capital gains and depreciation. A few do include metropolitan or state agency participation in "fair share" housing, environmental controls, or annexation. (See items marked 1—for intergovernmental on the table which follows).

5. From the very limited selection of cases reported here, it appears that

TABLE 7–1. Growth Management Methods.

General Category / Specific Technique or System Elements	Boca Raton, FL	Brooklyn Park, MN	Dade County, FL	Ramapo, NY	Fairfax County, VA	Loudoun County, VA	Montgomery County, MD	Prince George's County, MD	Boulder, CO	Petaluma, CA	Pinellas County, FL	Sacramento County, CA	Salem, OR
Public acquisition													
(1) Fee simple acquisition (park, open space, greenbelt)	*	*	X		X		X	X	*	*		*	
(2) Land banking			X[2]		O		X[1]		O				
(3) Compensable regulation									*				
(4) Less than fee simple acquisition				*			X						
Public improvements													
(5) Location of facilities to influence growth		*	O	*		*	*	*	*	*[1]	*	*	*[1]
(6) Access to existing facilities			O		*		*						*[1]
Environmental controls													
(7) Floodplains, stream valleys, wetlands, shorelands, slopes, mountainous areas		X	O		X	X	X	X	*	X			*
(8) Critical areas						X						*	
(9) Development of regional impact	X[1]		X[1]								X[1]	*	

(10) Other special protection areas												*	
(11) Pollution controls		O	X			*	*				*	*	*
Development rights transfer													
(13) Restrictive covenants and other agreements running with the land			X[3]										
Zoning Techniques													
(14) Conventional zoning	X	X	X	*	O	X	*	*	X	X	X	*	*
(15) Conditional zoning					X							*	*
(16) Contract zoning													
(17) Planned unit development (PUD)		X	O		X	O	X	*	*	X		*	X
(18) Flexible (cluster, average density) zoning		X		X	X		X	X	*			*	X
(19) Performance standards		X				X							
(20) Bonus and incentive zoning		X	X				*			X			X
(21) Floating zones							X						
(22) Special permit	*	X		*	X		X	X		*			
(23) Variance	*	X	X	*	X		X	X		X			X
(24) Conventional subdivision regulations	X	*	X	*	O	X	X	X	X	X	X	X	*
Zoning/Building Code/Subdivision regulations for permanent population control													
(25) Exclusive agriculture or non-residential zones		*								X		*	*
(26) Exclusion of multiple-family, mobile, modular, or industrialized housing				X[4]									
(27) Minimum floor area			X										
(28) Minimum lot size	*	*	X[5]	X		*	*	*			*	*	*

TABLE 7-1. *(Continued)*

General Category / Specific Technique or System Elements	Boca Raton, FL	Brooklyn Park, MN	Dade County, FL	Ramapo, NY	Fairfax County, VA	Loudoun County, VA	Montgomery County, MD	Prince George's County, MD	Boulder, CO	Petaluma, CA	Pinellas County, FL	Sacramento County, CA	Salem, OR
(29) Height restriction		*		X			X		*				
(30) Zoning or subdivision control relating to adequacy of off-site facilities		*		*	O	*	*	*		*		X	*
Exactions and other requirements													
(31) Mandatory dedication of land or capital facilities		*	O	*		*			*	*	*	X	P
(32) Money in lieu of land or capital facility		*	O	*		*			*	*		X	P
(33) Low/moderate income housing requirement					P		*		*	*			
Tax and fee systems													
(34) Urban and rural service areas									*		*		
(35) User and benefit fee													*
(36) Special assessment		X	X										*
(37) Preferential taxation (agricultural lands, etc.)		*	XI			*	*	*					*

Technique														
(38) Development districts		O							O					
(39) Annexation including timed and conditional boundary adjustments and servicing	*			*					O			*		*I
(40) Official mapping (roads, streets, parks, and drainage systems)			X⁶	*	O		X	X						X
(41) Capital programming process		O	O	*	O	*	*I	*K	*	*	O	O	*
(42) Plan or its elements	X	*	X	*	O	O	*	*	*	*	*	*	*	*
Geographical restraints														
(43) Longer-term limit line or serviced area (15–20 years)		*	O											
(44) Shorter-term serviced area (5–10 years)		O	O	*			*	*		*		*	*
Numerical restraints or quota systems														
(45) Total population charter provision	*													
(46) Annual permit limits														
(47) Population and employment targets					OI	OI	OI	O		*				
(48) Fair share allocations					OI	OI	OI							
Other planning and management techniques														
(49) Planning moratoriums and interim development controls	*	P		*	*OI	*OI	*OI	OI		*	P	P	
(50) Environmental moratoriums	P													
(51) Administrative processing and delay	*		O	O	O	O	X	X					
(52) Environmental impact assessment			O										
(53) Cost/benefit analysis			O										
(54) Impact zoning														
(55) Information, education, monitoring, and technical assistance	*		*		O	O	O	O		*	*	*	*

TABLE 7-1. (Continued)

* system elements
O emerging system elements
X other controls not in the system
I intergovernmental application
P used previously but abandoned

[1] Advanced land acquisition program with revolving fund of $3,000,000

[2] Advanced land acquisition but limited to low-income housing

[3] Dade gains agreement for restrictive covenant relating time phasing, low-income housing, and other restraints in lieu of PUD provisions

[4] While there is no provision for multifamily housing in the unincorporated area, multifamily housing is provided in the incorporated villages

[5] In agricultural zones to protect land

[6] Actually a special provision in the zoning code for protecting street right-of-way

Reprinted with permission from PAS Report 309–310, "Urban Growth Management Systems," by Michael E. Gleeson, et al. 1975. American Society of Planning Officials.

early involvement of elected officials, citizens, and a staff team consisting of administrator, planner, and lawyer is important. Because of a general lack of thoroughly documented evaluations on development management systems, the current requirement for high caliber staff people is critical.

6. In examining the various community approaches, it became clear that many described their systems as a public decision process in which plans and programs are major support elements. This process and program orientation is central to their controlling the timing and location of development. Schemes such as those in Ramapo, Petaluma, Boulder, Prince George's and Montgomery Counties place heavy emphasis on plan elements as policy and as a rationale for the operation of a program-oriented control system.

7. The use of absolutes, whether in geographic area or numbers, appears to be an early approach that is being set aside. Sacramento's original scheme defined a specific geographic area and referred to it as bounded by an urban limit line. It has now adopted the new terminology "urban service area." This new term relates the concept directly to its purpose and achieves a greater rationale for its existence.

8. Another observation is that exclusionary effects by and large have received little attention. The provision of low and moderate income housing, if mentioned at all, is something which is enabled but not pressed. The exceptions are Boulder, Montgomery County, and Petaluma. Fairfax County previously tried such an approach and lost in court. Boca Raton has no such provision and the strategies it is pursuing tend to work further against any provision of low and moderate income housing.

9. Perhaps the key conclusion in this examination is that the truly unique contribution many of these systems have made is in integrating control elements. One of the most common linkages is to combine the programming of capital improvements (41) with physical location of facilities (5), and a requirement for adequate public facilities (39) as a precondition to building or development permits. This approach puts the emphasis on programming and shifts the system from private initiative to public investment initiative as a basis for permitting private development.

A detailed description of the elements composing growth guidance systems as listed in Table 7-1 and mentioned in connection with the individual case descriptions is to be found in Section III of the University of Minnesota study. They are not described here because most of them have been described elsewhere in this chapter or in previous chapters.

The study also makes the point that the elements involved in a growth guidance system must be integrated by means of specific linkages into a planning implementation program if they are to be considered part of a system.[160]

Despite the shortcomings of the described systems pointed out in the study's conclusions, it is both remarkable and salutory that many local governments are taking steps to develop and carry out organized growth guidance systems in what seems now to be a political environment more favorable to the active implementation of land use plans.

CONCLUSIONS

The last two decades have been a time of increasing concern for improving the means and effectiveness of implementing land use plans, especially in systematically controlling the timing and location of development through what are increasingly being called *growth guidance systems.* There have been proposals by prominent professional planners and other urbanists, recommendations by commissions and committees of the national government and national professional organizations, pioneering and experimental state planning legislation often influenced by the above mentioned individual and organizational proposals, and the formulation by a number of localities of systems for guiding development which have been adopted and put into effect.

No single theoretical or practical approach to land use planning implementation programs is predominant in these proposals and experiments, but as previously commented, there has not yet been enough experience with these growth guidance systems to enable evaluation of their relative effectiveness in regard to alternative approaches and combinations of techniques.

The formulation of the American Law Institute's Model Land Development Code, for all its possible defects, is probably the most significant single event in the period because of its immediate influence on planning legislation passed in several states and the likelihood of its being a major point of departure for legislation in other states wanting to update planning enabling legislation based on the Standard Acts of the 1920s.

There is ample reason to suppose that the experimentation with and use of growth guidance systems will continue if they prove to be effective in ameliorating the difficulties which continue to be brought on by environmental, energy, housing, and local government financial problems—especially in areas where growth rates tend to remain high.

NOTES AND ACKNOWLEDGEMENTS FOR CHAPTER 7

1. Scott, Randall W., *Management and Control of Growth: Issues-Techniques-Problems-Trends, Vol. 1*, (Washington: The Urban Land Institute) p. 2; and Real Estate Research Corporation, *The Costs of Sprawl: Detailed Cost Analysis*, (Washington: U.S. Government Printing Office, 1974), pp. 1–24, *passim*; this latter report was commissioned by the U.S. Department of Housing and Urban Development.

2. Einsweiler, Robert C., Gleeson, Michael E., Ball, Ian Traquair, Morris, Alan, and Sprague, Diane. "Comparative Descriptions of Selected Municipal Growth Guidance Systems, A Preliminary Report," in Scott, *op.cit.*, pp. 284–85.

3. ———. *op.cit.*, p. 285.

4. ———. *op.cit.*, pp. 284–288.

5. ———. *op.cit.*, p. 285, reproduced with permission.

6. Fagin, Henry, "Regulating the Timing of Urban Development," from a symposium entitled *Land Planning in a Democracy* appearing in *Law and Contemporary Problems*, **20**, No. 2, (Spring 1955), pp. 298-304. Published by the Duke University School of Law, Durham, North Carolina, copyright 1955 by Duke University.

7. Chapin, Jr., Stuart, "Taking Stock of Techniques for Shaping Urban Growth," *Journal of the American Institute of Planners*, **29**, No. 2, (May 1963), pp. 76–87.

8. Reps, John W., "Requiem for Zoning," *Planning 1964*, (Chicago: American Society of Planning Officials, 1964), pp. 54–67, copyright 1964 by the Society, and "The Future of American Planning—Requiem or Renascence?" *Planning 1967*, (Chicago: American Society of Planning Officials, 1967), pp. 45–65, copyright 1967 by the Society.

9. Bain, Henry, "The Organization of Growth," in *The New City*, Donald Canty, ed., (New York: Praeger, 1969) pp. 135–43. Copyright © 1969 by Urban America, Inc.

10. So, Frank S., "Metropolitan Planning Policy Implementation," *Planning Advisory Service Report 262*, (Chicago: American Society of Planning Officials, 1970), pp. 40, copyright 1970 by the Society.

11. Canty, Donald, "Metropolity," *City, Magazine of Urban Life and Environment*, (March–April 1972), pp. 29–44. Copyright 1972. The Urban Coalition, 1201 Connecticut Avenue N.W., Washington, D.C. 20036. All rights reserved.
12. Fagin, *op.cit.*, pp. 299–303, reprinted by permission of the author and publisher.
13. Here he is probably referring to what is now commonly called "planned unit development."
14. Chapin, *op.cit.*, p. 77, reprinted by permission of the author and Journal.
15. ———. *op.cit.*, p. 78, reprinted by permission.
16. ———. *op.cit.*, p. 81, reprinted by permission.
17. ———. *op.cit.*, p. 84, reprinted by permission.
18. ———. *op.cit.*, p. 86, reprinted by permission.
19. ———. *op.cit.*, p. 83, reprinted by permission.
20. Reps, John W., "Requiem," pp. 56–67.
21. ———. "Future," p. 49, reprinted with permission.
22. Comsat is jointly owned by the federal government and several private communications corporations.
23. ———. "Future", p. 59, reprinted with permission.
24. Holbein, Mary Elizabeth, "Land Banking: Saving for a Rainy Day," *Planning*, **41**, No. 1, (January 1975), p. 19.
25. The American Law Institute (ALI). *A Model Land Development Code*, (Philadelphia: The Institute, April 15, 1974), pp. 253–280, copyright 1974 by the American Law Institute.
26. Bain, *op.cit.*, pp. 135–43.
27. ———. *op.cit.*, p. 137, reproduced by permission of Praeger Publishers, Inc., a Division of Holt, Rinehart and Winston.
28. ———. *op.cit.*, pp. 140–42, reproduced by permission of Praeger Publishers, Inc., a Division of Holt, Rinehart and Winston.
29. So, *op.cit.*, p. 1, reprinted with permission.
30. *Ibid.*
31. ———. *op.cit.*, p. 3, reprinted with permission.
32. ———. *op.cit.*, p. 17, reprinted with permission.
33. ———. *op.cit.*, p. 21, reprinted with permission; for an illustrative implementation program see So, *op.cit.*, pp. 33–38.
34. Canty, "Metropolity," p. 38, reprinted by permission.
35. ———. "Metropolity," pp. 39–40, reprinted by permission.
36. Fagin, Henry, "Organizing and Carrying Out Planning Activities within Urban Government," *Journal of the American Institute of Planners*, Vol. xxv, No. 3, (August 1959) pp. 109–114.
37. Canty, Donald, ed., *The New City*, (New York: Praeger, 1969) pp. 172–74. Copyright © 1969 by Urban America, Inc.
38. National Commission on Urban Problems (NCUP). *Building the American City*, (Washington: U.S. Government Printing Office, 1968), pp. 235–53.
39. Canty, *New City*, pp. 172–174.
40. The American Institute of Architects (AIA), "A Plan for Urban Growth: Report of the National Policy Task Force," from *Memo, Newsletter of the American Institute of Architects*, (January 1972/Special Issue), pp. 12.

41. International City Management Association, "Managing Growth: Report of the ICMA Committee on Growth and the Environment," *Management and Control of Growth—Issues—Techniques—Problems—Trends, Vol. I*, ed. by Randall W. Scott, (Washington: The Urban Land Institute, 1975), pp. 136–47; also *Public Management*, **55**, No. 9, (September 1973), pp. 8–10.

42. Advisory Commission on Intergovernmental Relations, *Regional Decision Making: New Strategies for Substate Districts, Vol. I, Substate Regionalism and the Federal System*, (Washington: U.S. Government Printing Office, 1974), pp. 339–74 (Hereinafter referred to as ACIR, R.D.M.). This report was completed and approved for publication in 1973.

43. ALI, *op.cit.*

44. The American Institute of Planners, "The American Institute of Planners Review of the American Law Institute Model Land Development Code—A Primer for Action," (Washington: The Institute, 1974), pp. 19 plus attachments (an unpublished report of the American Institute of Planners), hereinafter referred to as AIP, Code Review.

45. NCUP, *op.cit.*, pp. 236–39.

46. ———. *op.cit.*, p. 239.

47. ———. *op.cit.*, p. 243.

48. ———. *op.cit.*, p. 245.

49. Downs, Anthony, *Urban Problems and Prospects*, (Chicago: Markham Publishing Company, 1970), pp. 20–22.

50. Boley, Robert E., "Industrial Districts Restudied, An Analysis of Characteristics," *Urban Land Institute Bulletin No. 41*, (Washington: The Institute, 1961), pp. 36–38.

51. NCUP, *op.cit.*, p. 250.

52. ———. *op.cit.*, pp. 251–52.

53. ———. *op.cit.*, pp. 252–53.

54. Canty, *New City*, pp. 172–74, reproduced by permission of Praeger Publishers, Inc., a Division of Holt, Rinehart and Winston.

55. The Committee on Community Development (COCD), The Domestic Council, *National Growth and Development, Second Biennial Report*, (Washington: U.S. Government Printing Office, 1974), p. ix.

56. Canty, *New City*, p. 173, reproduced by permission of Praeger Publishers, Inc., a Division of Holt, Rinehart and Winston.

57. AIA, *op.cit.*, inside front cover, reproduced by permission.

58. ———. *op.cit.*, p. 4, reproduced by permission.

59. ———. *op.cit.*, p. 10, reproduced by permission.

60. The Committee on Growth and the Environment of the International City Management Association, Report of the ICMA Committee on Growth and the Environment, from *Public Management*, vol. 55, No. 9, (September 1973), pp. 8–10. Reprinted by special permission, © 1973 by the International City Management Association.

61. ACIR, *R.D.M.*, p. 348.

62. ———. *R.D.M.*, p. 354. The other mentioned recommendations and discussion of them are to be found on pages 363-74.

63. ——. *R.D.M.*, p. 366.

64. ——. *R.D.M.*, pp. 366–367.

65. "ALI Adopts Its Model Land Development Code." *AIP Newsletter*, **10**, No. 8, (August 1975), p. 10.

66. ALI, *op.cit.*, pp. 3–7, reprinted with the permission of the American Law Institute.

67. ——. *op.cit.*, pp. 8–9, reprinted with the permission of the American Law Institute.

68. ——. *op.cit.*, p. 18, reprinted with the permission of the American Law Institute.

69. Hagman, Donald G., *Articles 1 and 2 of A Model Land Development Code: The English are Coming*, (Los Angeles: Institute of Government and Public Affairs, University of California, Los Angeles, 1972), p. 1.

70. ALI, *op.cit.*, p. 126, reprinted with the permission of the American Law Institute.

71. ——. *op.cit.*, p. 139, reprinted with the permission of the American Law Institute.

72. ——. *op.cit.*, p. 177, reprinted with the permission of the American Law Institute.

73. ——. *op.cit.*, p. 180, reprinted with the permission of the American Law Institute.

74. ——. *op.cit.*, p. 195, reprinted with the permission of the American Law Institute.

75. Downs, *op.cit.*, p. 21.

76. ALI, *op.cit.*, pp. 203–09, reprinted with the permission of the American Law Institute.

77. Reps, "Future," pp. 49–50.

78. ALI, *op.cit.*, p. 257.

79. ——. *op.cit.*, p. 261, reprinted with the permission of the American Law Institute.

80. ——. *op.cit.*, p. 267, reprinted with the permission of the American Law Institute.

81. ——. *op.cit.*, p. 286, reprinted with the permission of the American Law Institute.

82. ——. *op.cit.*, pp. 286–87, reprinted with the permission of the American Law Institute.

83. ——. *op.cit.*, pp. 293–94, reprinted with the permission of the American Law Institute.

84. ——. *op.cit.*, p. 305, reprinted with the permission of the American Law Institute.

85. ——. *op.cit.*, pp. 305–06, reprinted with the permission of the American Law Institute.

86. ——. *op.cit.*, pp. 306–07, reprinted with the permission of the American Law Institute.

87. ——. *op.cit.*, p. 312, reprinted with the permission of the American Law Institute.

88. ——. *A Model Land Development Code—Tentative Draft, No. 3*, (Philadel-

phia: The Institute, April 22, 1971), p. 101, reprinted with the permission of the American Law Institute.

89. From AIP, *Code Review*, p. 2.

90. *Ibid.*

91. The review was prepared by Jim Childress, Assoc. AIP and AIP Government Relations Assistant, in consultation with Robert Einsweiler, AIP President; Maxine Kurtz, AIP, a planning lawyer; Bob Payslay, AIP; Ernest Bartley, AIP; George Raymond, AIP; John Joyner, AIP, Exec. Director of AIP; and Al Massoni, AIP Director of Government Relations.

92. From AIP, *op.cit.*, pp. 4–5.

93. From AIP, *op.cit.*, pp. 7–8.

94. From AIP, *op.cit.*, p. 8.

95. *Ibid.*

96. ALI, *op.cit.*, (1974), p. 146, reprinted with the permission of the American Law Institute.

97. Council on Environmental Quality, *Land Use*, (Washington: U.S. Government Printing Office, December 1974), p. 49.

98. Bosselman, Fred, and Callies, David, *The Quiet Revolution in Land Use Control*, (Washington: U.S. Government Printing Office, 1973), pp. 6–7.

99. Thompson, Myron B., "Hawaii's State Land Use Law," *State Government*, (Spring 1966), pp. 97–100.

100. Hawaii Department of Planning and Economic Development, *General Plan Revision Program, Part 1*, (Honolulu: The Department, 1967), p. 40.

101. Bosselman and Callies, *op.cit.*, p. 13.

102. Environmental Protection Agency, "Environmental Protection Agency—Air Programs: Approval and Promulgation of Implementation Plans—A Review of Indirect Sources, Part III," *Federal Register*, **39**, No. 8, (February 25, 1974), p. 7276.

103. Council on Environmental Quality, *Environmental Quality, The Fifth Annual Report*, (Washington: U.S. Government Printing Office, December 1974), p. 407.

104. *California Environmental Quality Act of 1970, as amended in 1972 and 1974*, Public Resources Code Division 13, p. 5 (mimeographed).

105. ———. *op.cit.*, p. 1.

106. Congressional Research Service, *Toward a National Growth Policy: Federal and State Developments in 1972*, (Washington: U.S. Government Printing Office, 1973) p. 75.

107. Bosselman and Callies, *op.cit.*, p. 108 and p. 292.

108. ———. *op.cit.*, p. 207.

109. ———. *op.cit.*, pp. 216–26.

110. ———. *op.cit.*, pp. 165–80.

111. Nordheimer, Jon, "Florida Seeks to Control Growth," *New York Times*, November 19, 1973, section 1, p. 2.

112. Rubino, Richard G., "Florida's New Land Use Law is Among Most Comprehensive in Nation," *AIP Newsletter*, **8**, No. 4, (April 1973), p. 11. Reprinted by permission of the American Institute of Planners.

113. Chapter 22F.1 and 22F.2, *Suppl. No. 30, Laws of Florida*, pp. 1–5.

114. Rubino, *op.cit.*, p. 11. Reprinted by permission of the American Institute of Planners.

115. "News Report," reprinted from *Progressive Architecture*, September 1975, pp. 26–27, copyright 1975 by Reinhold Publishing Company.

116. Schell, Steven R., "Summary of Land Use Regulation in the State of Oregon," in U.S. Senate Committee on Interior and Insular Affairs, *State Land Use Programs*, (Washington: U.S. Government Printing Office, 1974), p. 55.

117. ———. *op.cit.*, p. 56.

118. From Scott, Randall, "Oregon Supreme Court Says Cities Must Zone in Accordance with Their Comprehensive Plans," *AIP Newsletter*, **10**, No. 7, (July 1975), pp. 7–8. A publication of the American Institute of Planners.

119. Schell, *op.cit.*, p. 58.

120. ———. *op.cit.*, p. 62.

121. Bosselman and Callies, *op.cit.*, pp. 56–59.

122. ———. *op.cit.*, pp. 66–67.

123. ———. *op.cit.*, p. 77.

124. ———. *op.cit.*, p. 79–89.

125. ———. *op.cit.*, p. 262.

126. ———. *op.cit.*, p. 263–283.

127. ———. *op.cit.*, p. 267.

128. ———. *op.cit.*, p. 269.

129. ———. *op.cit.*, p. 282.

130. ACIR, *Regional Governance: Promise and Performance, Substate Regionalism and the Federal Systems, Volume II—Case Studies*, (Washington: U.S. Government Printing Office, 1973), p. 118, (Hereinafter referred to as ACIR, *Governance*).

131. ———. *op.cit.*, pp. 120–121.

132. ———. *op.cit.*, pp. 121–122.

133. *Ibid.*

134. "Metropolitan Reorganization Act," *Minnesota Session Laws—Laws, 1974, Chapter 422*, (St. Paul: Metropolitan Council, 1974), pp. 1–22, passim (mimeographed).

135. "Metropolitan Parks," *Minnesota Session Laws—Laws, 1974, Chapter 563*, (St. Paul: Metropolitan Council, 1974), pp. 1–5, passim (mimeographed).

136. "Protection Open Space," *Minnesota Session Laws—Laws, 1974, Chapter 359*, (St. Paul: Metropolitan Council, 1974), pp. 1–2 (mineographed).

137. "Metropolitan Housing and Redevelopment Authority," *Minnesota Session Laws—Laws, 1974, Chapter 359*, (St. Paul: Metropolitan Council, 1974) pp. 1–2 (mimeographed).

138. Metropolitan Council, "Summary of Metropolitan Significance Act," (St. Paul: The Council, April 12, 1976), pp. 1–2 (mimeographed).

139. Metropolitan Council, "Metropolitan Lands Planning Act Summary," (St. Paul: The Council, 1976), pp. 1–7 (mimeographed). Also letter from Ted Smebakken of the Council's Public Information Office dated April 6th 1978.

140. For more detailed evaluations see: ACIR, *Governance*, pp. 130–134; Bosselman and Callies, *op.cit.*, pp. 153–155; and Richard B. Spicer, "Increasing State and Regional Power in the Development Process," *ASPO Planning Advisory Service Report*, No. 255, (Chicago: American Society of Planning Officials, March 1970), p. 27.

141. Bosselman and Callies, *op.cit.*, p. 108, p. 291, and p. 293.

142. Gleeson, Michael E., Ball, Ian Traquair, Einsweiler, Robert C., Freilich, Robert H., and Meagher, Patrick, *Urban Growth Control Systems: An Evaluation of Policy Related Research,* (2 vols; Minneapolis: University of Minnesota, School of Public Affairs, 1974). Note: This is a mimeographed longer version than the later ULI publication cited in note 2 or the ASPO PAS Report 309–310 cited in note 157.

143. Gleeson, *op.cit.*, vol. 1, p. II-1, reproduced with permission.

144. ——. *op.cit.*, vol. 1, pp. II-16.

145. ——. *op.cit.*, vol. 1, p. II-22.

146. ——. *op.cit.*, vol. 1, pp. II-28 & II-29.

147. ——. *op.cit.*, vol. 1, pp. II-34 & II-35.

148. ——. *op.cit.*, vol. 1, pp. II-39 to II-41.

149. ——. *op.cit.*, vol. 1, pp. II-48 to II-51.

150. ——. *op.cit.*, vol. 1, pp. II-55 & II-56.

151. ——. *op.cit.*, vol. 1, p. II-63 to II-65.

152. "Petaluma Wins on Growth Control," *Planning,* **42**, No. 4, (May 1976), p. 6.

153. Gleeson, *op.cit.*, pp. II-67 to II-70.

154. ——. *op.cit.*, p. II-72.

155. ——. *op.cit.*, p. II-80 to II-82.

156. ——. *op.cit.*, p. II-81, reproduced with permission.

157. Gleeson, Michael E., et al., "Urban Growth Management Systems," PAS Report 309–310 (Chicago: ASPO, 1975) p. 24. Reprinted with permission of the American Society of Planning Officials.

158. ——. *op.cit.*, p. 25, reprinted with permission.

159. ——. *Urban Growth Control Systems*, pp. II-3 to II-6. Reproduced by permission of the University of Minnesota School of Public Affairs.

160. ——. *op.cit.*, p. III-1.

8

Concluding observations, evaluations, and suggestions

The previous chapters have dealt with the context in which urban planning takes place, the conventional American land use planning implementation tools and techniques, reforms and innovations in these tools and techniques, proposals for additional or new tools and techniques, and finally with both proposals for and experiments with integrating various implementation tools and techniques into organized implementation programs often described as growth guidance systems.

This chapter will touch on informal strategies, summarize previous findings and suggest the more likely and potentially workable directions for future reforms and innovations in the means for carrying out land use plans in urban areas.

INFORMAL STRATEGIES: SOME BRIEF OBSERVATIONS

In addition to the legal and organizational implementation means there exist a multitude of behavioral strategies which may be valuable for bringing the legal and organizational means into being, into use, and for influencing private and public decision-making regarding physical development. They involve the planner's relationships with the political decision-makers, other agency professionals at all levels of government, organized civic and professional groups, and with the citizenry. Because dealing with these complex subjects adequately is beyond the scope of this book they will be only briefly taken into account here.

Ranney[1] and Catanese[2] among others have examined the possible relationships between planners and local decision-makers. One role of the planner is that of the passive technician giving politicians the benefit of his expert judgment on more or less a "take it or leave it" basis. This role avoids risk on the part of the planner but his technical arguments must be overwhelmingly persuasive (and obvious) if he is to obtain political support. Another role is that of attempting to secure political support covertly either directly but informally and behind the scenes, or through friendly local pressure groups or prominent influentials before and/or during the decision-making process. This role entails less risk and is more frequently successful. A third role for the planner is that of political activist, promoting specific plans and policies directly and publicly in the political arena. This entails the most risk, often puts the agency planner in the position of biting the hand that feeds him, and the outcome of using this strategy is uncertain. The choice of which role to take may be dependent on the particular planning issue raised as well as the planner's personality as it affect the role or roles he/she is most comfortable with, and the attitudes and responses of the decision-makers with whom he/she is dealing. Many planners play all three roles from time to time as seems appropriate. However, it is certain that if planners are not willing to take some risks not much is likely to be achieved. It is also true that the development of frequent, friendly relations between planners and the politicians they deal with is essential to mutual understanding and the fostering of cooperation.

Interagency relationships also depend on frequent and friendly direct contacts and having the support of the respective agency heads and their superiors. Where there is a planning commission its members may be in a position to facilitate good interagency relations when interagency communication or cooperation problems arise. The chief executive of the local government involved may also be a key person in establishing and maintaining such relations, especially where the department form of planning agency exists. The creation of an atmosphere of mutual trust between the local government agencies in the area being planned for and between related agencies at all levels of government is necessary to the operation of a successful planning process and must constantly be nurtured by those responsibly involved.

The cultivation of organized civic and professional groups having a stake in the planning effort is necessary both for obtaining information and developing support. These organizations can help in the establishment of community priorities and goals, provide specialized local data, serve as a sounding board as critics of various planning alternatives and lend public support for planning programs at critical points. Good two-way communication with such groups is essential.

Citizen participation in the planning process must extend beyond civic and professional organizations and the elected and appointed officials, to the citizenry at large. Required public hearings, large public meetings, and token citizen committees are inadequate for the task. Public meetings which are issue-oriented and highly structured requiring individual participation are very useful, especially if they are followed up by surveys designed to elicit responses from citizens who tend to be nonparticipants in civic processes. No single approach to citizen participation has proven universally successful; there is room in this field of operation for much more experimentation. Nonetheless the value of citizen participation is increasingly being recognized, especially in view of the growing number of planning projects being delayed or defeated by citizen activists of various persuasions.

CONTEXT

The intergovernmental context in which urban land use planning takes place is extremely complex, especially in the larger metropolitan areas with their many, often overlapping, units of government. The seemingly intractable problems of central cities and the tensions between these cities and their suburbs serve to complicate the planning process and contribute to difficulties in the implementation of area-wide land use plans and policies. The techniques for carrying out plans each have various individual shortcomings and are difficult to integrate systematically into coordinated implementation programs. Even where such programs have been put together there often arise organizational, administrative, judicial, and/or political problems. Nevertheless professional planners, other urbanists, and governments at various levels are actively working toward the improvement of the techniques and processes for carrying out land use plans. In these endeavors they are supported by increasing public concern about the rate, quantity, and quality of urban development, especially in areas of rapid growth and where there are threats to the natural and/or man-made environment.

ZONING

Zoning, originated primarily as a means for controlling nuisances and protecting property values, has proven difficult to adapt as a tool for carrying out land use plans, especially in newly developing areas. Nevertheless it is a powerful tool and recently there has been a proliferation of zoning innovations designed to make it more flexible and responsive to the needs of the land use planning implementation process.

The problems of conventional zoning include the difficulty of relating it to long-range land use plans in the absence of stage development plans, its relative ineffectiveness in dealing with nonconforming uses, its inflexibility, its negative character as seen in its inability to encourage desired development, its lack of provisions for economic compensation when it restricts use so severely as to approach being confiscatory, its usual lack of coordination with other implementation means, and its misuse to perpetuate or promote socio-economic segregation, inequitable tax patterns and monotonous development patterns.

Some of the more significant recent innovations alleviating zoning's shortcomings have been the linking of zoning to short-range stage-development plans based on long-range land use plans, the amortization of nonconforming uses, increased reliance on density and design controls as opposed to the segregation of uses and building types, the introduction of special permits and individual project review for conditional uses and for planned unit development, the introduction of esthetic controls requiring design review in historic districts and other special areas, the introduction of transferable development rights and tax incentives as a means of compensation for severe use restrictions, and the introduction of density bonuses conditional on developers providing specified amenities.

SUBDIVISION REGULATIONS

Subdivision regulations continue to be an important tool for the implementation of land use plans in urbanizing areas. Usually intended for the control of single-family residential development, they often need extensive modification for application to the other types of land uses for which subdivision increasingly is taking place. Well-written regulations based on sufficiently high standards can go a long way to insure high quality in new development. In order to be effective in carrying out land use plans they must in use be carefully coordinated with the community facilities plan, major street plan, official map, capital improvement program, and all other relevant controls affecting land use. As part of such integrated planning implementation programs they can serve to help influence the location and timing of new development and keep its financial impact on local government resources manageable. The single most significant recent innovation in subdivision regulations, has been that of tying development permission to the adequacy of off-site facilities as exemplified in several growth guidance systems described in chapter seven.

SUPPLEMENTAL REGULATIONS AND TAX POLICIES

Because this miscellany of controls and devices cannot be readily generalized about as a whole it will be summarized in a series of statements on the individual topics:

Building codes are intended to insure safety of buildings as they are constructed so these codes affect land use only indirectly. The lack of uniformity in building codes from jurisdiction to jurisdiction has had the effect of limiting the market for manufactured housing and the introduction of new building products. This has prevented possible savings in construction costs and affected planning for low- and medium-cost housing. Recently, however, the states have taken action toward unified statewide codes and the federal government has undertaken new building product research designed to enable more frequent and uniform updating of building codes. These moves should help somewhat in housing planning.

Housing codes apply to existing housing and are intended to require that substandard housing be brought up to standard and that sound housing be well maintained. These codes are difficult to administer and enforce, especially when the costs of bringing a building up to code standards cannot be recouped through increased rentals, often leading to housing abandonment. This problem has been relieved in some places by scheduling repairs over longer periods, the use of tax incentives and through urban homesteading programs. The use of housing codes for upgrading and maintaining housing quality has been more successful in residential areas where housing is not severely deteriorated.

Health and sanitary regulations, especially those affecting sewage disposal and water supply, may be very important means for deterring development in unserviced areas or areas unsuitable for the use of wells and/or septic tanks thus helping control the location and timing of development. Sewer or water moratoria based on such regulations are an important feature of many of the previously described local growth guidance systems.

Licensing of businesses does not have enough effect on the location of uses to be of significance in implementing land use plans.

Tax policies do not lend themselves very easily to planning purposes even though they affect land use patterns. Income tax policies generally favor home ownership and hence encourage single-family residential development and, more recently, condominiums. The effects of real property taxes on land use patterns are neither consistent nor clear. Lower tax rates in the suburbs may have contributed to the flight from the central city but there were many other factors. Many planners and other urbanists favor the land tax as a deterrent to speculation and leapfrogging of development but case studies of this tax where used have been generally inconclusive. Preferential taxation, particularly of agricultural land and historic sites or districts, is now being more frequently used and may prove to be an effective way of preserving low density uses where development pressures are not extreme. There are persuasive arguments for selective taxation based on planning goals and purposes but the proposals made raise serious and possibly insurmountable questions of legality and the achievement of fair administration. Tax-base sharing as being tried out in the Twin Cities and Hackensack Meadows areas would seem to have great potential as a means of achieving more rational land use planning through reducing interjurisdictional competition for commercial and industrial development in multijurisdictional metropolitan areas.

FINANCIAL PLANNING AND CAPITAL IMPROVEMENT PROGRAMMING

Financial planning and capital improvement programming are increasingly being recognized as essential to orderly and more effective management of local government finances and the scheduling of public expenditures in order to keep expenditures within public financial capacity and coordinate related spending activities of the various units of local government urban areas. Private and public developmental expenditures can become more mutually supportive through careful scheduling of development in land use planning implementation programs which carefully link financial planning and capital improvement programming with stage-development plans and other land use controls as exemplified by some of the experimental growth guidance systems described previously.

SPECIAL DISTRICTS AND PUBLIC AUTHORITIES

While the use of special districts, especially single-purpose districts, should be avoided as contributing to the fragmentation of governments and compounding the coordination difficulties in the implementation of area-wide land use plans and policies, however, in the absence of consolidated area-wide government, multipurpose districts, such as those established to serve as umbrella multijurisdictional organizations charged with the responsibility for and empowered to coordinate the planning and development-related activities of many otherwise independently acting units of local government, can be a very useful organizational means for carrying out area-wide plans (as exemplified by the Twin Cities Metropolitan Council). Also useful are multipurpose state authorities empowered to participate directly in the urban development process at various scales, as are the Puerto Rico Land Administration and the New York Urban Development Corporation.

GROWTH GUIDANCE SYSTEMS AND INNOVATIVE LEGISLATION

During the last two decades there has been an increasing concern among citizens, planning-oriented professionals, and many of those in all levels of government for systematically improving the means for and effectiveness of implementing land use plans and policies. This concern has been expressed through growth guidance system proposals, organizational recommendations, and innovative legislation and programs for controlling the timing, location, and quality of urban development, especially at the state, regional, and local levels. At the federal level there has been an increased effort to coordinate federal programs which affect development. This has taken the form of interagency coordination agreements, interagency groups such as the Council on Environmental Quality, and legislative proposals to strengthen state and national planning.

This is a time of trying out new legal and organizational techniques for the implementation of land use plans and policies. The political climate is such that the amount and variety of experimentation is likely to continue until the relative effectiveness of the innovations can be properly evaluated.

CONCLUSIONS

The foregoing examination and evaluation of the tools and techniques for implementing land use planning and policies, current practices in their use, current attempts to strengthen the ability to influence land use and physical development decisions, innovative planning legislation, and the organization of integrated implementation programs (growth guidance systems) has shown that the limitations of the prevalent, currently available means are becoming more widely perceived and remedied.

Based on the information developed in the previous chapters and summarized here, recommendations for affirmative action by the appropriate levels of government toward the continued improvement of the legal and organizational tools and techniques for more effective land use plan/policy implementation are listed as follows:

1. *National Planning.* At the national level there is a need for the formulation and adoption of national land use and physical development objectives as part of a continuous planning process concerned with encouraging development where additional growth would be most beneficial to the nation; curtailing growth where it would contribute to overburdening natural and human resources; and preserving from development areas where in the national interest the natural environment should be left relatively undisturbed. The national plans and policies so formulated should serve as a broad framework within which state and local plans and policies could be evaluated for the purposes of allocating federal planning and development funds. They should also serve as means of evaluating the interaction between the various federal programs affecting state and local land use and development with the purpose of resolving conflicts and achieving better coordination.

While it has been the policy at the national level to encourage state, regional, and local planning there has been no recent serious effort to establish a national land use and development planning and policy framework within which national legislation could be coordinated and a rational allocation of resources achieved. Although the coordination of the programs of the various executive departments has been improved by the establishment of interdepartmental coordinating committees, this is simply not enough. What has been prescribed for the lower levels of government needs for the same good reasons to be required at the national level. The problems, needs, and opportunities are not geographically evenly distributed. Priorities and resource allocation clearly should be established on clearer views of national goals and a better basis than political horse trading.

A permanent national planning board attached to the executive arm of government should be established with adequate professional planning staff to prepare and maintain a long-range national land use development policies plan expressing national goals. It should also prepare programs for intermediate and short-range action including recommendations for implementing legislation. It would report to the President on a regular periodic basis and serve as an information gathering resource for both the executive and legislative branches, closely coordinating its research efforts with those of the relevant congressional committees and staff of the Library of Congress.

2. *State Planning.* At the state level there is a need in most states for increased planning efforts toward the formulation of state land use and physical plans and policies as a framework for coordinating state programs affecting patterns of land use and development at the state, regional, and local levels. Pursuant to these plans and under improved state planning enabling legislation the states should more actively guide planning at all levels of government in matters of statewide and multicounty regional public concern.

Although more states are undertaking to formulate at least some elements of statewide planning for land use and resource development there is a need for more intensive and extensive activity in this field to be undertaken by adequate professional planning staffs reporting to the governors with comprehensive long-, intermediate-, and short-range plan, policy and program proposals. Just as in the previous recommendation such strengthened planning activities could benefit governors in preparing their legislative programs and legislators by providing more extensive information for use in the decision-making process.

3. *State Subregional and Local Planning Legislation.* Most state planning enabling legislation is in need of updating, in respect to regional and local planning. This should be undertaken preferably somewhat along the lines of the American Law Institute's Model Land Development Code, especially as the Code affects state intervention in "areas of critical state concern" and "development of regional impact," the integration of zoning and subdivision controls into unified development codes specifying coordinated administrative procedures, and provisions for land banking. However, this code should be modified to require that development controls be based on long and mid-range comprehensive plans and short-range development plans and programs indicating the time sequence of development as reflected in the scheduling of the construction of community facilities in the capital improvement programs. Further, permission to subdivide and develop should be made conditional on the adequacy of existing community facilities, i.e. access roads, utilities, and drainage, or their provision by the developer if he is not willing to wait until local government provides them as scheduled. The states should also consider enabling the

use of transferable development rights as a means of compensating owners for providing specified development amenities or for restrictions such as those imposed on landmarks, for historic preservation or in special design control districts.

It is essential that land use controls be strengthened at the regional and local levels; that they be unified into more closely linked and coordinated development controls for more effective and rational growth guidance; that more flexibility in their administration be made possible by giving controls administrators more discretionary authority within the context of specific criteria and that the public be protected from administrative incompetence by mandating that these positions be filled only by *qualified* professional planners; that regulations involving esthetics and historic preservation be subject to review by planning staff and *qualified* review boards; that compensation by way of tax subsidies and/or the sale of development rights be provided in cases where controls result in unfair and severe economic hardship to property owners; and that a more effective means such as that proposed in the Code be instituted for dealing with incompatible existing land uses.

Furthermore state intervention in regional and local land development is clearly justified in cases where growth pressures are extremely great, the scale of proposed development is too large for the local government to cope with, or there is an adverse threat to a delicate ecological condition. The time is overdue for states to take a more active role in preserving and enhancing the quality of both their rural and urban areas.

4. *Umbrella Agencies*. In metropolitan areas where the creation of metropolitan general purpose governments as a means of coordinating urban development is not politically feasible, the states should create elective multijurisdictional umbrella agencies to undertake metropolitan planning which have the power to review, amend, and coordinate the planning and development controls of all local governmental units within their jurisdictions and also undertake to construct and operate or coordinate such area-wide services as mass transit, sewage lines and processing plants, or other functions appropriate for the individual metropolitan situation.

While most states have created multicounty and in some cases interstate regional planning districts in both rural and urban areas, many of which have governing boards made up of elected officials (councils of governments), for the most part these planning agencies are only advisory to their constituent governments and lack the power necessary to manage effective coordination and implementation of intraregional plans and policies, nor are these agencies directly responsible to the voters in regard to regional matters. These agencies need both strengthening and greater accountability to the citizens they serve, especially in metropolitan regions where the problems of development and renewal are both complex and extensive.

5. *Implementation Programs.* Local and regional planning agencies need to put more effort into formulating and carrying out systematic land use planning and policies implementation programs using the tools and techniques at their disposal. Where these are inadequate, they should seek improved state enabling legislation and more comprehensive local implementation ordinances.

The formulation of long-range comprehensive plans is only a first step in the development of viable plans and policies. For long-range plans to be useful they must be broken down into stage development plans for the intermediate periods reflecting priorities for development and other activities. What should happen in each time interval between the present and long-range planning time horizon must be determined more in detail for the earlier stages than the later.

Very detailed programs for the earlier stages must be developed including implementation strategies which make coordinated systematic use of all the implementation techniques which can practically be brought to bear on the problems of effecting the programs. This will involve the organization of growth guidance systems such as those described in the previous chapter and will most probably involve the adoption of more innovative legislation at both the state and local levels of government.

6. *Research.* More research is needed in the development, refinement, and functioning of alternative guidance systems for use in differing geographic and governmental settings and to meet needs of special situations. Such research would be an aid to professional planners, planning lawyers, and political decisionmakers in chosing the strategies and techniques appropriate to the land use problems they are dealing with. New ideas need development and testing and ongoing experiments need evaluation for their relative effectiveness.

As proposed in the ALI Model Land Development Code those universities in each state having urban research capacities could be very effective and appropriate resource institutions for state planning research activities in growth guidance system development and monitoring. In many research activity areas state government-university cooperation has already proven itself in partnership relationships in regard to both basic and applied research and the workshops, seminars, and publications necessary for the dissemination of research findings.

Carrying out these recommendations, distilled as they are from the many observations and conclusions of governmental and professional studies on which this book is based, would go a long way toward the improvement of the conditions under which land use plans and policies are formulated and their implementation takes place. It must be kept in mind, however, that the achievement of the important goal of bringing into being and maintaining a better urban physical environment depends not only on skilled and innovative professional planning endeavors but also upon securing strong and continuing public and political support.

NOTES TO CHAPTER 8

1. Ranney, David C., *Planning and Politics in the Metropolis*, (Columbus: Charles E. Merrill, 1969), pp. 179.
2. Catanese, Anthony James, *Planners and Local Politics: Impossible Dreams*, (Beverly Hills & London: Sage, 1974), pp. 189.

Bibliography

BOOKS, PAMPHLETS, REPORTS AND THEIR COMPONENT PARTS

Advisory Commission on Intergovernmental Relations. *Building Codes: A Program for Intergovernmental Reform.* Washington: U.S. Government Printing Office, 1966.

Advisory Commission on Intergovernmental Relations. *Governmental Functions and Processes: Local and Areawide.* Vol. IV, *Substate Regionalism and the Federal System.* Washington: U.S. Government Printing Office, 1974.

Advisory Commission on Intergovernmental Relations. *Performance of Urban Functions: Local and Area Wide.* Washington: U.S. Government Printing Office, 1963.

Advisory Commission on Intergovernmental Relations. *The Problem of Special Districts in American Government.* Washington: U.S. Government Printing Office, 1964.

Advisory Commission on Intergovernmental Relations. *Regional Decision Making: New Strategies for Substate Districts.* Vol. I, *Substate Regionalism and the Federal System.* Washington: U.S. Government Printing Office, 1973.

Advisory Commission on Intergovernmental Relations. *Regional Goverance: Promise and Performance Substate Regionalism and the Federal System, Volume II— Case Studies.* Washington: U.S. Government Printing Office, 1973.

American Law Institute. *A Model Land Development Code.* Philadelphia: The Institute, April 15, 1974.

American Law Institute. *A Model Land Development Code—Tentative Draft No. 3.* Philadelphia: The Institute, April 22, 1971.

Andrews, Richard. *Urban Land Economics and Public Policy.* New York: The Free Press, 1971.

Babcock, Richard F. *The Zoning Game.* Madison: University of Wisconsin Press, 1966.

Bain, Henry. "The Organization of Growth," in *The New City.* Edited by Donald Canty. New York: Praeger, 1969.

Bair, Frederick H., Jr. *Local Regulation of Mobile Home Parks, Travel Trailer Parks and Related Facilities.* Chicago: Mobile Homes Research Foundation, 1965.

Bair, Frederick H., Jr. "Modular Housing, Including Mobile Homes." *ASPO Planning Advisory Service Report,* No. 265, 1971.

Bair, Frederick H., Jr. "Special Public Interest Districts," *ASPO Planning Advisory Service Report,* No. 287, January 1973.

Banfield, Edward C., and Grodzins, Morton. "Some Flaws in the Logic of Metropolitan Reorganization." *Metropolitan Politics.* Edited by Michael N. Danielson. Boston: Little Brown, 1966.

Banfield, Edward C. *The Unheavenly City.* Boston: Little Brown, 1968.

Beal, Franklyn H. "Defining Development Objectives." *Principles and Practice of Urban Planning.* Edited by William I. Goodman and Eric C. Freund. Washington: The International City Managers' Association, 1968.

Bellush, Jewell, and Hausknecht, Murray. "Public Housing: The Contexts of Failure." *Housing Urban America.* Edited by Jon Pynoos, Robert Schafer, and Chester W. Hartman. Chicago: Aldine, 1973.

Benson, Philip A., and North, Nelson L. *Real Estate Practices and Principles.* New York: Prentice-Hall, 1947.

Billboard Regulation. Chicago: Chicago Plan Commission, 1952.

Bingham, Charlotte. "Regulating Public Uses." *ASPO Planning Advisory Service Report*, No. 228, November 1967.

Blair, Lachlin F. "Programming Community Development." *Principles and Practice of Urban Planning.* Edited by William I. Goodman and Eric C. Freund. Washington: International City Managers' Association, 1968.

Boley, Robert E. "Industrial Districts Restudied, An Analysis of Characteristics." *Urban Land Institute Bulletin No. 41.* Washington: The Institute, 1961.

Bollens, John C. *Special District Governments in the United States.* Berkeley and Los Angeles: University of California Press, 1957.

Bosselman, Fred, and Callies, David. *The Quiet Revolution in Land Use Control.* Washington: Council on Environmental Quality, 1973.

Brooks, Mary. "Bonus Provisions in Central City Areas." *ASPO Planning Advisory Service Report,* No. 257, May 1970.

Brooks, Mary. "Exclusionary Zoning." *ASPO Planning Advisory Service Report,* No. 254, February 1970.

Brown, G. G. and Others. *Land Value Taxation Around the World.* New York: Robert Schalkanback Foundation, 1955.

Buehler, Alfred G. "Revenue Improvements under Present Laws and Government Structure," in *Financing Metropolitan Government.* Princeton: Tax Institute, Incorporated, 1955.

Burchell, Robert W., and Hughes, James W. *Planned Unit Development—New Communities American Style.* New Brunswick: Rutgers University Center for Urban Policy Research, 1972.

Burke, William. "Public Improvements Program and Financial Planning." Unpublished paper, Purdue University, 1972.

Butler, George D. "Recreation Administration in Metropolitan Areas, Part 2: Authorization and Function." *Recreation,* October 1962.

Candeub, Fleissig, and Associates. *Route 1: A Highway Demonstration Study, Woodbridge, New Jersey.* Newark: Candeub, Fleissig, and Associates, 1968.

Cahn, Robert. "Where Do We Grow From Here?". *Management and Control of Growth.* Edited by Randall W. Scott. Washington: The Urban Land Institute, 1975.

Canty, Donald, ed. *The New City.* New York: Praeger, 1969.

Carter, Steve; Bert, Kendall; and Nobert, Peter. "Local Government Techniques for Managing Growth." *Management of Growth,* Vol. II. Edited by Randall W. Scott. Washington: The Urban Land Institute, 1975.

Catanese, Anthony James. *Planners and Local Politics, Impossible Dreams.* Beverly Hills and London: Sage Publications, 1974.

Clapp, James A. *New Towns and Urban Policy.* New York: Dunellen, 1971.

Clark, W. A. V. *The Impact of Property Taxes on Urban Spacial Development.* Los Angeles: The Institute of Government and Public Affairs, The University of California, Los Angeles, 1974.

Clawson, Marion, and Perloff, Harvey. "Alternatives for Future Urban Land Policy." *Modernizing Urban Land Policy.* Edited by Marion Clawson. Baltimore and London: The Johns Hopkins Press, 1973.

Clawson, Marion, and Hall, Peter. *Planning and Urban Growth.* Baltimore and London: The Johns Hopkins Press, 1973.

Clawson, Marion. *Suburban Land Conversion in the United States: An Economic and Governmental Process.* Baltimore and London: The John Hopkins Press, 1971.

Committee for Economic Development. *Modernizing Local Government.* New York: The Committee, 1966.

Committee for Economic Development. *Reshaping Government in Metropolitan Areas.* New York: The Committee, 1970.

Committee on Community Development. The Domestic Council. *National Growth and Development, Second Biennial Report.* Washington: U.S. Government Printing Office, 1974.

Congressional Research Service. *Toward A National Growth Policy: Federal and State Developments* in 1972. Washington: U.S. Government Printing Office, 1973.

Council on Environmental Quality. *Environmental Quality, The Fifth Annual Report.* Washington: U.S. Government Printing Office, December 1974.

Council on Environmental Quality. *Land Use.* Washington: U.S. Government Printing Office, December 1974.

Cowan, H. B. *Municipal Improvement and Finance.* New York: Harper and Brothers, 1958.

Crecine, John P. ed. *Financing the Metropolis.* Beverly Hills and London: Sage, 1970.

Crenson, Matthew A. *The Un-Politics of Air Pollution.* Baltimore and London: The Johns Hopkins Press, 1971.

Delafons, John. *Land-Use Controls in the United States.* Cambridge: The M.I.T. Press, 1969.

Domestic Council Committee on National Growth. *Report on National Growth 1972.* Washington: U.S. Government Printing Office, 1972.

Domestic Council Committee on National Growth. *Report on National Growth 1974.* Washington: U.S. Government Printing Office, 1974.

Downs, Anthony. *Urban Problems and Prospects.* Chicago: Markham, 1970.

Einsweiler, Robert C.; Gleeson, Michael E.; Ball, Ian Traquair; Morris, Alan; and

Sprague, Diane. "Comparative Descriptions of Selected Municipal Growth Guidance Systems, A Preliminary Report," *Management and Control of Growth*, Vol. II. Edited by Randall W. Scott. Washington: The Urban Land Institute, 1975.

Fagin, Henry, and Weinberg, Robert C., eds. *Planning and Community Appearance*. New York: The Regional Plan Association, 1958.

Faraci, Piero. "The Authority of the Zoning Administrator." *ASPO Planning Advisory Service Report*, No. 226, September 1967.

Federal Housing Administration. *Land Use Intensity*. Washington: U.S. Government Printing Office, 1966.

Fessler, James W. *Area and Administration*. University, Alabama: University of Alabama Press, 1949.

Finley, William E. "A Fresh Start." *The New City*. Edited by Donald Canty. New York, Washington, London: Praeger, 1969.

Finney, Graham S. "The Intergovernmental Context of Local Planning." *Principles and Practice of Urban Planning*. Edited by William I. Goodman and Eric C. Freund. Washington: International City Managers' Association, 1968.

"Forms for Performance Bonds." *ASPO Planning Advisory Service Report* No. 58, January 1954.

Friday, Richard E. *Summaries of State Legislation Dealing with the Preservation of Farmland*. Ithaca: Department of Agricultural Economics, Cornell University, October 1969.

Funk, Robert L., ed. *Municipal Finance Administration*. Chicago: The International City Managers' Association, 1962.

Gaffney, Mason. "Property Taxes and the Frequency of Urban Renewal." *National Tax Association Proceedings*. Harrisburg: The Association, 1964.

Gallion, Arthur B. and Eisner, Simon. *The Urban Pattern, City Planning and Design*, 2nd ed. New York: Van Nostrand, 1975.

Gans, Herbert J. *People and Plans*. New York: Basic Books, 1968.

George, Henry. *Progress and Poverty*. New York: Henry George, 1888.

Goldschmidt, Leopold A. "Zoning for City Housing Markets." *ASPO Planning Advisory Service Report*, No. 279, April 1972.

Goodman, William I. and Freund, Eric C., eds. *Principles and Practice of Urban Planning*. Washington: International City Managers' Association 1968.

Governmental Functions Committee of the Capitol Regional Planning Agency. *Governmental Organizations for the Capitol Region*. Hartford: The Committee, 1967.

Grad, Frank P. *Legal Remedies for Housing Code Violations, Research Report No. 14*. Washington: The National Commission on Urban Problems, 1968.

Green, Philip P., Jr. "Land Subdivision." *Principles and Practice of Urban Planning*. Edited by William I. Goodman and Eric C. Freund. Washington: International City Managers Association, 1968.

Hagman, Donald G. *Articles 1 and 2 of A Model Land Development Code: The English Are Coming*. Los Angeles: Institute of Government and Public Affairs, University of California, Los Angeles, 1972.

Hagman, Donald G. *Urban Planning and Controls: Problems and Materials*, Part II.

Los Angeles: Institute of Government and Public Affairs, University of California, Los Angeles, 1969.

Hagman, Donald G. *Urban Planning and Land Development Control Law*. St. Paul: West, 1971.

Hawaii Department of Planning and Economic Development. *General Plan Revision Program, Part 1*. Honolulu: The Department, 1967.

Hearings Before the Subcommittee on Urban Affairs, Joint Economic Committee of the Congress of the United States, Part 1. Washington: U.S. Government Printing Office, 1970.

Heeter, David. "Interim Zoning Ordinances." *ASPO Planning Advisory Service Report*, No. 242, January 1969.

Heikoff, Joseph M. *Planning and Budgeting in Municipal Management*. Chicago: The International City Managers' Association, 1965.

[Herman, Harold, and McKay, Mary Elisabeth]. *Community Health Services*. Washington: International City Manager's Association, 1968.

Heyman, I. Michael. "Innovative Land Regulation and Comprehensive Planning." *The New Zoning: Legal, Administrative and Economic Concepts and Techniques*. New York: Praeger, 1970.

"Hillside Development." *ASPO Planning Advisory Service Report*, No. 126, September 1959.

Howard, John T. "The Local Planning Agency: Internal Administration." *Principles and Practice of Urban Planning*. Edited by William I. Goodman and Eric C. Freund. Washington: International City Managers' Association, 1968.

Howard, S. Kenneth. "Planning and Budgeting: Marriage Whose Style." *Planning and Politics: Uneasy Partnership*. Edited by Thad L. Beyle and George T. Lathrop. New York: Odyssey, 1970.

Hutchinson, A. R. *Public Charges upon Land Values in Australia*. Melbourne: no publisher given, 1961.

"Installation of Physical Improvements as Required in Subdivision Regulations." *ASPO Planning Advisory Service Report*, No. 38, May 1952.

International City Managers Association. *Municipal Recreation Administration*. Chicago: The Association, 1960.

International City Management Association. *Municipal Yearbook, 1972*, Vol. 39. Washington: The Association, 1972.

Kaufman, Jerome L. "Varying Improvement Requirements." *ASPO Planning Advisory Service Report*, No. 174, 1963.

Kent, T. J., Jr. *The Urban General Plan*. San Francisco: Chandler, 1964.

Krasnowiecki, Jan. "Planned Unit Residential Development." *Urban Land Institute Technical Bulletin*, No. 52, May 1965.

Kusler, Jon A., and Lee, Thomas M. "Regulation for Flood Plains." *ASPO Planning Advisory Service Report*, No. 277, February 1972.

Lauber, Daniel. "Recent Cases in Exclusionary Zoning." *ASPO Planning Advisory Service Report*, No. 292, June 1973.

Leary, Robert M. "Zoning." *Principles and Practice of Urban Planning*. Edited by William I. Goodman and Eric C. Freund. Washington: International City Managers' Association, 1968.

Levy, Frank; Meltsner, Arnold J.; and Wildavsky, Aaron. *Urban Outcomes—Schools, Streets, and Libraries.* Berkeley, Los Angeles, and London: University of California Press, 1974.

Lieberman, Barnet. "Administrative Provisions of Housing Codes." *Housing Code Standards: Three Critical Studies, Research Report No. 19.* Washington: The National Commission on Urban Problems, 1969.

Louisville and Jefferson County Planning Commission. *Metropolitan Subdivisions.* Louisville: The Commission, 1969.

McKeever, J. Ross. "Business Parks." *ULI Technical Bulletin,* No. 65. Washington: The Urban Land Institute, 1970.

McNayr, Irving G. "Recommendations for Unified Government in Dade County." *Government of the Metropolis.* Edited by Joseph F. Zimmerman. New York: Holt Rinehart Winston, 1968.

Mandelker, Daniel L. "The Rosslyn Experience." *The New Zoning: Legal, Administrative, and Economic Concepts and Techniques.* Edited by Norman Marcus and Marilyn W. Graves. New York: Praeger, 1970.

Mandelker, Daniel R. *The Zoning Dilemma.* Indianapolis: Bobbs-Merrill, 1971.

Manvel, Allen D. "Metropolitan Growth and Governmental Fragmentation." *Governance and Population: The Governmental Implications of Population Change.* Washington: The Commission on Population Growth and the American Future, 1972.

Marks, Marvin and West, John Petit, III. "Urban Design Through Zoning." *Planners Notebook,* Vol. 2, No. 5, October 1972.

Metropolitan Study Commission. *Report on Seweage Disposal in the Milwaukee Metropolitan Area.* Milwaukee: The Commission, 1958.

Meyerson, Martin and Banfield, Edward C. *Politics, Planning and the Public Interest.* Glencoe, Ill.: The Free Press, 1955.

Meyerson, Martin; Tyrwhitt, Jacqueline; and Wheaton, William L. C. *Housing, People, and Cities.* New York: McGraw-Hill, 1962.

Miner, Ralph W. "Conservation of Historic and Cultural Resources." *ASPO Planning Advisory Service Report,* No. 244, March 1969.

Mood, Eric W. "The Development, Objective, and Adequacy of Current Housing Code Standards." *Housing Code Standards: Three Critical Studies, Research Report No. 19.* Washington: The National Commission on Urban Problems, 1969.

Moore, Woodrow L., Jr. *Governmental Reorganization and Metropolitics: Determinants Central to a Normative Theory of Metropolitan Planning.* West Lafayette: Purdue University/Indiana State Highway Commission, 1975.

National Commission on Urban Growth Policy. "Findings and Recommendations." *The New City.* Edited by Donald Canty. New York: Praeger, 1969.

National Commission on Urban Growth Policy. "Planning and Precedents." *The New City.* Edited by Donald Canty. New York: Praeger, 1969.

National Commission on Urban Problems. *Building the American City.* Washington: U.S. Government Printing Office, 1968.

Natural Resources Committee. *Our Cities.* Washington: U.S. Government Printing Office, 1937.

Netzer, Dick. *Impact of the Property Tax: Its Economic Implications for Urban Problems.* Washington: The National Commission on Urban Affairs, 1968.

New York State Urban Development Corporation. *Goals, Policies and Prospects.* New York: The Corporation, 1972.

"Organization of the Subdivision Ordinance." *ASPO Planning Advisory Service Report,* No. 116, 1969.

Ornstein, Gail. "Auto Centers." *ASPO Planning Advisory Service Report,* No. 219, February 1967.

"Performance Bonds for the Installation of Subdivision Improvements." *ASPO Planning Advisory Service Report,* No. 48, March 1953.

Pickford, James H., and Shannon, John. "Harnessing Property Taxes and Land-Use Planning." *Planning,* Vol. 38, No. 11, December 1972.

Pickford, James H. "The Local Planning Agency: Organization and Structure." *Principles and Practice of Urban Planning.* Edited by William I. Goodman and Eric C. Freund. Washington: International City Managers' Association, 1968.

Preserving Norfolk's Heritage. Norfolk, Va.: Norfolk Department of City Planning, December 1965.

Price, Waterhouse & Co. *A Study of the Effects of Real Estate Tax Incentives Upon Property Rehabilitation and New Construction: Summary.* Washington: U.S. Department of Housing and Urban Development, 1973.

"Public Open Space in Subdivision." *ASPO Planning Advisory Service Report,* No. 45, January 1953.

Pynoos, Jon; Schafer, Robert; and Hartman, Chester W., eds., *Housing Urban America.* Chicago: Aldine, 1973.

Ranney, David C. *Planning and Politics in the Metropolis.* Columbus: Charles E. Merrill Publishing Company, 1969.

Rawson, Mary. *Property Taxation and Urban Development.* Research Monograph 4. Washington: The Urban Land Institute, 1961.

Real Estate Research Corporation. *The Costs of Sprawl: Detailed Cost Analysis.* Washington: U.S. Government Printing Office, 1974.

Real Estate Research Corporation. *The Costs of Sprawl: Executive Summary.* Washington: U.S. Government Printing Office, 1974.

"Recommended Practices for Subdivision Streets." *Traffic Engineering,* Vol. 37, No. 4, January 1967.

"Regulation of Mobile Home Subdivisions." *ASPO Planning Advisory Service Report,* No. 145, April 1961.

Reps, John W. "Requiem for Zoning." *Planning 1964.* Chicago: American Society of Planning Officials, 1964.

Reps, John W. "The Future of American Planning—Requiem or Renascence?" *Planning 1967.* Chicago: American Society of Planning Officials, 1967.

Rick, William B. "Planning and Developing Waterfront Property." *Urban Land Institute Technical Bulletin,* No. 49, June 1964.

Rodwin, Lloyd. *Nations and Cities.* Boston: Houghton Mifflin, 1970.

Rody, Martin J. and Smith, Herbert H. *Zoning Primer.* West Trenton: Chandler-Davis, 1960.

Rogers, William B. "Clinic: Fiscal Planning and Capital Budgeting." *Planning 1954.* Chicago: American Society of Planning Officials, 1954.

Rose, Jerome G. "Recent Decisions on Population Growth Control: The Belle Terre, Petaluma, and Madison Township Cases." *New Dimensions in Urban Planning:*

Growth Controls, Vol. 1. Edited by James W. Hughes. New Brunswick: Center for Urban Policy Research, The State University of New Jersey, 1974.

Rosenthal, John. "Cluster Subdivisions." *ASPO Planning Advisory Service Report,* No. 135, June 1960.

Rossano, A. T., Jr. *Air Pollution Control Guidebook for Management.* Stamford: E.R.A., 1969.

Saltzenstein, Marvin A. "Industrial Performance Standards." *ASPO Planning Advisory Service Report,* No. 272, September 1971.

Sanderson, Richard L. *Codes and Code Administration.* Chicago: Building Officials Conference of America, Inc., 1969.

Schell, Steven R. "Summary of Land Use Regulation in the State of Oregon." U.S. Senate Committee on Interior and Insular Affairs. *State Land Use Programs.* Washington: U.S. Government Printing Office, 1974.

Scott, Randall W. "An Introduction and Summary." *Management and Control of Growth.* Edited by Randall W. Scott. Washington: Urban Land Institute, 1975.

Scott, Randall W., ed. *Management and Control of Growth.* Washington: The Urban Land Institute, 1975.

Scott, Robert L. "The Effect of Nonconforming Land-Use Amortization." *ASPO Planning Advisory Service Report,* No. 280, May 1972.

Scott, Stanley and Bollens, John C. *Governing a Metropolitan Region: The San Francisco Bay Area.* Berkeley: Institute of Governmental Studies, 1968.

Slavet, Joseph S. and Levin, Melvin R. *New Approaches to Housing Code Administration, Research Report No. 17.* Washington: The National Commission on Urban Problems, 1969.

Smith, Robert G. *Public Authorities, Special Districts and Local Government.* Washington: National Association of Counties Research Foundation, 1964.

So, Frank S. "Government and Community Facilities." *Principles and Practice of Urban Planning.* Edited by William I. Goodman and Eric C. Freund. Washington: International City Managers' Association, 1968.

So, Frank S. "Metropolitan Planning Policy Implementation." *Planning Advisory Service Report,* No. 262. Chicago: American Society of Planning Officials, 1970.

Spicer, Richard B. "Increasing State and Regional Power in the Development Process." *ASPO Planning Advisory Service Report,* No. 255, March 1970.

"State Building Code Profile." *Construction Review,* March 1972.

Stern, Arthur C.; Wohlers, Henry C.; Boubel, Richard W.; and Lawry, William P. *Fundamentals of Air Pollution.* New York: Academic Press, 1973.

Stone, Harold A.; Price, Don K.; and Stone, Kathryn H. *City Manager Government in the United States.* Chicago: Public Administration Service, 1940.

Subcommittee on the Planning Process and Urban Development of the Advisory Committee to the Department of Housing and Urban Development. *Revenue Sharing and the Planning Process—Shifting the Focus of Responsibility for Domestic Problem Solving.* Washington: National Academy of Sciences, 1974.

"Subdivision Regulations for Industry." *ASPO Planning Advisory Service Report,* No. 162, September 1962.

U.S. Bureau of the Census. *Governmental Organization,* Vol. I, *Census of Governments: 1962.* Washington: U.S. Government Printing Office, 1963.

U.S. Department of Housing and Urban Development. *Housing in the Seventies.* Washington: U.S. Government Printing Office, 1974.

U.S. Department of Housing and Urban Development. *Preserving Historic America.* Washington: U.S. Government Printing Office, 1966.

U.S. Department of Housing and Urban Development. *Subdivision Analysis and Procedures.* Washington: U.S. Government Printing Office, January 1973.

U.S. Water Resources Council. *Regulation of Flood-Hazard Areas to Reduce Flood Losses.* Washington: U.S. Government Printing Office, 1972.

"Waterfronts: Planning for Resort and Residential Uses." *ASPO Planning Advisory Service Report*, No. 118, January 1959.

Weber, Melvin M. "Comprehensive Planning and Social Responsibility." *Urban Planning and Social Policy.* Edited by Bernard J. Frieden and Robert Morris. New York and London: Basic Books, 1968.

Webster, Donald H. *Urban Planning and Municipal Public Policy.* New York: Harper, 1958.

Weintraub, Tina V., and Patterson, James D. *The Authority in Pennsylvania: Pro and Con.* Philadelphia: Bureau of Municipal Research, 1949.

Williams, Norman, Jr. *The Structure of Urban Zoning.* New York: Buttenheim, 1966.

Wolfe, Myer R. "Land Use Economics and General Taxation Policy." *Urban Land Use Policy.* Edited by Richard B. Andrews. New York: The Free Press, 1972.

Wolffe, Leonard L. "New Zoning Landmarks in Planned Unit Development." *Urban Land Institute Technical Bulletin*, No. 62, 1968.

Yearwood, Richard M. *Land Subdivision Regulation: Policy and Legal Considerations for Urban Planning.* New York: Praeger, 1971.

COURT CASES

Berman v. Parker, 348 U.S. 26, 75 Sup. Ct. 98, 99 L. Ed. 27, 1954.

Burlington Co. NAACP v. Township of Mount Laurel, 200 A. 2d 465, New Jersey Super. Ct. 1972.

Hadacheck v. Sebastian, 239 U.S. 394, 1915.

Village of Euclid, Ohio v. Ambler Realty Company, 272 U.S. 365, 1926.

People v. Goodman, 31 N.Y. 2d 262.

Ranjel v. The City of Lansing, 417 F. 2nd. 321, Michigan, 1969.

Southern Alameda Spanish Speaking Organization v. City of Union City, 424 F. 2d 291, California, 1970.

LEGISLATIVE ACTS AND ORDINANCES

California Environmental Quality Act of 1970, as amended in 1972 and 1974, Public Resources Code Division 13, (mimeographed).

Chapter 22F.1 and 22F.2, *Suppl. No. 30, Laws of Florida.*

City of San Jose, Ordinance No. 16251.

[Carl Feiss], *Planning and Zoning Code and Zone Map* (Village of Bratenahl, Ohio: The Village, July 1962).

Indiana Area Planning Legislation. Indianapolis, Division of Planning, Department of Commerce, State of Indiana, undated.

Metropolitan Council. "Metropolitan Land Planning Act Summary." St. Paul: The Council, 1976 (mimeographed).

Metropolitan Council. "Summary of Metropolitan Significance Act." St. Paul: The Council, April 12, 1976 (mimeographed).

"Metropolitan Housing and Redevelopment Authority." Minnesota Session Laws—Laws, 1974, Chapter 359, St. Paul: The Council, 1974 (mimeographed).

"Metropolitan Parks." Minnesota Session Laws—Laws, 1974, Chapter 563, Metropolitan Council, 1974 (mimeographed).

"Metropolitan Reorganization Act." Minnesota Session Laws—Laws, 1974, Chapter 422, Metropolitan Council, 1974 (mimeographed).

1974 Omnibus Housing Bill, Public Law 93-383, Title VIII, Sec. 809 (1974).

"Oakland Zoning Ordinance." *Oakland Tribune,* August 26, 1965, Supplement.

"Protection Open Space." Minnesota Session Laws—Laws, 1974, Chapter 359. Metropolitan Council, 1974 (mimeographed).

Public Law 93-383, 92rd Congress, 53066, 1974.

True Copy Act (No. 13), Commonwealth of Puerto Rico. San Juan: Puerto Rico Land Administration, 1969.

[Unigov Planning Legislation]. *Laws of the State of Indiana.* Acts 1955, Ch. 283, Sec. 68.

PERIODICAL ARTICLES

Abrams, Charles. "The Uses of Land in Cities." *Scientific American,* Vol. 213, No. 3 (September 1965).

"Agency News." *Planning,* Vol. 39, No. 6 (July, 1973).

"ALI Adopts Its Model Land Development Code." *AIP Newsletter,* Vol. 10, No. 8 (August 1975).

Bangs, Frank S., Jr. "Urban Land Policy: Some Proposals for Change." *Planning,* Vol. 38, No. 4 (May 1972).

Canty, Donald. "Metropolity." *City* (March–April 1972).

Cassidy, Robert. "The Last Oregon Story: Preaching the Good Life." *Planning,* Vol. 40, No. 9, October 1974.

Chapin, F. Stuart, Jr. "Taking Stock of Techniques for Shaping Urban Growth." *Journal of the American Institute of Planners,* Vol. XXIX, No. 2, May 1963.

The Committee on Growth and the Environment of the International City Management Association. "Report of the I.C.M.R. Committee on Growth and the Environment." *Public Management,* Vol. 55, No. 9, September 1973.

"Community Development." *AIP Newsletter,* Vol. 10, No. 1, January 1975.

Corby, Linda L. and So, Frank S. "Annual ASPO School Survey." *Planning,* Vol. 40, No. 1, January 1974.

Davidoff, Paul and Rosensweig, Linda. "Entire Township Zoning Ordinance Struck Down as Exclusionary." *AIP Newsletter,* Vol. 6, No. 11, November 1971.

"Density Lowers Demands in a Time of Power Shortage." *Planning,* Vol. 39, No. 9, October 1973.

Duggar, George. "Local Organization for Urban Renewal." *Public Management*, Vol. XL, No. 7, July 1958.

Environmental Protection Agency. "Environmental Protection Agency—Air Programs: Approval and Promulgation of Implementation Plans—A Review of Indirect Sources, Part III." *Federal Register*, Vol. 39, No. 8, February 25, 1974.

Fagin, Henry. "Organizing and Carrying Out Planning Activities Within Urban Government." *Journal of the American Institute of Planners*, Vol. XXV, No. 3.

Fagin, Henry. "Regulating the Timing of Urban Development." *Law and Contemporary Problems*, Vol. 20, No. 2, Spring 1955.

"Fiscal Disparities Bill." *Planning and Developmental Newsletter*, Dakota County Planning Advisory Commission, Vol. 1, No. 4, August 1971.

"Florida Mandates Local Planning." *AIP Newsletter*, Vol. 10, No. 8, August 1975.

Friedman, John. "The Public Interest and Community Participation: Toward a Reconstruction of Public Philosophy." *Journal of the American Institute of Planners*, Vol. 39, No. 1, January 1973.

Gaffney, Mason. "Land Planning and the Property Tax." *Journal of the American Institute of Planners*, Vol. XXXV, No. 3, May 1969.

Gleeson, Michael E., Ball, Ian Traquair, Einsweiler, Robert C.; Freilich, Robert H., and Meagher, Patrick. *Urban Growth Control Systems: An Evaluation of Policy Related Research*. 2 Vols. Minneapolis: University of Minnesota School of Public Affairs, 1974. Note: This is a longer version than those published later by the Urban Land Institute and American Society of Planning Officials.

Haar, Charles M. "In Accordance with a Comprehensive Plan." *Harvard Law Review*, Vol. 68, No. 7.

Hagman, Donald G. "A New Deal: Trading Windfalls for Wipeouts." *Planning*, Vol. 40, No. 8, September 1974.

Hartzer, Timothy J. "Comprehensive Plans Edge Zoning Ordinances as Legal Documents for Development." *AIP Newspetter*, Vol. 10, No. 9, September 1975.

Holbein, Mary Elizabeth. "Land Banking: Saving for a Rainy Day." *Planning*, Vol. 41, No. 1, January 1975.

HUD News, No. 74–254, July 31, 1974.

International City Management Association. "Managing Growth: Report of the ICMA Committee on Growth and the Environment." *Management and Control of Growth—Issues—Techniques—Problems—Trends*, Vol. I, Edited by Randall W. Scott. Washington: The Urban Land Institute, 1975. Also in *Public Management*, Vol. 55, No. 9, September 1975.

Israel, Barry. "EPA Promulgates Land Use Regulations to Control Air Pollution." *AIP Newsletter*, Vol. 8, No. 7, July 1973.

Jacobs, Scott. "The Housing Allowance Program in Kansas City Turns into a Notable Failure." *Planning*, Vol. 39, No. 9, October 1973.

Lash, James E. "Renewal: Area Problem." *National Civic Review*, Vol. LI, No. 4, April 1962.

Lyall, Katherine C. "Tax Base-Sharing: A Fiscal Aid Towards More Rational Land Use Planning." *Journal of the American Institute of Planners*, Vol. 41, No. 2, March 1975.

McCahill, Ed. "Ecozoning: Wrong Approach, Right Idea." *Planning*, Vol. 39, No. 8, September 1973.

McGivern, William C. "Putting a Speed Limit on Growth." *Planning*, Vol. 38, No. 10.

Mayer, A. J. and Abraham, P. L. "New Morality." *Newsweek*, Vol. 85, March 10, 1975.

Meyerson, Martin. "Building the Middle-Range Bridge for Comprehensive Planning." *Journal of the American Institute of Planners*, Vol. XXII, No. 2, Spring 1956.

Meyerson, Martin and Terrett, Barbara. "Metropolis Lost, Metropolis Regained." *The Annals of the American Academy of Political and Social Science.* Edited by Thorstein Sellin, Vol. 314, November 1957.

"Microcosms of Urbanity." *Progressive Architecture*, December 1975.

"Municipal Real Estate Taxation." *Yale Law Journal*, Vol. 57, 1947.

Mylroie, Gerald R. "American Law Institute Last Month Voted No to Mandatory Land Planning and Regulation." *AIP Newsletter*, Vol. 9, No. 6, June 1974.

National Policy Task Force of the American Institute of Architects (AIA). "A Plan for Urban Growth: Report of the National Policy Task Force." *Memo, Newsletter of the American Institute of Architects*, January 1972/Special Issue.

"News Report." *Progressive Architecture*, September 1975.

Nordheimer, Jon. "Florida Seeks to Control Growth." *New York Times,* November 19, 1973.

"Petaluma Wins on Growth Control." *Planning*, Vol. 42, No. 4, May 1976.

Pratter, Jerome and Ward, Richard. "A New Concept in Residential Zoning." *Urban Law Annual*, 1971:33.

Prentice, Perry, ed. "Financing Our Urban Needs." *Nation's Cities*, reprint, March 1969.

Ridings, Don. "Floodplain Zoning Study Underway." *The Courier Journal and Times,* Louisville, April 25, 1971.

Rodwin, Lloyd. "Land Economics in the United States." *Town Planning Review*, July 1950.

Rubino, Richard G. "Florida's New Land Use Law is Among Most Comprehensive in Nation." *AIP Newsletter*, Vol. 8, No. 4, April 1973.

Scott, Randall. "Oregon Supreme Court Says Cities Must Zone in Accordance with Their Comprehensive Plans." *AIP Newsletter*, Vol. 10, No. 7, July 1975.

Scott, Randall. "The Petaluma Decision: Another Sign That Federal Courts Don't Want to Get into Land Use." *AIP Newsletter*, Vol. 10, No. 10, October 1975.

"Securities—A Moral Issue." *Time*, Vol. 105, March 10, 1975.

Stegman, Michael A. "Housing Finance Agencies: Are They Crucial Instruments of State Government?" *Journal of the American Institute of Planners*, Vol. 40, No. 5, September 1974.

Stevens, David Ross. "How a U.S. Law May Sharply Change Planning Here." *The Courier Journal and Times*, Louisville, June 9, 1974.

Stollman, Israel. "Remapo." *Planning*, Vol. 38, No. 6, July 1972.

Svirsky, Peter S. "San Francisco Limits the Buildings to See the Sky." *Planning*, Vol. 39, No. 1.

Thompson, Myron B. "Hawaii's State Land Use Law." *State Government*, Spring 1966.

Tomson, Bernard and Coplan, Norman. "New Trends in Zoning Laws." *Progressive Architecture*, March 1973.

Walker, Mabel, "Tax Responsibility for the Slum." *Tax Policy*, Vol. 26, 1959.
"What's Behind the UDC Debacle?" *Business Week*, March 24, 1975.
Williams, P. R. "Pittsburgh Pioneering in Scientific Taxation." *American Journal of Economics and Sociology*, Vol. 21, No. 2, 1962.
Wilson, James Q. "The War on Cities." *The Public Interest*, No. 3, Spring 1966.
Woodruff, A. M., and Ecker-Racz, L. L. "Property Taxes and Land Use in Australia and New Zealand." *Tax Executive*, Vol. 18, 1960.

UNPUBLISHED MATERIALS

American Institute of Planners. "The American Institute of Planners Review of the American Law Institute Model Land Development Code—A Primer for Action." Washington: The Institute, August 1975. (Mimeographed Draft).
Larsen, Peter A. "Arden, Delaware—Utopian Experiment in Single Tax and Success as a Planned Community." Unpublished paper presented at the 1973 Confer-In of the American Institute of Planners in Atlanta. (Mimeographed).
Legler, John B. *Some Critical Comments on Property Taxation as an Alternative to Site Planning*. St. Louis: Institute for Urban and Regional Studies, Washington University, 1970. (Mimeographed).
Letter from Dale R. Gatlin, Director of Code Research, Indiana Administrative Building Council, Indianapolis, May 28, 1974.
Letter from Ken Reddick, Public Information Office, Twin Cities Metropolitan Council, June 2, 1976.
Letter from Gene A. Rowland, Chief, Office of Building Standards, Center for Building Technology. Washington, D.C., August 8, 1974.
Letter from Robert Wehrli, Chief, Architectural Research Section, National Bureau of Standards. Washington, D. C., July 15, 1974.
Marcinkus, Betsy Ross. "Planning for an Island Metropolis." Washington: American Institute of Planners, 1972. (Mimeographed).

Index

337

Public improvement programs (*see* Capital improvement programs)

Special districts and public authorities, 23, 165–90, 316–17
  financial and functional advantages, 166–67
  functional characteristics, 171–89
    air pollution control, 176
    education and related functions, 175–76
    health facilities and services, 176
    housing, 179–83
    land banking, 186–87, 285–303
    planning, 187–89
    public safety, 179
    public utilities, 171–72
    recreation and open space, 173–75
    solid waste, 178–79
    state authorities, 180–82
    transportation, 172–73
  general characteristics, 165–70
    coordination of, 169–70
    definition of, 165–66
    formation of, 168
    funding of, 168–69
    governance of, 168
development standards, 93, 98, 101–07
  F.H.A. insurance standards, 98, 102
  local design and construction standards, 101–07
    compulsory dedications, 103–04
    lotting out, 95, 97, 99, 102–03
    parks and recreation, 104
    payments in lieu of dedication, 104
    required improvements, 104–05, 107
      timing and financing, 105–06
    streets, 101–02
    utilities, 102
extraterritoriality, 94
growth guidance systems, 109–10
legal basis, 94
planned unit development, 99
problems of control, 106–110
  enabling legislation, 106
  evasion, 108
  fragmentation, 107
  hillside sites, 108–09
  inadequate enabling legislation, 108
  nonresidential subdivisions, 109

  unconventional designs, 108
  waterfront sites, 109
purposes, 93
state intervention, 94
Suburbanization, 4–9, 20
  costs of sprawl, 7–8, 20, 194
  inner suburbs, 9

Taxing power, 21–22
Tax policies, 113, 130–44, 315–16
  abatement, 140
  income taxes, 130–34, 315
  property taxes, real estate
    land (only) taxes, 135–37, 315
    land vs. improvements, 134–35, 315
    preferential taxation, 137–41, 287, 289, 293–94, 315
    selective taxation, 141–42
    multijurisdictional, 248–52, 320
    proliferation of, 169
  purpose for creating, 166–68
  problems with
    coordination, 169–70
      fragmentation of functions, 171, 173, 174
      kind and degree of dependence, 169–70
    proliferation, 169
Special permits, 72, 83 (*see also* Growth guidance systems and Zoning, conditional uses)
Spending power, 21–23
Standard City Planning Enabling Act, 17, 27–28, 92, 94–95, 252, 266, 303
Standard Zoning Enabling Act, 17, 27–28, 252, 266, 303
State Concern, areas of critical, and development of regional impact, 253, 258–59, 263–64, 273–74, 283–84
  wetlands, 272–73
Subdivision regulations, 21, 92–112, 314
  administration of, 99–100, 106, 110
  amateur developers, 107–08
  appeals, 100
  approval process, 96–106
    fees, 100
    preapplication, 99
    preliminary plan or plat, 99